THE DRAMA KING

MR SORKIN,

A SMALL TOKEN OF MY
ESTEEM FOR YOUR WORK.
YOU'VE BEEN AN INFLUENCE
LONGER THAN I KNEW (PG 191)
CONTINUED SUCCESS

BEST,
CARL
De Gregorio

THE DRAMA KING

BY CARL DE GREGORIO

Los Angeles / Saint Petersburg

Carl De Gregorio is an actor, writer, and comedian, this is his first book.
http://www.carldegregorio.com

Alligator Suitcase Press, Saint Petersburg, Florida
first print edition published 2015

Printed in the United States of America
9 8 7 6 5 4 3 2 1
ISBN: 978-0-9961224-6-7

Library of Congress Cataloguing in Publication Data
The Drama King
Copyright number:
TXu-792-781
Claimant:
Carl DeGregorio 2011

For my father, George D., our Champion.

1

IOWA

I've been to Iowa twice; the first time was in eighth grade attending the Future Problem Solvers International competition. I'm not sure how Cedar Rapids pulled such a plumb event, but I think it had something to do with it being Cedar Rapids. It was my first plane trip, and it was my first time away from home without family, and it was preceded by my first appearance on television.

Cable television was in its infancy and my teammates and I appeared on a low-rent-low-tech local show that was barely viewed by the people in our families. My restless legs never stopped moving during the interview, and I told the creepy host my future plans were either sports or the arts. The sports never worked out and the arts— we're still working on that.

What is a future problem solver? It is a kid who is sure to spend his high school years being thrown into lockers, but at the time I wasn't thinking about my social status. A problem solver is a kid who was in the gifted and talented program in grade school like a Mathlete or an Olympian of the mind.

I spent a day a week outside of my regular classroom to hang out with some hyper, but verbal, fellow students who had tested into a program for smart kids. How this pays off down the line, I'm scared to find out.

Competitive problem solving started with a fuzzy situation. This situation could be a social or moral event, or development in the future that is posed to the group—stuff like genetic engineering, or prisons in outer space. We met the lifers at Rahway State Prison for research. They started their scared straight speech, not caring, or maybe not being told, that we were the "good kids." I think I had to give up my shoes and sit in a corner while the trustee frothed at the mouth and told us how to avoid having your manhood taken in the shower.

Competition consisted of the problem solvers wasting a Saturday and doing a group report, voluntarily, in an empty classroom at a local school. Judges graded the report and scores were compared. We won our region and then our state. We got our invite to Iowa like getting into the NCAA tournament, minus cheerleaders and any chance of ever getting laid.

I was unable to attend the state competition because my oldest brother was getting married, and when my team won I was relegated to alternate and lost my captaincy to my best friend Jimmy Carver. I still got the free trip and didn't have to sit through the think-tank part anymore, so I wasn't complaining. I could have saved us all some time by titling the chapter Nerds Take Iowa.

I was a lost soul at this point in my life. My personality was beginning to emerge and a few issues were popping up. While I exhibited intelligence, I was not setting my academics on fire. I was also debating in myself what kind of life I hoped to live—a normal, expected life, or an off-the-beaten-track kind of life. It's also when I began to seek approval in my search for romance.

The chaperone for our group threw down a challenge at the closing night dance.

"I'll give you twenty dollars if one of you can bring a girl over here and introduce her to me." She said.

We looked at each other like she asked us to build a hydrogen-fueled rocket. I had my eye on a cute blond with glasses who caught my attention at the skit portion of the competition. Twenty bucks and bragging rights were a big motivator and so was fear of humiliation and failure. I was angry at the proposal because it put me in a pressure zone; I had to be the one to pull it off. I stalked the gym floor looking for the girl who caught my eye and found a wave of bravery that I didn't know I possessed. Would I have made the approach without the nudge? It's hard to say. It's hard to say because the answer would have been no.

"Hi, I'm Carl, do you want to help me win a bet?"

"What's the bet?" She said.

"My teacher wants to meet a girl." I replied.

"What?"

"No, she wants one of us, her students, to introduce her to a girl."

"That doesn't sound right."

"I get twenty bucks if you say hello and dance with me." I say.

"Oh, I get it."

"What do ya say?"

"OK."

I bring the girl back to the chaperone more quickly than she expected. Maybe she didn't think it would happen with the geeks she was looking after. I got my twenty bucks and danced with the girl of my dreams. She would spend the rest of the dance in the arms of others and I was asked to dance by a redhead from Nebraska. It was heartbreak and rebound all in the space of a few hours on the court where the Coe College Kohawks played fundamentally sound basketball in the wilds of Iowa.

We don't place in the competition and I found out I would have to compete as a single person, meaning I would have to crack a blue book and work alone. I guess you have to pay to play. I didn't place either. We were a team again, bonded over the travel and our mutual lack of success.

Years later (my second time in Iowa), I am in my trailer on location for a film starring Ray Liotta of *Goodfellas* fame. We are outside of Des Moines. I should be clear—I am in one fifth of a trailer and have to wash my hands with a gallon jug of water. I can't flush the toilet because it has been so cold that the pipes and portable septic tanks have frozen. My name is on the door written in masking tape, and it makes me feel important. There is a knock on the door and the production manager comes into the trailer and hands me an envelope and has me sign some papers. He leaves and I open the envelope, and it holds one hundred ninety five dollars cash. I look around, count it several times, fan it out on the table, and pose in the mirror holding the cash like a gangster in a rap video. I add the amount to my money clip. Despite my best efforts to escape the clichés associated with my heritage, I still find myself using a money clip. That the money clip often holds less than it's worth is something I need to work on.

Through some back channels and being at the right place, I finagled a small part in a movie, and I have three lines. I am grateful, but when I set out almost twenty years ago, I was sure I would be farther along than this. Acting prodigies who aren't child stars don't get noticed unless they work. Now, I am sitting and freezing my ass off in a trailer in Iowa and a little too excited to be holding just shy of two hundred bucks.

The name, Walter, is taped to the mirror and affixed to the hangers on my costume. My character is a schlub-used-car-dealer, and the clothes match those attributes, every shade of beige. These aren't clothes I will take home as mementos.

There are three days left of shooting and the crew has suffered through a historically bad winter. Most of them are Canadian and know from bad winters. I'm excited to make a movie, and they want to kill someone, so I try to keep my enthusiasm under wraps. Nothing enrages the disgruntled more than enthusiasm.

They are ready for me on the set, and I am driven to a muddy parking lot with a crummy looking shack that will play the role of my shitty office. I know the director, and he looks relieved to see me. I am a friendly face in a sea of a burnt out and stressed out cast and crew. I am introduced to Ray Liotta who is polite and a bit distant—I try not to try too hard to make a connection. The director tells his star that I work in a restaurant that Ray has been to many times. I want to kill my pal, the director. Can't I have one day where I am just an actor at work? I shake it off and I enter the office, which is being lit for my scene. I meet the leading lady, who will be in the scene with me, and I try not to react to her attitude, which is haughty and bothered.

The film is about a woman on the run with her kids. She has taken them on the lam to escape an abusive ex-husband. They are helped by Ray Liotta's character and are trying to make it to Canada. The mother needs another car, and she steals one from my character, promising to send me money when she gets her life back together.

She has a gun drawn on me and has me tied to my shitty chair at my shitty desk. This is the scene.

> JOCELYN
> *I'm going to send you a check for sixteen hundred, right?*

> WALTER
> *Twenty-six hundred.*

> JOCEYLN
> *Walter, you know that car is not worth more than sixteen hundred.*

> WALTER
> *They're gonna be so mad at me tomorrow.*

JOCELYN
You had a gun to your face. What
were you supposed to do?

WALTER
Somehow, it's always my fault.

This is the extent of my involvement in the film. We are up against the clock with lunch looming in half an hour. I had fantasies of being able to improvise some more lines for myself, but when I saw the time, I knew the only way we would come back to this scene after lunch was if I totally fucked up.

I tried to take the saying that there are no small parts, only small actors, to heart. My take on the scene was to play against the peril of being robbed at gunpoint and play up the fact that I was going to be in the shithouse with my boss. I figured I hadn't sold a car in a long time and now a car was being stolen—a zero sum screw-up. It added some comedy that I was still trying to get my price if she actually came through and paid me back—playing the eternal optimist.

We wrapped up, and I was done for the day. I was done for the duration. I was hoping to hang out with the cast and crew over drinks, but they were shooting through the night. I had per diem money burning a hole in my money clip, and I wanted Iowa to know I was back in town. Back at the Chase Suites, the apartment style hotel commandeered by the production, I have nothing to do. I call my girlfriend and give her the blow-by-blow account of my major motion picture debut. She is thrilled; it is a day I don't have a laundry list of laments about my career, and we celebrate over the phone.

I am itchy to hit the streets, but these are the streets of Des Moines, Iowa. I want to blow some money on a good meal. That turns out to be harder to do than one might think. I have a choice of Applebee's or a place called Cheddar's. I go with Cheddar's - my mistake. When you regret not going to Applebee's, you know it's a tough town. The lights are so bright that I think the place is trying to close for the night. There are booths against the wall and a horseshoe shaped bar in the middle of the room that's empty. Waiters are congregated at the service side of the bar, and some are counting their money before kicking off for the night.

At Cheddar's I have a couple of beers and some awful boneless Buffalo chicken strips. In truth, they were bad; also in truth, I cleaned my plate. I try to engage the bartender in conversation because I want to tell him about me being in the movie, and he couldn't give a shit.

"I'm not from around here." I say.

"That right?"

Nothing. He gives me nothing.

"Yeah, I'm from LA." I say.

"That right?"

This guy is a rock.

"Yeah, I'm here working on a movie." I say.

"That right?"

I pay my bill, which is criminally inexpensive, and ask where a bar named Bradley's is located and if it's walking distance.

"It's about a mile or so. It's on the other side of the bridge." He says.

"That right?" I say.

There is snow on the ground and large piles of it at intersections. The land is flat and, while there are sidewalks, it is not common ground for pedestrians. The bartender was right; it was a mile or so, and I have crossed a couple of bridges. I start to think he was fucking with me and sending me out in the middle of nowhere. I almost turn back, but as my paranoia peaks, I see a strip mall with people standing out front. I've made it to Bradley's. It's loud and carpeted with a pool table by the door and one of those mechanical dartboards that never work. It's packed with mostly college kids and couples who look like they're doing time with each other. I feel like the record stopped when I enter the room. I can't find a seat at first, which is brutal, I order a beer and stand alone in the bar area. I'm that guy. It is the opposite of a friendly neighborhood bar. I'm yearning for Applebee's. I get a bar stool eventually, and I start writing in my Moleskine reporter notebook. Now I'm that freak drinking alone and writing. I'm wearing a leather jacket and look like Serpico in the wrong movie.

This is one of the better days I've had, and I still can't shake the feeling of loneliness and isolation. In your battle for your soul, the negative thoughts creep in and have to be fought back. An outsider could say, "this is the sum total of your shitty career," but I have to be grateful and glad and remind myself that this is a difficult pursuit, and there are thousands of actors who woke up today without a job and would kill for even three lines. I'm being paid for my efforts, and I celebrate this small beginning alone. I order another beer and I drink to my good fortune. I turn my chair out and face the room—a smirk on my face, like I know a secret: "You guys don't know it, but you are in the same room with a movie star."

2

A KICK IN THE DICK

June 29, 2010: I am younger now than my father was when he had me. He was raising his three kids, my siblings, with my mom for thirteen years before I showed up. As I write this I am not on the doorstep of fatherhood myself, but I am on the doorstep of losing my father.

It's not as if I'm sitting vigil by his bedside right now, but there is a door down the hall we can all see. He's eighty two and that's a good old age to make it to, but with an older brother trucking at ninety two years old and a mother who made it to 102, it's been a kick to the groin to find out he has a really bad cancer and we're talking months not years.

A few weeks ago, I was sitting at the kitchen table, in the house I grew up in, as my dad read from my laptop the words he's been putting together for a memoir. I was tired. We've been sleeping downstairs on the sofa bed since my dad got sick and we re-fitted the dining room into a room for my dad. My dad told me to look at his files and see if there was something there I could help him with. I should have been honored. My dad worked for the *New York Times* for thirty-nine years, wrote a book about Joe DiMaggio, and still writes poetry. Just this year he self-published a book of poems entitled *Zerilda's Chair*, which refers to a chair he inherited from his mother-in-law that is the only chair that alleviates his back pain and sometimes allows him to get his only sleep. It was recently restored, and it's where he spends much of the day.

My qualifications to help him are not overwhelming. I wrote a play that he helped me produce in New York. I have a couple of languishing screenplays and about an hour of stand-up comedy that I've been lugging to the stages of LA and road gigs for years. I think I'm funny, and a few other people do too. I got myself on TV a few times and got a small part in that movie, but my dad is a real writer. He paid my way through college, and my brothers' and sister's way through college with the tip of his pen. Now he's asking me to check out his work.

I couldn't focus on the material he was reading. He had a burst of energy and was enjoying the sound of his words as I scrolled to the next page when necessary as if I were turning pages of sheet music for a pianist. It's good prose, and it tells me things about my family that I didn't know, but I was beat and sad, and I didn't know what to do.

I had an idea—maybe I could tie in the pages of my dad's life with the pages of mine. The only problem is I don't have any pages. I now have a project I'm not sure I'm up for and a gimmicky idea that I'm stealing from the *Godfather Part II*.

Stranger things have begun from less auspicious beginnings. I'm not saying my saga stands up to the sagas of film and literature, but it might be familiar to someone who's seen the peaks and the valleys that come to a striving artist.

My dad is a writer; my mom is a reader—a good match that has been together for 53 years. Maybe I can create something to bridge the gaps that send some of us to the stage, some of us to the bottle, or some of us to the shrink, where we work this shit out in front of strangers, with the bottle at our side, and the shrink ever elusive like the health insurance you'd need to go to one.

The preceding was an earlier opening for this story. My intention was to have a back and forth narrative of my father's life and my life at similar stages. As I read my father's pages and thought about what to write, I started with me becoming an actor mostly out of vanity, but also because I needed a distraction. Going back in time three hours a day took me back to a time when thoughts of my father's mortality were buried deep and possibilities were ripe.

I also had the notion that if I wrote quickly and got a draft done, it would, in some tenuous way, help my dad hold on. Maybe we could have a project together.

Being the son of a writer, I had to make decisions on narrative, and that took me down the path of a coming of age tale. Not being able to shut out the issues at hand, I interrupted the harkening back and talked about what was going on in the present.

It gave my process urgency. Five pages a day being less of a guideline, but more of a high-stakes necessity, I was writing against the clock. Maybe all writing is that way.

3

PURPLE HAZE

Janey Mays is jocking me, bro," I told Jimmy Carver.

"She doesn't even know who you are, dickhead," Jimmy replied.

"I'm telling you, bro she's flirting with me at rehearsal, I wouldn't lie about that."

"We're talking about Janey Fucking Mays, asshole," Jimmy yelled through the phone.

"That's what I'm telling you, Janey Fucking Mays is on my jock. She's always talking to me when we take a five," I said.

"A five?"

"That's what we say in the theater, take a five." I explained.

"We'll see, dude, if she says hi to you in the hallways, maybe that'll prove she thinks of you as a fucking cute little brother or some shit." He said.

"I'm just telling you what I'm getting." I said.

"Janey Fucking Mays …"

"Janey Fucking Mays …" I said and hung up the phone.

Janey Mays was a senior, and I was a sophomore. Janey Mays was the co-captain of the cheerleading squad. Janey Mays was a stone cold fox with huge breasts. She competed in beauty pageants. She looked like one of those hot guest stars on the *Love Boat*. She had brown curly hair; by today's standards, she had puffy hair, like one of the Landers sisters who were frequent guest stars on the afore-mentioned Aaron Spelling monstrosity. I was a late-developing sophomore who sat out two seasons of basketball because I blew out both knees. I spent my freshman year on crutches and wore tear-away pants over a cast. Sponge bathing before school didn't exactly give me the confidence that I needed to make my introduction to high school.

We had a song we used to sing, it was called "Janey Mays." It was in the tune of Jimi Hendrix's "Purple Haze."

It had similar lyrics: "Janey Mays all in my brain/ lately things just don't seem the same ..."

We were clever enough to switch her name for the hallucinogenic that Hendrix was referring to, but her narcotic effect was no less mind blowing. It was 1986, and I had a part in the senior musical, *Guys and Dolls*. It was my first play. I was playing Arvide Abernathy, the missionary uncle to the leading lady, Sarah Brown, who is pursued by the dashing gambler Sky Masterson. You have to love high school theatre—I was younger than my niece and younger than everyone in the play, but I had a song, grey hair spray, and a reason to get out of the house on a school night—and a reason to be in the same room with "The Mays."

Janey Fucking Mays was playing one of the Hot Box Girls— sometimes life writes the best punch line—the girls had a few dance numbers and were basically there to torture the pubescent flashes of the young student body.

I had a recent awakening in my life. I signed up for Theater I as my elective that year. My teacher, Mrs. Becker, was a real deal Broadway veteran. She was in the original cast of *Man Of La Mancha*. The class consisted of mostly senior girls needing credits to graduate and a couple strange dudes who lived for Monty Python. I was there because I had a performance Jones.

This was also the year I discovered cologne. I was lucky enough to fall upon a killer fragrance known as Racquet Club. I can't recall the smell, but I should have realized that day that God was a friend of mine. For some reason the senior girls in the theater class loved the smell of my drug store cologne and would ask to smell my neck. After a couple of weeks they stopped asking and took tokes off my neck like it was the best weed wrapped in strawberry rolling papers.

It was during this season of cologne that I found out that I was a good actor. When other students would get self-conscious and stop the scene or the exercise, I would stay with it, and the reaction was strong. I wasn't really doing anything more than committing to the moment and not pulling out of something to avoid embarrassment. It gave me a feeling of power. It also shot my social status through the roof. Senior girls were sniffing my neck and calling me Joe Actor in the halls. As they say on the streets—my name was ringing out.

Someone else was directing the senior musical, but Mrs. Becker encouraged me to audition. I had to sing the song from the show. Just a factoid about the song—it is usually cut from most productions. It does nothing to further the plot and is painfully dull and slow. It was perfect for me.

Normally, an affinity for the theater and performing in school plays is a ticket to outcast status in high school. I was lucky to be on the basketball team, even though I was injured, and this afforded me a little more leeway. Plus, that Racquet Club was like a magic spell protecting me. The only time I got thrown against a locker was when a liberated woman wanted to get a whiff.

What kept me from getting cocky was the fact that I was still a virgin, and at fifteen, in New Jersey, I was in jeopardy of looking like a freak. I'd made out with a couple girls even a couple good-looking ones. I was just clueless about how to pull it over the top. I don't know where this pressure came from. Every guy is obsessed with sex and losing their virginity, I suppose I was hoping it would be a magic pill that would make all my insecurities disappear or give me the direction that I was looking for. Early exposure to pornography also made it feel like a fever that had to be quelled or repressed, like a werewolf on a full moon.

How would I have been expected to seduce a woman? I didn't have a car or a license, my parents never went anywhere on the weekends, and I had to be home at eleven o'clock.

It was also during this period that I met one of my early mentors. Pete Vespoli was a college student who happened to be a substitute teacher at RHS. I've been in a classroom where the students tied a "Sub" to her chair, so it was no small feat that Pete even registered as an entity in the school. He was a student at NYU, majoring in theater. He was also an RHS alumnus, and his brother went to school with my brother. He took over the theater class for a month when they needed someone to fill in. His classes were more intense, and it was a quantum leap for my training.

Pete was in a theater company that performed at high schools and colleges. It was called "Good Clean Fun" and was an educational, improvisational theater company. The company was run by another early mentor of mine, Curtis Kline, and I was gung-ho to get involved. I rehearsed with the group and got really pretentious back in school. It's when I started spelling theatre with the "re" instead of the "er."

I earned my first paycheck as an actor with Good Clean Fun when I was fifteen; it was for two hundred bucks. I was sure the checks would keep coming, and this was what I wanted to do with the rest of my life. While the paychecks have been sporadic, they have come from time to time, and I'm still on that early morning path I set out on at fifteen.

On opening night of *Guys and Dolls*—the Rutherford High School version, not the Broadway opening, in case you were confused—I don't recall having nerves. That only means I don't remember, not that I didn't have them. A trip to the supermarket stresses me out, so I'm sure there were nerves. I don't remember much about the performance. I remember being as relieved as the audience when my song was over, not because I was bad, but the song, "More Than I Can Wish You" is painful. It's about an Uncle hoping the best for his niece. At fifteen, with a huge bass drum to lug around on stage, I had other things to worry about than my character's motivation, not to mention what little grasp I had on method acting; I didn't have the depth of character to pull from.

It's funny not to have a clear recollection of my first play. If I were this natural I kept thinking I was why wouldn't my debut be the stuff of folklore? What could I really do with a part I wouldn't be right for until I was sixty-three years old? The fact that I had balls to do it was probably the biggest lesson.

The real reason I have faint memories of the play itself is that the memories of the cast party are the kind of memories that get men through military prison. After the performance my family and friends congratulated me, and my mom started a tradition of bringing me flowers. I was wearing make-up, had just finished performing musical theatre, and now was holding a bouquet of flowers. That I survived without a beating by my peers is still a miracle.

The cast party was at Dave Cordova's house. Dave was a senior to whom I never said a word. He was one of the jocks who played a gangster in the dice game number, "Luck Be a Lady." As a sophomore I would have been barred at the door, but as a cast member, I was tolerated. The Cordova's had the classic New Jersey finished basement. My basement at home still had asbestos pipes exposed. The idea for the party was to watch a replay of *Guys and Dolls* on the VCR. This kid had all the accoutrements of 1980s technology. I was sitting between Janey Mays and Mallorie Hedgeberg - the two reigning co-captains of the cheerleading squad on the pool table. I think there was beer and by think, I mean—I was four-beers-deep.

We watched the tape of the play, and everyone is heckling

everyone. I think Dave Cordova yelled out, "you suck" during my song. I actually toasted the air in his direction in agreement. It would be, the only contact I ever had with Dave Cordova. While everyone is having fun abusing each other on the video, I am actually able to get my arm around Janey Mays. I am also getting some looks from Mallorie Hedgeberg who is now talking to Sky Masterson, the lead. The looks from Mallorie seemed to say, "holy shit, he might actually pull this off," and not the look that preceded two girls about to take the pizza boy on the pool table in my fantasy. Still, I had my arm around JFM, and the co-captain giving me eye contact, I was truly crossing over. We could stop there and it would have been a good night, but somehow I manage to fully engage Janey in a straight up tongue kissing make-out session on the pool table. And I'm talking about in full view of everyone and right next to Mallorie Hedgeberg and Sky Masterson. The whole time I'm thinking THEATRE IS FUCKING AWESOME.

At fifteen, making out is amazing, but at fifteen making out with the object of your longing from afar is otherworldly. I was going to say surreal, but if I hear that word used again to describe things that aren't surreal I'm going to punch a wall. My watch wasn't melting, so surreal didn't apply in this case. It was exciting and new, arousing and sweet tasting, not the most flowery descriptors, but that's what it was.

There was a cosmic pay-off. I wasn't misreading the signs in rehearsal. She was digging me; Jimmy Carver would have to eat his words. It was public domain. The other fact remained that I liked the Janey I was now getting to make-out with. She wasn't just a Siren of the hallways. She was right there in my grasp, and it was crazy, but not surreal.

I've always thought that my newfound confidence in acting was informing the rest of my life. The more I studied, the more confidence I had in other places. I would not have had any confidence before. I would not have given off the right energy, or vibe or whatever it was that made me attractive to Janey or any other girl. It's why it's so important for kids to find something they're good at, and even one class a day can change a kid forever. I was lucky. I felt like I was saved, and it paid a direct dividend: I got the girl. In the play, Sky Masterson gets the girl. In this story, the corny old uncle gets her.

My curfew was a sore spot for me. My parents wanted me home at 10:30. I eventually negotiated 10:45 and was often coming in at 11:00. I'm a rebel sometimes. I would yell at my folks, "I'm not a girl! I'm not gonna come home pregnant." My parents were older than my friends' parents, and they were using the 70s rulebook on an 80s kid. My siblings hitchhiked home to make curfew. I was just trying to be out past the late news. This all got blown to bits thanks to that cast party at Dave Cordova's house.

Eventually, even Dave's permissive parents shut down the party, and it was time to go. I was holding onto Janey like a bank robber with a hostage in a standoff. I didn't want this night to end. Not having a license actually helped me out. Janey had a car and the documentation to operate it, so I had a ride home. Somehow, Mallorie Hedgeberg and Sky Masterson were in the mix, and we drove around town.

"Do you need to get home?" Janey asked.

"Hell no." I replied.

I suppose I had a shred of fear about being late, but sometimes the right decision and the wrong decision are the same thing. Again, I don't remember much in the way of dialogue I just remember getting to the field where they played football and ran track. We walked around and tried to distance ourselves from the other couple. We made out in the high jump pit, and eventually the four of us were making out in Janey's Subaru. It wasn't a weird wife swap thing. We just coupled up in the car, each doing our own thing.

I hopped out of Janey's Subaru at five o'clock in the morning. This was six hours past my curfew, and I didn't give a shit. When the front door opened without the need for my key, I knew I was cooked. The problem was I couldn't care less. I had to fight the urge to smile as my parents stared at me in anger. I tried to explain where I was and who was there, but it was sounding a lot worse than it was to my folks. My dad told me to go to bed, and we'd talk in the morning. I was think-ing, "This guy should be hi-five-ing me," as I climbed the stairs to my room.

The next day I called Jimmy Carver.

"What did I fuckin' tell you?"

"You're full of shit." Jimmy replied.

"Jim, I'm telling you …"

"Un-fuckin-believable." Jimmy ranted into the phone.

"Crazy, right?" I said.

"I don't know what to say." Jimmy said.

"Don't say anything, OK? I don't want her to think I'm bragging about it." I said.

I think I could hear Jimmy muttering to himself as he hung up the phone.

My punishment never came, just an awkward conversation with my dad. He said, "You know older girls expect things."

I responded, "Yeah, dad, like sex," and kept waiting for him to come to his senses and congratulate me. What was with this guy? Didn't he know that I had just pulled off something even a John Hughes movie wouldn't dare tackle? I leap-frogged to the head of the line, my reputation was made in one fell swoop, and I didn't have to get arrested to do it.

Monday rolled around and I was eager, if a little groggy, to get to school. Truthfully, I was eager to see Janey and see if she were still cool with what had transpired. I guess I hadn't thought about whether this would be something she had to live down, or something we could build on.

The first person I saw in the hallways was Miss Budig, a gym teacher. I said hello as I walked by. Over my shoulder I heard her say, "Five o'clock in the morning, huh?" I stopped and turned back in her direction as she weaved her way down the hall. How the hell did she know? I hadn't told anyone but Jimmy. I didn't think about the fact that Janey and I were seen at the party going at it, but how would a teacher know? Later in the day I was in the locker room getting ready for gym class and Mr. Roucks, the wrestling coach and gym teacher, pats me on the shoulder and says, "Janey Mays, huh?" This was getting creepy.

There was never a conversation with Janey about what went down; we just started hanging out. She drove me to tennis practice after school everyday. It was my first season playing tennis, and I found out what people meant when they said that tennis is a mental game. My temper got me in trouble with the coach and with friends. I hit Jimmy Carver in the back with a ball as he walked back to the line to serve because he was beating me in a playoff match.

I started carrying my cologne in my gym bag. This was the secret to my success. I had nabbed the girl because of this magic scent. I didn't want to be too far away from my source of power. On a ride to practice the bottle of Racquet Club broke, and Janey's car smelled like me for weeks. Talk about having a presence.

At this point I was a full-fledged theatre geek, reading books about acting and renting only important films. I became obsessed with Robert DeNiro and Marlon Brando. I also started hanging out with Pete and Curtis and their whole crew. They were in their mid 20s and we would go to Manhattan. My curfew was now a thing of the past. I'm sure my parents wondered if they should clamp down or let it be. I wasn't up to much but seeing plays and, yes, drinking beer in bars that didn't bother to ID me.

Pete's father owned a strip bar out by Giants Stadium. It was called the Half-Way Go-Go. I actually went there with Pete, his date, Curtis and his wife, and Janey. I thought I was hot shit. I was with my hot older girlfriend and was dragging her into a titty bar for a date, all at the ripe age of fifteen. I pretended to be mortified at the whole thing. It was just a quick stop on our way to the city. Pete actually wanted to visit his dad, and it just so happened to be at the Half Way Go-Go. Thinking about it now, my parents would have been dragged in for allowing this kind of behavior if they had any idea.

4

BRAND NEW CADILLAC

My choir teacher, Mr. Garibaldi, had come up with the idea to do a variety show at the school. Yes, I was in choir and gave up my lunch hour to do it. I was not in the band, so I was still able to keep myself from taking a beating socially. Mr. Garibaldi called his idea "The Popcert"; it was a talent show without the prizes. It was more musically based than the plays the school did. It was a chance for singers, piano players, and dancers to perform. It was almost an independent production. If you had a song you wanted to sing you brought it in and worked on it.

I'm not sure how it came to pass, but I was going to be the emcee for The Popcert. I was probably given the task because I was hard to embarrass. I was going to read off index cards, wear a tux, and keep the crowd focused. There was a preview performance that would highlight a few of the acts in the show over the weekend. It was an assembly during school hours, and it was before the entire student body and faculty. Things were going along well until a band had a technical difficulty, I was about to introduce the act when Mr.

Garibaldi stuck his head out from behind the curtain and told me to "stretch" for a couple of minutes. As terror shot through my body, I turned back to the crowd and started talking. I had an idea.

I started talking to the crowd as if I were David Toma. If you never heard of David Toma, it's probably because you didn't grow up in New Jersey in the 1980s. David Toma was a cop in Newark in the 1960s and 1970s. He worked undercover and developed techniques like decoys and dressing as a woman to apprehend criminals. He was the inspiration for two TV shows, most notably *Baretta*. In his retirement from the police force, he became a motivational speaker. He would go to high schools and talk about drugs and staying straight. He'd yell at kids' parents and was a pretty passionate speaker. He also had a local TV show on WWOR, Channel 9, in the New York market, that I watched avidly.

I developed an odd fascination with David Toma. I read his autobiography, *The Compassionate Cop*, and found his style funny, but hard to take your eyes off. He's a zealot, but he's trying to do something positive, and I connected to it.

I turned to the crowd and, in Toma's intense voice, I started going into a rant. I told the crowd to close their eyes.

"How many of you kids are out there doing the weed, the Mary Jane, the wacky tobacky, huh? How many of you are doing the ups, the downs, reds, greenies, the coke the blow, the nose candy?" I asked in Toma's pained cadence. The crowd went wild.

"WHEN'S IT GONNA STOP?" I bellowed, using Toma's catch phrase.

"I been there. I did the coke, the 'ludes, the herb, the Mary Jane, glue. I did it all, but I found the light and want you to know you can get there too. I love you guys," I continued. I was in a-lather and a zone I would understand better years later. Then I shifted to the parents in the room following the Toma script.

"Do you wanna know how many of your little darlings, by the time they were fourteen, have been doing the pot, the Mary Jane, the coke? Do you wanna know?"

"WHEN'S IT GONNA STOP?" I screamed again.

It was a near riot. Mr. Garibaldi poked his head through the curtain and the next act was finally ready. It was probably five minutes, but I was fired up and wanted to keep going. I did the rest of the assembly as David Toma. When the show wrapped up and we went on with the rest of the day, kids were telling me how funny I was. "When's it gonna stop?" they kept shouting in the hallways. I wasn't into drugs and that wasn't the point I was trying to make. I just thought Toma was hilarious and kind of endearing; he was doing good deeds. I dug David Toma. The bit worked so well because even "the burnouts" who hate everything the school presents thought it was classic. I was a crossover artist and I felt like I was harnessing a natural and positive thrust.

The Popcert was Friday and Saturday night and I was excited to keep going with my newfound stage act. I was the Eddie Murphy of my school. Mr. Garibaldi approached me before the show.

"You can't do Toma." He said.

"Why?" I asked.

"The administration thinks it's inappropriate. You're making fun of drug abuse." He said.

"No I wasn't. I was making fun of David Toma," I said.

"Either way you can't do it."

"I'm being censored." I said and tried to duck a punch that never came from the pretentious police.

I was pissed that I couldn't do my bit. I had another song to do later in the show, and I figured I would come up with something funny along the way. As I parted the curtain and faced the full house, the crowd chanted.

"Toma, Toma, Toma."

I didn't take the bait and started the show. Each time I came out I heard the crowd call for Toma. I waited until the end of the show. I parted the curtain and the crowd started chanting.

I said in Toma's voice, "I can't do it, guys, the school says I can't do it. But, I love you guys." The little taste was enough and the show ended on an up note. I was feeling confident in my new identity as a performer. I was working with Pete and Curtis and taking my acting seriously. I was gaining a reputation. Being called crazy was a compliment in New Jersey. Kids would say, "You're fucking crazy, man," and I loved it. Normally, you were called crazy for diving into a pool from the roof or giving teachers the finger when they weren't looking. I was being called crazy for having the balls to pull off performances that others enjoyed. I was completely sprung on my course as an actor.

Pete and Curtis had a job teaching at Oberlin College in Ohio. They were to be instructors at the Oberlin Theatre Institute. It was a summer conservatory for college students wanting more intense training. The institute was also bringing in two actors from the Royal Shakespeare Company who would perform two plays and teach during the day. With my progress and enthusiasm, Curtis said he could get me a scholarship for the six-week program. It would normally cost $2000, but he could get me a spot. All I had to do was fly there. It would be worth college credit and a chance to take this acting stuff seriously.

I was torn. Janey was graduating, and the summer was all the time we'd have before she went off to college. I would be giving up making out in her pool and maybe unburdening myself of the virgin yoke. We were having a good time, but I had neither the means nor the know how to properly date a girl. I took her to the Bronx Zoo; it rained and we made out by the exotic bird pagoda. I was worried I wouldn't be able to pull off the whole shebang. Her experience was intimidating. I suppose we could have had an open conversation about sex and our feelings, but this was Jersey in '86, and I still have trouble having open conversations in relationships.

There was talk of me going to the senior prom. I think with Mallorie Hedgeberg, not as a date, but to be there with Janey who decided to honor her word and go with a guy who asked her a long time ago. I was cool with a lot of the seniors and it sounded like a good idea. This sounds a bit sketchy now and probably was then, but it made sense. I should be there to keep an eye on my girl, by having another girl on my arm. What was hard to understand about that? The problem was proms cost money. It wasn't my prom, and money was something I didn't have. I tried asking the folks, but they were worried I would have a great time having sex and doing drugs. They couldn't get past the idea that I was a sophomore and she was a senior, and it was inappropriate for me to go. I kept looking around for a referee to come out of the wall and throw a flag on my parents.

"Interference, obstructing. This kid is on fire, buy him a car, brag to your friends, let him go," he'd say. It's really hard to avoid the age disparity and feel like a stud when you have to tell a girl, "My parents won't let me."

The next hurdle for me that spring was getting the OK to go away for the summer, to study acting with these guys who bought me beer on the weekends. I couldn't figure out what could possibly be the downside to the situation.

I told my dad about the scholarship and met with some resistance. He kept thinking there would be a hidden fee. I suppose the plane fare and miscellaneous cash was more than he wanted to spend for the summer. Truly, there was no other expense. It was free room and board plus the classes. I lost my patience. Why was I being handled with such care? Did I have a heart condition nobody told me about? True, I did hang out in the city and drink beer with twenty-something actors, but my parents knew these guys. I wasn't date raping and drag racing on Route 1 and 9, or starting fights with kids in Secaucus. As my mind cycled through some of the assholes in my school, and as I was met with more resistance from my dad, I lost my cool. I got angry and stormed up the stairs.

As I climbed, I shouted the lamest thing ever uttered. I screamed, "I'm the best kid I know," and slammed my door.

The next day I came downstairs embarrassed not by my anger, but for the *After-School Special* dialogue I chose to use the night before. My mom and dad had spoken and decided that after they talked to Curtis and Pete that I could go to Ohio. Has anyone been more excited about a summer in Ohio before or since?

As the end of the school year approached, I was filled with a sense of melancholy that was oddly familiar. I was dreading the graduation of the senior class and most notably Janey. I had come to dread goodbyes. My two brothers and my sister had left for college in rapid succession when I was little and I hated seeing them go. More than the loss of Janey was a feeling of being left behind – that I was better suited to be with older people and was held back by my youth.

Held back by my youth, can you imagine feeling that way now? As the summer came, I only had a couple of weeks to hang out with Janey before I left for Oberlin. Most of the time I'd go to the batting cages and meet Janey under a tree. It was all sweet and innocent, and I was holding on like Harold Lloyd hanging off a ledge, doing his own stunts, in the silent movie era.

As the school year winded down there was another substitute teacher who made his presence felt in the hallways of RHS. He was no theatre major, but a wrestling coach about two years out of high school. While my buddy Pete was popular for the way he made his classes interesting or his quick wit, this "Sub" was popular for his fully developed musculature. It was hard to feel tough with my convex chest and my tennis shorts.

5

THE UNFORGETTABLE FIRE

As I made my way to Ohio, there were rumors that this *Vision Quest* extra of a substitute teacher was "making time" with the Mays. I sent a feeble letter trying to get the issue resolved and received tepid pen pal replies from Janey. By now, I was immersed in my new environment. Oberlin College is an idyllic campus; is there any other way to describe a campus? It was at least different from anything else I'd seen, so my trauma back home was blunted. I was away from home for the longest time yet and lucky for me I had a single room. This was the summer I learned that theatre people are freaks. While I might have been an odd bird in Rutherford, New Jersey, I was practically an ROTC candidate to the students at the institute. I guess you don't shoot hoops *and* do plays everywhere else in the country. I was the freak for a different reason out there—I was painfully normal and out of my element.

I clung to Pete, Curtis, and another instructor who came out, Dan, for the first few days. They were the teachers, so it was a bit awkward for me to be able to hang out at their rented house. There was a curfew at the dorms, and I'd often blow it off. The resident tech had to warn me, but it was all done with a wink. It wasn't the best way for me to socialize with this new group.

Part of my discomfort was that my ability to grasp Shakespeare was low. I'd stare at the pages double-checking whether it was in English or not. The other students were rattling off quotes like they were Springsteen lyrics. Without sounding pretentious, Shakespeare is taught as if it were literature (which it is), but not as theatre (which it is also), in high school. So most kids' eyes glaze over because it sounds weird, instead of getting fired up about how good the story is, or dare I say how dramatic it is. It took a while for me to get my head around the material. I was the youngest student at the institute and had not been exposed to serious theatre. I thought I was hip because I sat through the *Deer Hunter* on VHS.

I had a breakthrough in class one day. We were working on the sonnets, and it was my turn to perform. The instructor was Lisa Harrow of the Royal Shakespeare Company. I was working on Sonnet 30, which starts, "When to the sessions of sweet silent thought/ I summon up remembrance of things past." The last part of that line is the title of a Proust novel. I was butchering my way through the sonnet sounding like Ralph Macchio playing Hamlet when Lisa stopped me.

She was this hot lioness of a woman with an English accent, and the women I grew up hearing didn't sound like this. I was agape. She broke down the words and asked me to paraphrase them in my own way. We went through it line by line until I understood what I was saying. Then she told me to taste the words and use someone specific as the recipient of those beautiful words. She grabbed my face and said go. I ripped into the text, and it made sense. When I got to the couplet—"And if the while I think on thee dear friend/ All losses are restored and sorrows end"—I was feeling pretty good about myself.

I had used my brother as my image, with a little Jimmy Carver and some Janey thrown in, it was still hard to use that acting technique; how can you be talking to someone who isn't there?

I was now totally enamored with Lisa Harrow while all the female students were spun out by the other visiting artist, Patrick Stewart. Yes, that Patrick Stewart, star of *Star Trek: The Next Generation* and the *X-Men* films. His classes were more showcases of how great he was. He would talk about a play and then rock a soliloquy. I thought Lisa really taught us something. But, again, at fifteen what use did I have for a bald Englishman. Maybe my judgment was clouded by teen longing, but I thought Lisa Harrow rocked. This theatre shit was growing on me.

"I got laid." Jimmy Carver said into the phone.

"No Shit?" I said.

"Yeah the other night," he replied.

I think that I muttered fuck to myself as I hung up the phone. This was not good. Sure it was, for Jimmy, but for me it was a disaster. I'm not sure when I became a terrible friend. I just knew that I had lost. Who gets competitive about this shit? I did.

About this time, as luck would have it, I had made special friends with a girl at the institute. That sounds like we met wearing hospital gowns, chain smoking, and swatting away imaginary insects. From now on we'll call it the program, which makes it sound like a brain washing clinic. Kate was a student at Oberlin College. She was a junior heading into her senior year. She was petite and blonde, like a small Meryl Streep, with a soft voice. We met at a barbeque. I was hanging out with Pete, Curtis, and Dan at the house owned by the head of the Oberlin theatre department. Kate was there, and we hit it off. I didn't really think there was a chance with her. I was more of a mascot, but I was making the usual precocious impression which is either totally annoying or charming depending on the person you're trying to impress. For example, the head of the theatre department probably found me annoying, wondering what the hell I was doing on his porch. Somehow Kate found it charming.

Conversation revolved around music and how I listened to what my older brother listened to which made me weird to my peers, but hip to a college chick. Neil Young was a big subject and Crosby, Stills and Nash. We're talking about Oberlin, which I learned is a liberal lighthouse to wayward wanderers of the Midwest. Some of the Freedom Riders were students at Oberlin. It also happened to be the first institution of higher learning to grant degrees to women and most notably the first African American woman, making her the first African American to receive a four-year degree. It is a special place. There was spontaneous harmonizing to classic songs and it was thoroughly embarrassing to recall. U2's *Unforgettable Fire* was big too. It was atmospheric and romantic. It was make-out music for white people.

A week or so later, Kate and I took a long bike ride. Pete had driven out my Schwinn Le Tour (my prized possession), and I was good to go. I remember the terrain being flat for most of the ride, and it was the first time I saw a rock quarry other than in the movie *Breaking Away*. It was a great day, the kind of day that can't be manufactured, a day when a soda at a Dairy Queen is the best thing you ever tasted, a day when you wonder if you'll ever see the like of again when you're really down in the dumps.

Nothing major happened on that day, just a bike ride and a lot of conversation. And sometimes there's nothing better.

Of course I was falling for Kate, but my recent résumé wasn't on display. Kate wasn't a cheerleader from New Jersey. She was a college girl from Connecticut—worldly and into theatre. I still didn't need a razor—I used one, but I didn't need it. We started spending time together and eventually there was a kiss, then, there were knocks on my window and Kate would climb in it and we'd make-out all night. I pulled the two mattresses in my room to the floor trying to create a king size bed, but it doesn't really work. You wind up with two twins on the floor and you try to trick yourself by lying across the seam. I'd sneak out sometimes and head to her place. God was smiling at me, again, with a ground floor room. I was sneaking in and out instead of flouting the rules at the dorm.

It was all so mature—the conversation, the independence, and the fact that I was about to turn sixteen. I never thought it was odd from her perspective—she being twenty, me being fifteen. It was at this time that I learned a little lesson about the theatre. There aren't as many guys into it in the early stages. Of those guys who are into it, some are not into girls. This can leave girls in the theatre with slim pickings in terms of companionship. This gives the straight male, even a fifteen year old, some sway in these matters. It could also be the Racquet Club cologne, but I doubt it. What I know now is that sex complicates things, and the fact that I wasn't having sex yet kept things simple. Maybe it was a relief for Kate to have a relatively chaste summer fling with a guy who didn't have a clue how to get over. We kind of had an affair of the heart as nauseating as that sounds.

This didn't help me beat Jimmy Carver to the Promised Land, but I now had some evidence of romantic entanglement. I called Jimmy and lied my ass off.

"What's up, Jim, still getting some?" I said.

"Yeah, man, all the time," he replied.

"It's great isn't it?" I lied.

"Who are we talking about?" he asked.

"Me, bro, I had sex too," I lied again.

"Good for you, who with?"

"This girl, Kate, she's in college," I said.

"You're on a roll," he replied.

"Right? Anyway, I gotta go, I'll talk to you soon."

I hung up and didn't feel much remorse for lying. I could produce photos and phone numbers, and no one really knew what went on behind closed doors. My ego was so out of control I had to one-up my friend because I hadn't beaten him to the punch. Maybe I thought I was on a higher rung of the social ladder or that I was crossing over to a different life and wanted credit for it. It was pathetic—I admit. I didn't admit any of this to Jimmy until fifteen years later when I told him I lied in the parking lot of Giants Stadium before a Springsteen concert. We were about to enter the arena and Jimmy wanted to make a toast. He was drunk and emotional and said, "There is no place I would rather be than right here, right now, with you guys." We put our hands in like a basketball team coming out of time-out. I felt it was a good time to tell him that I had been lying for years.

"Jim, this is stupid, but I never slept with Kate in Oberlin. I lied because I didn't want you to beat me." I said.

"I'm impressed you kept up the lie that long." He said.

The truth of the matter is that I didn't have the courage to tell any girl what must have been painfully obvious. How do you tell a girl you're a virgin; the guy is supposed to have the experience. Admitting that truth would be admitting a major flaw. In my mind, everyone I knew back at school was in double-digits with lovers. That can't be possible, but that's what I thought. Jimmy Carver was making it happen; everyone was doing it but me. Maybe I could have said, "You know I've never done this. I'd like to, but I'm a bit out of my depth. If you were game to take this a little further, I'd be all for it." Essentially I'd be asking for a little help when your ball crosses into another court or you hit a ball over a neighbor's fence. That's not sexy. So, I became the greatest dry-humper in the country.

Perhaps, Kate was being kind by not letting things go too far. Or perhaps she was being smart. Her senior year would have been a nightmare with a crazy heartsick high school boy-toy cramping her style. But, we were spending a lot of free time together, I was totally in her snare, and I found myself sharing things I never would have with anyone else. I was growing up.

We talked about what we wanted to do with our lives. Kate was closer to the impending real world. I still had to learn to drive and take the SATs. It was mind-expanding to be able to be myself. I had grown up with older siblings and older parents. I got along with older people. I didn't exactly get along with girls my own age and had a very short array of topics to share with them. With Kate, I could just talk and not feel like I was losing her attention or that I was weird. There was also a college boyfriend home for the summer that would soon visit and mess up my flow.

There was work to do. It wasn't play camp; it was theatre camp. I had scenes to memorize and fake swords to wield. It was serious business. There was also wiffle-ball and touch football. We actually had Patrick Stewart out there on the football field, and in the huddle, we discussed how to proceed.

"I say we go at Stewart, exploit his defense."

"That's not cool he doesn't know the game." I said.

"Is he gonna take it easy with us on stage?" Pete said.

"Good point; let's light him up."

I was assigned a scene from David Mamet's *Sexual Perversity in Chicago*. It's the play that became the movie *About Last Night*, much to Mamet's dismay. It was a break-up scene with cursing. I had to wear a towel but was too worried it would fall off, so I wore underwear underneath it—not very slick. I remember how awkward it was to be in front of people with my shirt off and my pants for that matter. It helped to have a scene to take my mind off it. My scene partner was a lot older than I was and the scene had her yelling at me and telling me what a terrible lay I was, and I was screaming stuff back, and it went pretty well. Kate told me my back did something sexy, and I think that was a good thing. She also said it was distracting seeing my underwear under the towel, but I was not ready to show my vitals on stage. I was showing some potential and gaining some status in the group. There were a couple of students who were in Kate's class, and I was a source of curiosity to them.

One guy, in particular, couldn't get his head around the whole situation. He was a student at Oberlin and had a reputation as one of the hot actors in the class. That cracks me up today. He had a swagger, and I think he wore scarves even in the heat of summer. He was the epitome of cool, as oxymoronic as that could be at a summer theatre program. He'd see Kate and me hanging around.

"What is it about this guy?" he'd ask as if I wasn't there.

"What are you getting at?" Kate would respond.

"I don't know, what's he got going for him?" he'd persist.

I'd sit there taking this shit from him because my inner response was "I'm fucking awesome and that's why she's digging me, you fucking pretentious hack." He'd lose interest as soon as he realized the subject of the conversation wasn't him and move on. This is when things started to intensify. When Kate would defend our relationship or tell people to mind their business, it made me feel like we really had something - that the age thing was fading, and I really stood a chance of keeping her in my life.

There was a cement base in front of one the buildings on campus. It was like a foundation for a statue, but the statue never got built. Students would congregate on it, and it was the center of our down time. One night we were hanging out and Pete was there. This is an era when the game Truth or Dare was everywhere. Was there ever an era when the game wasn't? In New Jersey this game would lead to making out in the woods or showing your ass, no one ever took Truth. In Oberlin, the game was more mental, and no one took Dare. The questions were probing and overwrought. The answers were sometimes wordy and ponderous.

"Truth or Dare?"

"Truth," after a dramatic pause.

"Have you ever fantasized about being with someone famous?" someone would ask.

Big pause, "Yes, but I'm not proud of it …"

I was sitting there thinking this is the worst game ever. You people suck. Someone should have chucked a moon by now, shown a bra strap, not this horseshit. Then people started to loosen up. Someone would ask a person to list the people they had thought of sleeping with at the institute. I got a couple of mentions and was puffing up like a game bird. I also felt rage when Kate made a couple of lists. There might have been a kiss here or there. The game was improving until it was my turn and I chose Truth.

"Are you still a virgin?" Pete asked.

"Et tu Brute," I thought. "What are you trying to do to me? I thought you were a friend." I'm tensing up; I'm sitting next to Kate, and I don't have a lot of time. My options are to tell the truth and expose myself as a colossal pussy to the group or to lie and expose that fact to myself.

"No." I say.

"Who was it?" Pete follows up.

"What the fuck, dude," I'm thinking. I'm avoiding looking in Kate's direction and I'm trying not to look flustered. I'm too far in to turn back now. I remember hearing that the best lie has a little truth to it. It makes it easier to remember.

"Maureen Callahan," I say. It was a good cover. I had made out with her at Amy Fortunado's house a couple of times. I felt like a heel. Who would care? We were in Ohio, so none of this mattered.

There was never a conversation about the game. I'm sure my lie was transparent to Kate. Maybe she found it endearing. Maybe she found it telling about my character. I doubt she believed me. Part of me was hoping it would come up, so I could come clean and maybe broach the subject of our consummating our summer fling and getting me on the books. Getting me on the books? I had watched too many Mob movies. I was never sure what was on her mind. God forbid I ask her directly. This was one of my first relationships. I was new to this. It's where the age difference was most pronounced. I would have been better served dating a girl my own age and stumbling through the mating rituals as a neophyte with the girl, sharing in the inexperience and discovery.

It was harder to pull off back in New Jersey. I didn't have an open forum with my parents to talk about this. My folks wanted me to stay focused on school, and dating wasn't something that made that easier. I had this feeling that away from home, in this cocoon of independence, is where I stood the best chance of being free, being myself, re-creating myself. Part of my problem or maybe part of all our problems is that we are result oriented. Instead of basking in the glow of learning and loving and freedom, I was trying to get laid, trying to write a story—a story I could tell the world or at least the humps in my high school. I suppose drive is a good thing, but my failure to lose my virginity was a manufactured failure and something that kept me from being in the moment. From a tactical standpoint, it was a bad play. If I said to Kate, "I'm a virgin," she might have taken the bait and worked with me on it. I was afraid of losing Kate, and surely sleeping together would have bonded us more deeply. But, by clouding my thoughts with prideful self-protection, I made a barrier where there should have been an open field. Let's just say it took me a while to shake off that game of Truth or Dare.

If it sounds like I was sitting in the corner with blue balls and Shakespeare flash cards, it wasn't like that. I was having a better time than when I first arrived. Some of the theatre freaks were growing on me. I was hanging out with my friends and I was gaining more confidence. I was acquiring knowledge that would make me a pretentious monster back in the hallways of Rutherford High School. If there are moments of clarity for the addict, then there are moments of objective overview for the youngster. I knew this was a special time while I was going through it, a time that would imprint me like a brand. I knew I could ride a bike all day and at a rapid pace, and I knew that "Take My Breath Away" by Berlin was the greatest song ever written.

6

HELPLESSLY HOPING

There was a party celebrating the opening of *The Tempest* starring Patrick Stewart as Prospero. It was the event of the summer, the culmination of the institute. The teachers had roles in the play, as well as some of the college students. Kate had a small part. It was the weekend for family and friends to come and see what we were up to. One of the visitors was Kate's college boyfriend. It was a tough time. The nosy actor dude was all a-titter with the gossipy aspects. Kate was in a tight spot. The party was at the rented house of my buddies. I had a few beers and was trying not to fall apart. Kate would not be there; she had her business to attend to. The party was a blast for most, and I was doing my best acting of the summer pretending to have a good time. I was holding court in the kitchen when Kate walked in alone.

"Hey, what are you doing here?" I asked.

"It's the opening night party." She replied.

"What about what's-his-face? He on his way?"

"No. I broke up with him." Kate said.

"Are you serious?" I said.

"Yeah, it wasn't working and I didn't want to put you through any unnecessary pain." She said.

"Wow, I don't know what to say. You just made a guy very happy."

"Good, let's have some fun," Kate said. We embraced and made our way through the party as a couple—for the time being. I wouldn't trade that moment for anything—it was Kate saying—this may be weird and not practical in any way, but for now I'm going to honor it. I felt like a champ. Almost on cue, we bump into nosy actor dude with the scarves, and he starts prodding us for details about what had become a mini story line in the hallways.

"What's up with you guys? Your boyfriend here?" he asked.

"Yeah, he's here, he's just not *here*." Kate said.

"Is he on his way?"

"No. He won't be coming tonight." Kate said.

"Are you serious?" he asked, as I put my arm around Kate and walked with her into another room.

"What is it with this kid?" actor-boy said to the empty space as he took in the plot twist he never saw coming. Chalk one up for Carl D.

As the remaining days ticked off, I caught a bad flu, with chills and fever. I rested at Kate's apartment, not even bothering to check in at the dorms. What were they going to do? Send me home with only a few days left? Even though I was sick, I was glad to have Kate as a nurse. It was an odd way to wind down our time together. There was that moment in the kitchen where she forswore the other guy for me. That was our crescendo. The drama wouldn't hit me until I was back in New Jersey, knowing it would never be the same for us: no over-nights, no bubble to protect us from the realities of our stations in life. It was a melancholy time. It was that sweet ache of missing someone. It was time to get back to my life which woe for me was the life of a high school junior. Kate would be figuring out what to do after college, things like a job and housing.

The mood swings of adolescence were now fueled by my newfound flair for the dramatic. There wasn't a sad-sack song I didn't have in heavy rotation. It was all ballads all day. I was sullen and sleepy. I had nothing to do but write and mope. Jimmy Carver was busy banging away with his girlfriend, and I was missing Ohio. It was going to be a long couple of years.

I spent my time writing letters to Kate. I would create works of art that were eight pages long. I would instruct Kate to put the letter down mimicking the hours I wasn't writing. These things were days in the making. I made tapes. Not just mix tapes, but talking tapes. When she would reply, I'd read the letters over and over. It was completely ridiculous.

I actually got to see Kate at the end of the summer. I took a bus to Connecticut and had an awkward weekend. I met her family and slept in the basement. We couldn't go to bars, so we just hung out and her family treated me like a foreign exchange student—very nice, but not sure what to do with me. Kate snuck downstairs and we made out. It was great to be with her, but it wasn't like it was in our own little world back in Oberlin.

I was sure I would wait out my days in school find a way to stay in touch as I went to college and find a way to be with Kate. To say it was youthful exuberance would have enraged me to hear, at the time, but it would have been the truth. We did give it our very best shot. There were letters and phone calls and those horrific audiotapes I made. Curtis and I made a trip to Oberlin during the school year. I had earned some money doing some construction with a friend and spent it on a plane ticket. Another good visit, and Kate was great, but when you're not navigating sexual politics, you really don't have anything to navigate.

To this day, we would have no issue with each other. We were friends. There was no break-up, no hurt feelings, and no shattered expectations other than a little kid's wish to play grown-up. She taught me how to treat a woman and maybe I learned a few tricks that would help me later in the dating game. I also had the cover I needed and a story to add to my supposed reputation. I had moved up to college girls and I was going to be a holy terror in the hallways as I took to carrying a book of sonnets everywhere I went. Again, I don't know how I avoided getting punched in the face. I just thought I could protect myself with iambic pentameter.

7

PLEASE, PLEASE, PLEASE LET ME GET WHAT I WANT

I had one other previous engagement that summer. As vice president of the student council, I had to go to leadership camp with the president of the student council, Courtney Gallecki. She was a senior and the captain of the basketball team. She was tall and athletic with blonde streaks in her up-to-date hairstyle. I don't think I said word one to her. Nothing against her, but she was in an uber-popular clique, and I was busy trying to learn how to serve overhand and market my own cologne.

Courtney was going to drive us to the camp. I think it was a week before school started. We arranged the trip the previous year after we won our respective elections. By then, I knew I'd be spending my summer at Oberlin and when I got in her car, she asked me about it.

"Did you date anyone this summer?" Courtney asked.

"As a matter of fact I did." I was too eager to share.

I went on for 45 minutes; we may have even missed a turn because I was just too eager to spill the beans. Telling Courtney about my summer fling was ensuring it would get around the hallways of school.

The camp might have been interesting and transformative if I weren't so sure it was beneath my previous experience of the summer. I was probably over-stimulated and needed time to process, but instead I took on an annoying air of superiority. There was a talent show and I performed a monologue. I almost had to slap myself after that one, but I was still in my indoctrinated state.

You'd think leadership camp would be a bastion for the serious minded, but people were hooking up all around me. I think Courtney met another chief executive officer type at the camp. I was probably burnt out from all this fucking self-discovery and sharing. I was missing Kate and the Oberlin gang. I needed a nap and a good game of wiffle-ball. This encountering stuff was tiring. I needed to catch up with Jimmy Carver and destroy a bag of Doritos, and a two-liter of Coke.

The camp concluded and it was time to get back to Rutherford. We hopped into Courtney's car and hit the road. She had found love, or something like it, at the camp. It was her turn to talk on the way home. I was glad for her. I remember the guy she met was always wearing a cut-off t-shirt or a tank top. If I was ever going to get laid, I needed to start doing some push-ups.

Hopping out of the car, back home, I felt good about having gotten to know Courtney in a different way. I wasn't sure we'd be close friends, but I knew we'd have something that bonded us. I walked into my house and slept for fourteen hours.

At some point I reached out to Courtney or she reached out to me. It was cool, she had a car and I needed to get out of the house.

Courtney's running mate was Maria Castillo. She had dark hair, dark eyes and pale skin. She dressed in a fashionable Goth style; they were part of a crew that had been tight for years. I had never really floated in their circle, but Courtney and I had a bond in common, and I found myself hanging out with Maria and her. We'd go to a Chinese restaurant and order egg rolls and drink as many pots of free tea as humanly possible.

Beyond our experience at the camp, Courtney and I had something else in common. She was missing the guy she met, and I was missing Kate. We would commiserate and bore the hell out of Maria. I was milking this summer fling for all it was worth.

The fall play was approaching, and it was decided the play would be *Arsenic and Old Lace*. It was the senior play, so roles would go to the seniors, and I was sure I would be able to snag a lead. I'd been doing theatre in my underwear all summer who was going to deny me? I will attempt to describe the play without bringing this story to a screeching halt. *Arsenic and Old Lace* is about two elderly sisters who run a boarding house and murder their boarders. Their nephew is trying to keep his crazy aunts from killing again and keep the police away. There is a crazy brother who lives with his sisters and thinks he's Teddy Roosevelt, not exactly the kind of stuff that gets the teens going. It wouldn't have been my first choice, but they tend to shy away from David Mamet in high schools.

Auditions were held, and I had to fight the urge to wear a scarf and a sport coat. Courtney and Maria auditioned and were cast as the spinster sisters. I was cast as Teddy Roosevelt. I was pissed that I didn't get the lead. The director told me that she needed the strongest actor to play the hardest role. I was still immature in my training and was still counting lines, but I thought you should have the strongest actor on stage as much as possible. It took me a few days to talk myself into being excited to play the crazy brother.

With rehearsals and student council stuff, Courtney and I were spending a lot of time together. One night as I was about to hop out of her car, I summoned up the strength to attempt to kiss Courtney. I wasn't rebuffed and it was a decent first kiss. I'm not sure this is where it was heading all along, but we were there now. Rehearsals were entertaining because we were playing brother and sister, which was creepy and funny. As the set was built, we found places to make-out between scenes. It was more exciting during the performances. I had abandoned all the pretense of serious acting. She was wearing a gray wig, and I was wearing a pith helmet and we were going at it between cues.

We still managed to be a trio most of the time. Courtney, Maria, and I were always hanging out. I had to be careful to keep the pretentious meter from running high. We were hanging out in Courtney's basement—everyone in New Jersey finished their basement, everyone but my family, but my folks put three kids in private colleges, so I should give it a rest—and we were listening to music. Maria had a more alternative taste in music, real morose stuff like The Smiths and Siouxie and the Banshees. Courtney liked what she liked.

"Do you like Billie Holliday?" Courtney asked.

"Oh, yeah, totally." Maria responded.

"Yeah, he's great." I chipped in.

"Billie Holliday is a woman."

"I knew that," I lied.

I am aware that this scene appears in Amy Heckerling's *Clueless* almost verbatim, but I couldn't have been the first one to make that mistake when I tried to pretend I knew jazz, and I won't be the last. I had to remind myself that I wasn't the only person who knew things. I didn't have the corner of the market on ideas and interests. It was moments like this when I knew I had to keep myself in check. It was also where I had to let preconceived notions of people fall away. Courtney may have been the All-American girl, the jock, but it didn't mean she had no depth. She was my girl now. It was a surprise to both of us.

We may not have been well matched; I was prone to dark moods and rants. I was also coming up to that place where I didn't know how to make the next step physically. It wound up being disconcerting for Courtney. She didn't understand how a guy who'd spent the summer making it happen with a college girl would be taking his time. She wondered if I was pining over Kate. I had painted myself into a box with my fictionalizing. I was giving mixed signals because I needed the girl to take the lead if we were going to take it all the way. I wanted to, believe me. I just couldn't assume it was in the offing. It started to erode our relationship.

I found myself spending more time with Maria. We had more to talk about. On top of being a theatre geek, I was also an art nerd. I had spent many weekends in New York going to the Met, MOMA, and the Guggenheim. I was into Van Gogh like every other kid at the time that was into that sort of thing. Maria liked art and was hoping to go to college in Washington D.C. As Courtney and I drifted apart, I floated into Maria.

There was this crazy project that I had to do for a math class. This had long been my academic Achilles heel. The project involved equations that you had to prove and explain in space and show in this box that you had to make and then use yarn and graph paper. I had no idea how to do it and still don't. I asked Maria for help, which entailed her doing it for me while I distracted her. We hung out in her room and she told me how to sew the lines into the box. I mean this thing was so hard that it's impossible to explain.

I remember it being a great night. I didn't make a move. I still hadn't resolved the matter with Courtney. Maria and Courtney were good friends. It could get sticky. I was having a good time. I was at ease with Maria; she had a cool room. I remember noticing how comfortable I was being on her bed. It was my first movie moment, that scene where a boy and a girl go up to one of their rooms to do homework. Somehow, in my mind, it was intimate and normal to be in Maria's room, perusing posters and stuffed animals. The assignment was an after-thought. I kept thinking, "I can't believe I'm in Maria Castillo's room, I think she likes me." She was laughing at my jokes and pretending to be exasperated with my lack of focus on the project. There was a shift in the tide, and you knew we were headed in a certain direction, but it was going to take a minute, an exquisite minute. The project was finished. I wouldn't fail the class. I'd learned nothing about the project, but I was learning more about Maria, and liking what I was learning.

I hadn't talked to Courtney for a while. It was this dangling wire that neither of us would connect. I took that lack of communication as a green light to take a step with Maria. I'm not proud of it. If Maria and I got together, it would hurt Courtney. I wasn't about to ask permission to do it. Maria was where I wanted to be.

It's a lesson that I should have taken sooner. You may think you're the guy who isn't good with girls, or you may think you're the odd ball reading Shakespeare, but we are all capable of doing things out of our own selfish drives. You aren't excused because you're a sensitive soul, and people aren't bullet proof just because they have a car and a finished basement. I don't regret making it happen with Maria, and I'm not saying Courtney spent a minute missing me or being mad at me. I'm just saying I knew it was a dick thing to do, and I did it anyway.

It was starting to become a signature move for me, riding shotgun with a girl and making a grand gesture of trying to kiss her for the first time. I would ask her if I could kiss her, which was bold and scary, but I thought it showed flair. Later I would learn you don't ask you just go for it. I'm not sure if this is how Maria and I had our first kiss. But, I was riding shotgun a lot with Maria, still a year away from getting my license and I was feeling at home with her.

We made a few museum trips, and she bought me Shakespeare's complete works and inscribed it with a Sonnet. It was what I had been hoping for - someone my own age or a year older, who I could see every day, who was in my area code—it was Maria. I suppose the recent wave of activity was limiting my ability to see clearly. I was girl-crazy. I might have been drunk with my recent ability to procure female attention.

This was different. Maria was a triple threat: smart, pretty, and her house was across the street from the high school. I got along with her mom and felt like it was my first real relationship. We would kiss in the hallways, and it doesn't get more committed than that.

We were headed into the holidays. This was a first for me, having a girlfriend around Christmas time. I loved Christmas. The tree at my house was always a thing of beauty. We had decorations going

back generations. My mom had an eye for the unique ornament—
miniature trumpets, crystals from an old chandelier, Muppet finger
puppets in a basket, hand sewn three wise men, at least one art class
hold over from each of our childhood's—it was a dangling museum
of our family. My dad and I had a tradition since I was the last one of
the kids still home. We'd go pick a tree from the same place over in
Montclair, always a balsam. We were the final arbiters of the selection.
We'd bring it home and put it up and usually find a way to argue as we
strung the lights up on the tree. Once it was up it would inevitably be
the best tree yet. We never picked a dud, each tree better than the last
even if the trunk had scoliosis or it was thin near the bottom. This year
I was bringing Maria home.

The one picture of Maria and me is a picture taken in front of the
Christmas tree. I had bragged about it for weeks. I remember the visit
being pleasant if a bit perfunctory. She had family to get back to and
we had board games to play. It was important for me to get a picture
—some kind of proof of coupling. I'm not sure where this need came
from. Clearly, insecurity was at the root, the feeling of waiting for the
other shoe to drop. The picture made it official. We were together.
It may also have been part of what I think is a bit of a family shared
desire to collect. A collection of pictures of past loves is odd but could
be one hell of a collection if you're lucky. But, if you are in collecting
mode are you really present with the person you're so sure you can't
do without? Who are you going to show these pictures to? I heard
someone say that having many lovers is a way to acquire something
without having to keep an object. That's farther along than I was. I just
wanted a picture with my girl. I was happy with Maria, and she was
happy with me. She got along with Jimmy Carver. It was going to be
a great year.

My gift to her for Christmas was tickets to a Van Gogh exhibit at
the Metropolitan Museum in New York. Later in life, I learned there
are three gifts to buy a girl—jewelry, purses, or shoes, but mostly jewelry. Buying $12 tickets that put you in a room with four hundred

people might not have been the wisest choice. Her mom and my brother came along, not exactly romantic, but I thought it went a long way in bringing these two households together. I was, perhaps, getting ahead of myself.

Any time in the City was quality time for me. Once I got used to the trip and got familiar with the trains, I would never skip a chance to cross the river. My dad commuted everyday and would always tell me we lived nine miles from Manhattan "as a crow flies." Good for the crow, he didn't have to suffer Port Authority.

I remember sitting in the cafeteria of the Met with Maria, and her mom, and my brother, thinking that I was on my way. Look what I've managed to bring to my life. A few years ago, I was a pituitary case with no torso, and now I'm taking in art with my sexy girlfriend who digs the same things I do and digs me. It was a happy day, not as grand as the day at the rock quarry with Kate, but this was New York, baby.

Maria's mother was going to be out for New Year's Eve. Maria was going to have a couple of people over. It was a tame affair. She wasn't trying to roll a keg in the back door as her mom walked out the front. We were going to do our best grown-up thing - cheese and wine and some cheap champagne. I don't remember who else was there, but Jimmy Carver, Maria and me. This was a pre-designed night for us. We were going to capitalize on her mom being away and we were going to finally sleep together. Part of what made this weird other than the fact that I used the term "sleep together" is that Jimmy Carver was helping me do reconnaissance. Maria and Jimmy were becoming buddies. They'd talk on the phone, and it was helpful and totally passive aggressive of me to elicit Jimmy's help in getting information. Let's just say, for whatever reason, I knew tonight was the night.

Tonight was the night. It came down to this. Somewhere along the line Jimmy was gone. Maria and I had the run of the house and the rest of the night. I was in a dual state of euphoria and abject panic. This is about as good a scenario as you can get for these things—New Year's Eve, good music, good lighting, bad champagne. I knew guys who lost their virginities in station wagons with hookers by the Javits Center in New York. I was in a perfect setting with Maria Castillo. There was nothing to fear but not getting it done.

At some point, we made our way upstairs to her room, the same room that Maria helped me with my math project. It didn't look like the same room. It was going to serve another purpose. Maria put on some music. It was a mix tape. The Smiths figured in heavily and a Dire Straits song "Romeo and Juliet." I think there was a scarf over a lampshade, or it may have just been a candle, but it was dark, a warm darkness, but too dark to read. We got on the bed and kissed. I was still OK, and since I had this part mastered, I could do this all night. Since I knew tonight was the night, I was a bit more bold in removing Maria's clothes and then mine. We were naked, and the feeling of skin on skin was powerful. I remember thinking that I need to make this look good. I wanted to look like a pro. I knew the mechanics. I wasn't Amish; I had just never done it before. My strategy was to keep the foreplay going – or what I understood foreplay to be at the time. When I finally managed full contact, I remember feeling bliss and I remembered that most first times don't last very long. A sure sign of inexperience is a two-stroke performance. I didn't do much better, but I hung in there. It was sweet and sexy, and it was with a good person, and it was New Years, and it was all I could think about—a dopey grin now permanent on my face.

We had another party to go to after we had our moment. It was at a mutual friend's house, and I remember stuffing beers into my winter coat and trying to sound *with it* as we made it past the parents and down into the basement, again finished. Maria and I were all over each other, and the night was perfect.

The next day I woke up thinking, "I can fuck anyone I want." I'm not sure where that falls on the abnormal psychology scale, but that's what I felt. "I can fuck Kate, now, I can fuck anyone who will fuck me." I walked around town thinking I had joined a club or a religious sect. "Hey did you hear the good news? I just fucked." The only problem was I couldn't really share any of this euphoria with anyone. I wasn't going to tell my mom over waffles. Jimmy knew it was a big deal but not how big a deal. Maria didn't really talk about it. I'm not sure if she knew it was my first time or not. My performance showed inexperience, not blindness, so she could attribute it to that. All I knew was that I was official now, and I needed to see Maria immediately.

Basketball had started, and it was the first year I was healthy enough to play. I had earned some respect the year before practicing, but not playing, as my knee would swell up to twice its size. This year I was good to go. My body was filling in, and I gained a lot of coordination thanks to all the movement stuff I was doing in the theatre classes. At one practice, we had convinced the coach to let us play music for part of the warm-up. We had a boom box on the bench, cranking Kurtis Blow's "Basketball," and we started the three man weave drill. The weave is a drill where three guys pass the ball and traverse the length of the court in a weave as they run toward the other basket. The ball is not to touch the floor, and you pass it until the last guy takes a lay-up. As the basket is made, another group of three men head in the opposite direction toward the other basket.

With the music blaring and the guys goofing off, there was some confusion as I got on the court with my group, just as another group was heading our way. Looking back to catch a pass, I didn't see Kyle Pritchard as we smashed into each other, head to head, at full speed. Stumbling to the back of the line, I was a little groggy and I noticed guys pointing at my head. I reached up to my temple and felt a knot the size of a racquetball. Kyle had the same thing happening on the other side of the gym. Practice came to a halt, and the coach was "telling us so" about the music, and the paramedics came to take us to the hospital. It wasn't that bad, just a mild concussion, but when ambulances show up at a high school, it's a big story. I was released in a few hours. My folks came to get me, and I had to go back to the gym to get my stuff. I bumped into Courtney who had heard about the collision during her practice. She ran up and gave me a hug.

"Are you alright? I heard you split your head open." She said.

"I'm fine, I think Kyle got it worse." I replied.

"Well, I'm glad you're ok."

"Thanks, Court."

I wanted to say more. I wanted to apologize or be sure she didn't hate me, but I let the moment pass. I remember thinking what a class act Courtney Gallecki was. I had taken up with her best friend and never said a word to her about it, and here she was offering me comfort. It was more than I would do. It's a lesson I often fail to remember, but it's a good one.

That night my parents and I went to Roy Roger's, and I had one of everything on the menu.

Of course I milked the sympathy card with Maria, as my knot turned every color of the spectrum as it healed. I was tempted to ask her for cover-up make up when it started turning snot yellow, but I was a man of the theatre, not a cross dresser.

Most of the time Maria and I would watch TV and make out until her mother came downstairs signaling it was my time to leave. We'd hop into Maria's Ford Escort, and I would shift the manual transmission from the passenger seat. We'd park in front of my house and make out until it was time to head in. This was all good with me. We made love, and I was getting to know my way around which in most cases meant we were communicating in a physical way, not that I was getting better at navigating a public transportation system.

Once again, I was with someone who was on the doorstep of a life change and that brought some stresses. Maria was worried about her college applications and hoping to get into her first choice, which was George Washington University. I think she was looking toward international studies. She was Latina and had an eye for travel. Knowing how stressed I would be the following year; it was selfish of me to add to her grief.

They say we choose our patterns. I was playing the cards I was dealt. I didn't think it made sense to stop a situation and find a girl my own age because I wasn't sure I'd have the opportunity. There is a lack of balance when the prevailing feeling that you have in a relationship is gratitude. "Thanks for being with me" is a great sentiment to which we should all aspire; but it has to be reciprocal. I'm not saying I was a lap dog. I'm just saying I was in a clinging mode against which one should always fight.

In a bit of poetic justice, Maria and I were not hanging out. I had enough ego and self-preservation not to beg or stalk her, but calls were not returned and plans were hard to make. She was moving on, and eventually I discovered another dude was making her days. It was a crushing blow, especially if you could see the haircut on this guy. He was more of an alternative looking type. I had eclectic tastes but dressed conservatively. I thought you shared your interests and didn't have to wear them. It's my beef with tattoos. Do you really read Aramaic or Chinese—or do you just want to make sure people know you believe you should fucking "carpe diem" or live with integrity? I was not well adjusted about this development. There was never a break-up or a fight. The whole thing just drifted out with the tide.

When you are left to your own devices, you tend to look for reasons why people leave. I thought part of the issue was that I got along with Maria's mother. I'd sit in the kitchen and talk with her while waiting for Maria. I liked talking to her mother. I was one of those exasperating kids who liked to keep the ball in the air conversation wise. My buddies would say, "Can you not talk to my parents too long? I want to get out of here." Once I saw the goofball she chose, I thought she wanted more of a rebel, and someone her mother would not approve of. I met her dad and enjoyed talking to him also. I think he was a professor or something. Her folks were divorced but amicable, and I was in full student council mode at that dinner. It's when I learned that, for a time, and for some girls, being a proper young man is not what they always want. As thin as this theory was, I could cling to it.

I could tell Jimmy Carver that she dumped me, and he would be a good shoulder to lean on, but I couldn't tell him it was my first time, and I was falling apart. Of course I could have told him, but I was an egomaniac, and I would have had to tell him I lied, and that was more than I was willing to do. I didn't feel comfortable sharing any of this at home, so I just internalized it and walked around like a zombie listening to morose music and carrying my book of sonnets. Somebody take the shot. It was sweet agony, and I was wallowing in it, but seriously, if you could see the haircut on this guy.

I had my answer to the sex riddle or at least accomplished the elusive goal. I was right about one thing: it was phenomenal to be with someone you cared for in that way. It felt like I joined a club, but in the fall-out, I knew I had opened myself up to a different set of pleasures and pains.

I've heard women say that they were disappointed by their first times. I think men finally understand why they were so obsessed, in the first place. Maybe I was attention starved, and you can't get more attention than when you're engaged in the act. I was on another course.

8

THE BED'S TOO BIG WITHOUT YOU

It was this year that I made a decision that at the time seemed ground shaking. I was in the middle of my first healthy basketball season since eighth grade. I was playing OK and was enjoying the physical activity. It got my mind off things. At this time, the announcement for the senior musical came and it would be *Damn Yankees*. I know it's a musical, but it's about baseball and having heart, not to mention the Dr. Faustus angle. My dad had interviewed Gwen Verdon years before when she was starring in the stage version. He worked for the *New Haven Register* in his hometown, and that's where plays previewed before going to Broadway. There are photos of my dad with Gwen Verdon, and it was always fun to bring it up and hear my mom say my dad was falling all over himself flirting with the actress.

I was having a good year on the court but not good enough to be allowed to miss practice for play rehearsal. Mrs. Becker was directing, and I think it was safe to say that I was her prized pupil. I knew I'd have a big role. I went for the role of Applegate, the Devil who deals for the lead's soul. Gwen Verdon played Lola, the devil's assistant who does the dirty work for the devil. Applegate was the acting role and not the singing role, and this time I was glad to have it.

I had to quit basketball. It was an easy decision on the surface, but I had worked hard to get my legs back, and at one time basketball was my first love. The other issue was I remember being in the house as a child when my brother quit baseball his senior year to play tennis. To hear my dad tell it, my brother Steve had potential to play at the next level. He was 6'3" and hit multiple homeruns in games. The reason he wanted to play tennis (other than wanting to) was that his girlfriend was so good at tennis that she played on the boy's team in the same season as baseball. My dad, the sportswriter, was not happy with his decision, and there was arguing about it.

My dad was a yeller. He would get worked up, and the house would rattle. As a kid, it would jar my nerves. He didn't sound like himself, and the rage almost wiped away the affection that he usually exhibited. Unfortunately, I inherited this trait and can diagnose the symptoms. It's like what I've heard described as the onset of a migraine headache. Something stirs, and the anger almost pulses, and you can't be talked down until you've blown your steam. In fact, any effort to be talked down only stokes the fire like squirting lighter fluid on a barbeque. My brother and father had, at times, some rousing scenes in the house. Car trips could also ignite into a firestorm when my dad made a wrong turn and blamed my mother for not navigating up to an impossible standard. My brother, the doctor, tells me there is a recently coined syndrome called Intermittent Explosive Disorder (IED). My dad had it, and I have it now. My worry about quitting basketball might have been irrational, but understandable, when an outburst could ensue.

I was not as good an athlete as my brother, so I wasn't leaving much on the table. I had trepidation because I didn't want to let my dad down or replay a scene from my brother's day or get yelled at. It was much ado about nothing. I had already shown a propensity for being in the theatre, which my dad supported. I told my dad, and he was cool, so I had to tell the coach. I walked into his office and told him I had to quit because I had a role in the play and acting was what I was going to do with the rest of my life. If I heard him say "pussy" under his breath as I shut the door, I wouldn't have been surprised and I might not have disagreed. It wasn't the choice I made that embarrassed me; it was that dramatic proclamation I made about the rest of my life. By the way, Coach was very cool and supportive – he did not hurl any epithets my way as I left the office.

I mentioned earlier that I didn't beg or stalk Maria since we parted. That's only partially true. I never begged, but I had Jimmy Carver do some stalking. It was very subtle and probably didn't have the landing effect that I was looking for. Flashing back to New Year's Eve—I thought it was the height of sophistication to bring Gouda cheese to the party. Now, as my sullen days grew more sullen, I was compelled by some pathetic force to purchase some Gouda cheese, and I asked Jimmy to put it on Maria's front porch. This was not quite the horse's head in the *Godfather* but disturbing in its own way. I don't know how I wanted the scene to play out or what I thought would happen. I had my delusions. Maria opens the door, wearing a robe or better yet a kimono, and notices a small wheel of Gouda; she picks it up and begins sprinting through the streets of Rutherford knocking old ladies to the ground as she makes her way to my house. She bangs on the door and pushes past my mother, climbs the stairs, and kicks my door in and we make love. Or she picks up the cheese, walks into her house picks up the phone, and says, "Hey freak, did you put fucking Gouda cheese on my doorstep?" Neither of these things happened. I'm not sure if she even caught the reference, or whether her mother picked it up thinking Hickory Farms was trying to drum up some business. Maybe the mailman thought it was a tip. It was a feeble attempt not to be forgotten. "Hey remember we had this cheese when we had sex

62

that night? Does this make you want me back?" I was a mess and I owe Jimmy Carver a beer for doing my dirty work. To this day, all he has to do is say the word Gouda and all my facades fade away. Knowing someone a long time is like a blessing with potholes.

I bought some boosters for the yearbook, at a dollar a line, saying nice things to Maria. Somehow they managed to be misplaced by the yearbook staff. Maria got the chance to revise her yearbook blurb. She erased all evidence of our time together, and the dude with the haircut got the mention. I was losing my shit. It was bad enough to be dumped, but when your initials are deleted from the record, it stings. Back then, the yearbook was the only record that counted, and as a junior I had no place of my own to say what I wanted to say. Plus, Maria had the yearbook staff under her thumb. I was fucked.

There was a fundraiser at school where you could buy candy and send it to people in their homeroom. Of course, I sent something to Maria, but she was on vacation in Mexico and wasn't there to receive the candy. I remember feeling ripped off for two reasons—the candy not getting to her and me not getting to see her tan lines when she got back.

It was not my first instinct to look for a new girl; it was my instinct to recreate the music and mood of my depressed spirit every waking hour. This was getting to be a bad music video—slow motion, black and white, rain-slicked streets and all. I needed something to get my mind off of things. Mrs. Becker told me about a state program called "The Governor's School." It was a chance to spend a month at a college and study your particular discipline. There was a science and math school at one college, the arts school at another. You had to audition for the acting program, and I went for it.

I was hoping I would spend another summer with the gang in Oberlin, but there would be no scholarship. It didn't look good and what would I be going for but to hang out with Pete and Curtis. Plus, the Governor's School was gratis.

My dad took me to audition at Drew University in Madison. This is why it bugs me when people clown New Jersey. Have they seen towns like Madison and Princeton Junction, even Rutherford? It was Long Island that started the pre-fabricated development bullshit that everyone attributes to suburbia. Heard of Levittown? OK, we have Toms River the original white flight town, but Jersey has Boroughs and Counties and farms and yeah, Newark and refineries and Camden and Bayonne, but, shit, it isn't Cleveland or Bakersfield and the whole snobbery thing is uncalled for anyway. Not everyone can be born in Marin County or the Upper East Side. All people do is get born, they shouldn't pat themselves on the back because the womb they came out of was in a good part of the world. This is how the famous Jersey chip on the shoulder gets developed.

Drew University is an idyllic campus; is there any other way to describe a campus? I was armed and dangerous. I had two monologues that were probably too mature for me. I managed to talk myself out of using a sonnet, showing some restraint. I walked into the room with a lot of confidence. I was playing with house money. I wanted to go to Oberlin and still held out that hope. This was going to be a fall back situation.

"What have you brought in for us today?" the auditor said.

"I'll be doing a dramatic interpretation of the Star Spangled Banner." I quipped.

I was so loose that I had jokes. Who was this guy and how do you stay like this? They laughed, and I did my two pieces. They thanked me, and that was it. My dad and I were back on the road. A few weeks later there was a letter informing me that I had a callback. I had revised my attitude about the school. I had done some research and found out that almost two thousand students auditioned, and they were taking eleven in the acting tract. I also found out that there would be singers, painters, writers, and most importantly dancers at the Governor's School. I wanted in bad.

The callback was at another college, a bigger one. It could have been Rutgers; I'm not sure, but I was nervous for this one. I was hanging out with my dad, and we met a father and daughter and we hit it off—the fathers and us kids. It was a relief valve and it helped my nerves. I remember how outgoing this girl was, and I knew I had a friend. With the odds of acceptance, there was no guarantee either of us would get in, but as we waited and eventually auditioned, I knew we'd be seeing each other that summer.

The sting of the break-up or the drifting apart was fading. I checked the mail one weekend, and there was a cream colored envelope with a state seal on it. I was fairly sure I wasn't wanted for the Gouda incident, so I knew my answer had arrived. It was good news. This was actually a bigger deal than Oberlin. In that case, I knew somebody who knew somebody, and I got an opportunity. This was an accomplishment. I wouldn't have been noticed if it weren't for my previous experience. I had taken the proverbial journey, stood and delivered and was rewarded for the leap of faith. I would have been a lost soul were it not for these gifts. There is the story Bruce Springsteen tells of feeling like he wasn't alive until he saw Elvis on the *Ed Sullivan Show* or that he felt his life began when his mother bought him a Japanese guitar. I felt that at some point these were the days that I became myself. I had no clear idea what I wanted to do with my life. I knew I had to do things to make a good account of myself in school to go on to college like my brothers and sister. I had no idea how I was going to accomplish that. My grades weren't all A's. I was more of a sum total of my parts. I always felt this pressure to put a good sticker on the back window of our lime green station wagon. When I was little, I would see the decals—Duke, Michigan, Boston College. When I started high school, I realized what it would take to join that sticker club and was starting to panic about my options. Getting into this program started me thinking that I could bring this ship in to shore and slap something respectable on the back of the Townsman edition Chevy.

9

THE GREAT GIG IN THE SKY

The Governor's School was housed at Trenton State College. Trenton State is not an idyllic campus, but it was going to be home for a month. It is no longer called Trenton State but The College of New Jersey. The science and math school was at a seaside college. I guess they knew that the crazy artists would have torn that campus apart, and they wouldn't be able to control us with a beach nearby. Our loss, but we managed to turn Trenton State into the Sorbonne, as far as we were concerned, and there were dancers.

I was unpacking my stuff. I would have a roommate for the first time, I don't remember much about the guy. He was Asian and quiet. My dad was helping me unpack and he was going through a bag. I had packed an industrial size box of condoms since I was fucking now. I lunged at the bag, and my dad caught on.

"Let's just hope you get to use them." He said.

All I could do was smile and hang my Van Gogh prints and other pretentious accoutrements.

During my first class, I had the temerity to say that I dreamed of playing Hamlet and that I was really here for the dancers. I was coming out of my shell, and I was putting on all the stops. The best class was with this real earthy hippie type woman who was probably just out of college. She was kind of sexy but never crossed over into flirtatious. Most of her class was about improvisation and breaking into who we were as artists or performers or people. It was not something you could explain in a syllabus. We shared a lot as brutal as that sounds. We talked about what we did and didn't like about our bodies. We talked about our insecurities. We bucked each other up if we were too self-critical. I haven't thought about that class much until now. Thinking about it makes me see that this teacher was giving us some of the basic tools. All kidding aside, the tools an artist needs are found in moments where you dissect some of the things that make you tick. It was also the bonding that a company needs to deepen its connection to the group.

It was one of the first times I was surrounded by like-minded peers. It was the first time that I actually recognized and was inspired by other people's talent. It was humbling in the way that it's good to play with better players in a sport. Hitting with a better player in tennis is the only way to get better. All these kids were the theatre geek of their respective schools. More than that, they had the strength of personality to make an impression on people. Thinking about it now, it seems like I lost a lesson I learned so long ago that almost came to us naturally. In the real world of acting, the ability to make an impression is the most important ability. It's more important than knowing how to do dialects or how to walk with a limp.

One of the other blessings was the fact that there were other artists at the school, visual artists and musicians and of course dancers. It was utopian, and the other cool thing is that it was New Jersey. It was a true melting pot. There were hard edges everywhere. We had a collective attitude that this was artsy, but we still had heart, our art school could kick your art school's ass. Things were coming at me fast. I don't know how, but I started wearing a bandana. Here's the horrifying thing, I didn't wear it on my head like Tupac or a Lynyrd Skynyrd roadie. I wore it around my neck like a cowpoke or some rough trade for Andy Warhol.

My neighbor in the dorm was a guy named Tom Perry. He was a tattooed, longhaired, scary motherfucker who looked like he would beat you to death with a pool cue in a biker bar. He was also a talented artist and the nicest guy on the planet. It would have been too syrupy in a movie to have us be friends—the biker and the basketball player. We hit it off instantly, and I co-opted his leather Harley vest and cut-off shorts. I dressed like an Indigo Girl the rest of the summer. I think I stole his bandana too. We would sit in his room and rock out to some classic rock and some heavy metal. Tom was into Iron Maiden and, thusly, so was I. We would take over a room, and air-guitar the shit out of the song "The Trooper." Real head banging.

Friday nights at the school were a blast and it's where I did my first stand-up comedy. There was a thing called the coffee house where every discipline would get together in a common room and perform. It was outside the purview of the classroom. We could do anything we wanted. We would perform as a group and improvise. We'd do these games called freezes; two actors would start a scene, and when you felt like it, you would yell, "freeze," and tag one actor out and begin another scene and so on. I performed a soliloquy from Hamlet, and one week I sang. It was an artistic free for all and it was liberating.

The night I was attempting to do comedy, I watched as a polished magician did his tricks and his act. This kid had done this before. He was making shit disappear and doing jokes. I was on-deck and was sure I was going to get crushed. I wanted to kill this kid; he was funny and doing magic. I had one prepared bit and it was weak. I had a boom box, and after class I had the actors come over to my room and I recorded them laughing. The idea was that it was a portable laugh track. I would tell a bad joke and then save it by pressing play on the boom box, the portable laugh track providing the much-needed laugh. That was the prepared material. The rest I was going to wing. I remember the magician wrapped up, and I was introduced. My plan was to go high energy. I recalled my Star Spangled Banner joke from my audition months ago. I said the band at my high school was so bad they played "Oh, Canada." I tried my laugh track bit. There was a mirror above a mantel that was too high to see myself, so I checked my hair in the mirror by jumping up and down and trying to comb it while I was up in the air and able to see it. I killed. I didn't know that term back then, but I did well, and I think the fact that I wanted to beat the magician was part of it.

Competition figures into the arts. I think that is lost on a lot of artsy types, but sport isn't the only place to try to achieve an edge. It would serve the artist to harness some of that competitive spirit. More accurately, you need to be competitive with yourself. That magician kid was better than I was, and his jokes were written. He had tricks and cards. My act was a hodge-podge and barely tied together, but I wasn't going to go down without a fight. The fact was that we were both well received. There was no declared winner, but the fact that my ego or competitive spirit popped up saved me from being knocked out.

The classes were rolling along and were fast becoming a distraction from all the things we wanted to do away from class. There was a strict no drinking policy and a couple students were expelled when they were caught with booze. It never crossed my mind to party that way at the Governor's School. By my junior year we were partying pretty hard back at home, but rules aside, it never crossed my mind that summer. There was a natural high pervading the campus. I've met people from other states who went to their respective Governor's Schools and they said the same thing. It's painfully earnest and corny to say, but we were high on life or arts or being together, or clinging to our youth or whatever it was that would get us knocked out, back at our schools, but it was true. I remember at one of the mass assemblies that I got up and told everyone to stop being so cool because I needed to get some sleep. Sleep was an interruption, and the classes were starting to infringe on our time.

I was able to procure the company of one of the targeted dancers. Her name was Tori. She was short and busty and wore next to nothing. She didn't have the classical dancer body, but she had the body a teenager usually doesn't possess and one that males wanted to possess. She was a girl from the shore. She knew how to use her body, and I was conversant with my new found sexual awakening. There were rules about girls and boys in rooms after hours. The counselors for the school were former students, now in college, who were not exactly in the business of discipline. Days would go by without me seeing a counselor. It wasn't total chaos, but with a roommate, it was difficult and a little creepy to try and get it going with your girl. My roommate was not a social butterfly, so he was always in the room.

There were two wings to the dorms, a girl's side and the boy's side. The students were housed on the first and second floors with the third floor rooms all locked up. One night Tori and I were looking for some place to make out. We were up on the third floor and started trying all the doors. As we were about to settle for the hallway floor, we tried one more door. It was open. It was an empty unoccupied dorm room. It had linens, and we were the only people who knew about it. It was a gift from the heavens. Tori and I had a room where we could be alone. We could lock the door and have at it, and have at it we did. Tori had a lot more experience than I did, and I was ok with that. I wasn't a virgin anymore, so it wasn't a big impasse to cross. I had a few things to learn, and I was going to learn them in this room with dormer windows and linoleum floors.

There was a lot of learning going on at the Governor's School. Most of it was learning about oneself, and I learned a bit about my shallow nature. Maybe it's a male trait. I realized there was only a month to meet someone and get something going. Of course we were meeting people everyday. We were forced to meet people, and I remember hitting it off with a girl who was an artist. She was smart, and it was easy to talk to her. She was cute, and I could see wanting to know her better, but I was here to meet a dancer, and I had four weeks.

Tori and I had a lot less in common, but we were doing it, and that's what I wanted at the time. What other sixteen-year-old drama nerd had a girl doing a choreographed dance to Prince's "Do Me Baby"? I was feeling good about my decision.

The other lesson was that time management is a bear when you're juggling a girl, classes, and social life. I wanted to have as much sex as I could, but I had these friends I wanted to hang out with and moments I wanted to share with everyone. Artists had projects that they would work on all night in the common areas. They were using actors as subjects, and we had collaborative performances we had to write and memorize. Early on we realized that we had very little time together, and at the same time we realized this was a life altering experience. It was like MTV's *Real World* without the cameras and the train wrecks. I wish everyone could have that kind of transformative experience. I wish it didn't have to be a game show that gave people a chance to get to know what they are capable of doing. We were basking in our good fortune and trying to soak up every moment.

It was during this month that I first told my dad that I loved him. It's gross I know, but this wasn't the normal exchange in my house, so it was big. He came down to see one of the coffee shop performances. We went out for a quick bite, and before I hopped out of the car, I told him I loved him and bolted. I sang a song from *Godspell* and mentioned my moment with my dad before I sang. It was a bit over-the-top touchy-feely, but I was accepting the new me, and my sappy tendencies

I think you have a moment where you meet yourself, and the Gov's School was that moment for me. You spend the rest of your life trying to meet that guy again. You see him when you make a toast at a wedding or when you're particularly charming on a date. You see him when something goes your way or when you're a little flush. The key to growing up or not growing up, as it were, is to stay in touch with that guy you met. That's who you are, and that's the spirit that will seep out of your body when you pass. The dark days that you face are the days when you don't know where that guy went. It's not glory days or nostalgia, better days come and go, but who is at the helm of those days. Let's hope it's you. Let's hope you can stay like that guy or gal you already are. It's just that shit gets heavy; you have to pay your bills, manage your hair loss; and don't have a 32-inch waist anymore. Yeah, you need to save money and think about a 401k, but do you have to do it in khakis? Fuck that, remember who you are. It's who you were meant to be. That summer I met myself and I was cool with that guy. I'm still pretty cool with that guy, but he's out of town from time to time. You just have to make sure you stay in better touch.

What made it so special was I think everyone was meeting him or herself that summer and meeting each other—sounds like mass schizophrenia. It was the first time anyone called me a scholar, and it felt good. The classroom was where the template was placed. The time away was the growth time; a lot of immersion based studies work on an overload basis. They give you too much to learn in too little time, and you don't really process it until sometime down the line. We did care about our studies, and we weren't just strumming guitars and boning. Well, I was, but it's not nice to gloat.

The time was ticking and the end was near. We had a picnic. We went to some orchestra thing in a nice outdoor festival park. We were staying up around the clock. There was a ceremony to end the summer. We were goofing off before it began, sitting in the auditorium trying to stave off our sadness for the school concluding. I think there were awards given out. I didn't receive one, and it didn't matter. The whole month was a prize, a gift, and it was coming to a screeching halt.

The ceremony was scheduled so that parents would know when to come and retrieve their kids. When the director of the Governor's School concluded his speech, it was over, and it hit like a ton of bricks. People were hugging and bawling like gunshot victims. I was a complete mess. A torrent of tears poured out of me. I was shocked by my reaction. I didn't cry much as a teen. I remember feeling bad when my grandmother passed away and feeling guilty that I couldn't come up with any tears. This was a meltdown, and I wasn't alone. We were clinging to each other and slobbering through our goodbyes and promises to stay in touch. I had to part with Tori and that meant an end to my sexual awakening and our bond. I had to say goodbye to all the actors who felt like family. I said goodbye and cried with people whom I wished I'd gotten to know better. It was a bloodbath of emotion.

I suppose there was some joy mixed into those tears. We just had the time of our lives, and that was something to be happy about, but it stung to be leaving the bubble. We could see each other, but it would never be the same. This couldn't be recreated, only remembered, and that was what hurt. It was a place where crying like a baby wouldn't get back to anyone at home, so we were free to wail. Tom Perry disappeared. He was nowhere to be found. I asked everyone if they had seen him; he was a ghost. I felt deprived of a chance to let him know how I felt. I had a bandana to return, now that I had come to my senses and had stopped wearing it in public.

My father and sister were there to pick me up. I was a basket case. I sat in the back seat and stifled my tears, and by stifle I mean I blew snot all over the Malibu. I was inconsolable and was only able to eat one quarter-pounder when we stopped to eat.

My sister had a new job, and it was in New Hope, Pennsylvania, which is just over the border from Trenton. My dad and I helped her move into her new digs. I remember blubbering as I lugged boxes into her apartment. I just wanted to lie down and crank some Pink Floyd or any other depressing music that I could find.

I finally got home to north Jersey. I climbed the stairs and collapsed. My mom told me I had a couple of messages—one from Tori, which made me smile, and one form Alicia, who was the girl I met with her dad at the auditions all those months ago. I called them back, and it was really about hearing them breathe on the other end of the line. There wasn't a lot to say. I called Tom Perry and asked him what happened to him. He said he had to take off because he hated goodbyes. I understood completely. If I had the self-respect to bolt after the ceremonies, I would have avoided people seeing me blubber like three year old with a wet diaper. It's good to be in touch with your emotions, but a little restraint wouldn't kill you.

10

THE YEAR OF THE DOG

I lie about my age. If this ever sees the light of day some very close friends will discover that I'm a liar. Of course, you could Google me and find some evidence of my actual age, but I've even skewed the search by changing my DOB on certain unofficial web sites. Why do I do this? I'm vain and in a panic about death and aging. I also only shave off three years. My mother never told me how old she was, so it's a family trait. When I told her I was fibbing she said, "Good for you, it's nobody business." We had a surprise dinner for my mother about fifteen years ago and my father described it as "a significant milestone birthday," so you can see where I get it.

I think it has to do with living in Los Angeles. I'm not about to use botox or get rhino-plasti, but I have succumbed to some of the pressure. If you start out as an over-achiever, in some aspects, and then have a hard time making your mark later on, you worry about the age thing. It's also a strange place for me. I grew up trying to keep up with older people, hanging out with older people, dating older people. I'm not the precocious kid anymore. It's a silly vanity, I know, but I have to get through the day the best I can.

Certain greasy spoon Chinese restaurants use those paper place mats that feature the Chinese Zodiac signs. It goes by year instead of month, so while I'm a Leo in our Zodiac chart, I'm the Dog in the other. I'm good with both of those. I think they have a chicken and a rat in their chart, and that would suck. I know very little about the Zodiac, but a classic Leo/Dog trait is egomania and whatever sign a girlfriend happens to be is usually unstable, so there must be some validity to it.

I don't have a ton of childhood memories. I'm sitting here trying to find an anecdote, but how would I have an anecdote from before I was conscious? I wasn't trying to score chicks. I wasn't buying music, and I wasn't verbal—I was just soiling my diaper and trying to walk. I like to tell a story that I was reading since birth. It's a joke that I have with my brother. We get competitive about who was the ideal child. I say I was reading first, and he says he was doing long division before he was potty trained.

I was born in Passaic Hospital in New Jersey. I am the only native of New Jersey in my family. My parents were born in Connecticut, as was my oldest brother. My other brother and my sister were born in Ohio. The family lived in Toledo before I was born. My dad worked for the *Toledo Blade* and covered the Notre Dame beat for the sports section of the newspaper. From what I can gather, it was a tough time and a foreign land for the folks. My mom had three little ones in about three years, and it was a lot. There was terrible pizza and bad Chinese food in Ohio, and they had no extended family.

My parents met at the University of Connecticut. My dad went to school on the G.I. Bill and my mother worked her way through college because her dad said, "Girls don't go to college." My dad missed the war by a couple of years but was stationed in Japan for the occupation. My dad was older than my mom and graduated a couple of years before my mother in 1952.

Like I said in the beginning, I am the youngest of four, by ten years. I say thirteen to keep my story straight. I have the personality of an only child, with the starved for attention personality of the baby of the family. It's great for my intimate relationships. I need to be left alone and also need constant attention. It's that push and pull that makes me seem complicated when I'm really a simple lug. My oldest brother who is thirteen years older than I am left for college when I was five years old, and two years later my middle brother followed; the year after that my sister completed the exodus.

Each car trip to drop my siblings off at their respective schools was long, filled with cigarette smoke, and sadness. The car would be unloaded and the physical emptiness of the cabin was small compared to the emotional emptiness that I felt.

I should say that I was lucky, because my brothers and sister enjoyed me. They put up with me and gave me a lot of attention. I didn't grow up like them, having sibling rivalry or having teachers comparing me to one or the other. I didn't have to share clothes or a bathroom as a teen. I would have looked like a pimp if my mother saved their clothes from the 1970s for me. What I didn't know at the time was why they were gone.

I vaguely understood the concept of college but didn't understand what that lump in my throat was all about when I said goodbye. Knowing how ready I was to get out of New Jersey when I left for school, it seems silly to think that they were anything but excited to try their way in the world. What I got instead of a house full of siblings was a tight bond with my parents. That doesn't mean I could bear to be seen in public with my folks during those teen years when parents are speed bumps on the wobbly road to cool. I catch myself saying *my mom* and *my dad* around my siblings instead of saying mom and dad. I got used to not having my siblings around and thought that my parents were my parents alone.

My middle brother, Steve, thought I had the ideal childhood, and in a lot of ways, I did, but, I felt the age gap acutely and was eager to grow up and keep up with my brothers and sister. We grew up in

Rutherford, New Jersey, which is in Bergen County. Which is nine miles outside of New York City, and walking distance from Giants Stadium, now the New Meadowlands, which is in East Rutherford, an entirely different town. People who don't know the area cannot make the distinction, when they ask, "Where are you from?"

"Rutherford, New Jersey," I reply.

"Yeah, East Rutherford, I know exactly where that is," they say.

"No, just Rutherford, different town altogether," I say.

"Yeah, by the stadium, I know."

"Rutherford is a different town, East Rutherford isn't a description."

"I know exactly what you're talking about," they say.

"Yeah, but ..." I respond and give up.

It's as big a difference as East and West Germany. One was communist, and the other wasn't. Wait, which was which? I'm not sure, but that doesn't make it OK to get my anonymous hometown confused with an eastern bloc regime. I grew up in the shadows of the City and Giants Stadium. New York City was twenty minutes away without traffic on the 190 NJ Transit bus line or by car. When you grow up outside of the city, you have to hammer home how close it is. It takes the sting out of being from New Jersey.

I was brought home from the hospital on July 30th (sometime in the 70s) to 175 Mountain Way. My brothers were playing in the street as my folks brought me into the house. My sister might have been more interested in my arrival. I wonder if she was upset about losing her status as the baby of the family? I would have been. I like to imagine my siblings as three amigos who ruled the school and the neighborhood with a benevolent hand. That probably wasn't the case, but I had my vision.

As a very small child I would insist I remembered things that happened before I was born.

"I was there, too." I'd say.

"That was before you came." I was told.

"But, I was there ..."

That might be a recurring issue in my life, that desire to be part of something I could not be part of, either by the finite nature of time or by an impasse of age or impatience. I would say I had a happy childhood, but I always had this unnerving feeling that my timing wasn't right. How do you have brothers and a sister you don't really know so well? Where did they go? Don't siblings stay together in the same house? Why can't I go with them? What do you mean, I can't have a beer because I'm six?

Once the house was empty I did feel alone. It's where my toys became companions. I would lose myself in the stories I was creating with my toys. My mom would be in a different part of the house and would hear my sagas.

"What did you say, who are you talking to?" my mother would ask.

"Nothing, I'm playing, mom," I would say.

I'd be flustered at the interruption and embarrassed that I was so lost in a story that it sounded like someone else was in the house with me. I don't think I liked being a child. I never knew my siblings as children. I had friends my own age, but they weren't family. My siblings were teens by the time I knew who they were. I liked that. I could see wanting to be *that*. I liked all the activity in the house when they were around. They had friends and my sister had a boyfriend who was really nice to me. Can you imagine being a teenage girl with a little brother who wanted to go on your dates with you? Can you imagine being the dude? "Get this kid away from me, I want to make out, not baby sit." This guy was actually really cool and I remember going to see a movie with them and it was about as happy as a kid could get.

My brother, Steve, was a little more sullen and into his music. He had a cool girlfriend whom I never saw enough. He had the coolest stereo and wooden milk crates filled with records. Once in a while, I'd get to look at the album covers, but the stress of watching a kid mishandle his collection would shut that down pretty quick. Barry, the oldest, was busy getting straight A's and trying to build a steam engine in the basement—realizing soon that wood is not the best material with which to construct a piston.

The newspaper business is tough on a family. The hours are not nine to five. The paper's late-edition deadline is around 11pm or midnight. The Sports Department had to wait for late games to end. My dad would head into the city around two in the afternoon and would be home after midnight. During the week, I wouldn't see my father. It almost felt like being raised by a single mother. For most of his career, my dad's days off were Thursday and Friday. My siblings reminisce about Friday night family bowling outings. I remember having to sit in a different chair at dinner on my dad's days off.

It was important for my dad to make a priority of family time on the only weekend night he had off. When I was the last kid left, Friday nights would be just him and me and a movie. I would come home and recite the lines of the movie for my mom. It was our thing, and eventually we ran out of kid's movies to see, which didn't stop my dad's plan even if the movies might have been borderline appropriate for a child. It's not a very original realization, but it's probably the first time I thought that I might perform some time down the line and when a love for movies began.

11

LAUGHTER IN THE RAIN

Awhile back I was telling a friend a story about being on Nantucket with my parents and how it was just my folks and me—no siblings, no friends, just a twelve year old and some fifty year olds. I was about to explain how it was tough when my new friend stopped me and asked, "Did you just start to tell a sad story about being on Nantucket?"

"I guess, why?" I said.

"Oh, I don't know I didn't go on vacation as a kid, and Nantucket comes up in books about the most beautiful places on Earth." She said.

"Yeah, but I had no one to hang out with. We'd sit in cocktail lounges listening to a dude with a Casio keyboard sing Neil Sedaka songs; it was brutal."

The point was well made. Maybe everything in this story could be filed under, "You had it pretty good, what are you complaining about?" But, we all take meaning from early memories, good or bad. We had family friends, who were Nantucket natives, and we rented, and this was before the Gordon Geckos bought the place up. I haven't set foot on the island since I was thirteen, but I do have childhood memories of Nantucket. The dunes were so big that you could jump off the top and not fear a long fall to the bottom, just a soft landing every few feet as you hopped down to the beach like a kangaroo. It was my first exposure to the beach—the waves, the undertow, the incessant crabs nipping at your feet, which almost took the pleasure out of the water. I loved it there but developed an aversion to sand; I've often said I'd like the beach much better if it were carpeted.

I remember the fog at night so thick that it looked alive, the dark night drives back from town with my dad using his high beams to see better, and the etiquette of high beams that I learned as my dad clicked his way back to the house. I lived for hero sandwiches, which New Englanders call grinders, at a place called Henry's. It was the first stop after the two hour boat ride.

The boat ride was a good memory, but getting the trip underway was terrifying. The thing about a ferryboat that carries cars and trucks is those cars and trucks have to drive onto the boat. When a truck fires its engine, the noise would scare the hell out of me, and this would be followed by the sound of the boat's horn, which would jar my nerves and start me crying. I remember being embarrassed at my reaction, but I was powerless to stop it. Once on the boat with a deck of cards, I was fine. Landing on the island was magic, and I knew that a sandwich was minutes away.

One of the best memories I have from my childhood centers on the car trip to get to Nantucket. My father insisted on driving through the night to make the early boat. It must have been when I was six or seven years old, maybe earlier. I know this because my brothers and sister were all together. It was a family trip. We had a lime green station wagon that was as big as Delaware, and the back was packed with our luggage. I was wedged between my brothers in the back. We were six, so I think my sister was forced to sit in the middle in the front seat between my parents. These were the days of bench seats. It was three AM, and I was alert. We had a six-hour drive to Hyannis at the tip of

Cape Cod. I was thrilled, but everyone else was bracing for a long ride, packed in a car like clothes in a carry-on bag when you're trying to pack for a week instead of the prescribed three or four days. This was the last time in my childhood that I remember us traveling en masse. The feeling of the car moving and the cramped space was a comfort. I'm sure I was chipper and excitable while everybody else was grumpy and groggy.

There were a few stops along the way and maybe an argument or two that my memory hears as music. I felt lucky. Thinking about it now I feel like even at that moment, I was trying to savor the experience. I'm not sure if it's the sepia hue of memory or an actual feeling I recall. I was quite literally wrapped in the embrace of my family, and I never wanted to let go of it.

A lot of kids have a blanket. Many keep it for much of childhood. I held onto mine well into high school, not really, but I held onto it for a long time, long enough to feel shame about it and to closet my time spent with it. I'll leave it to the world of psychology to state the obvious: I had a habit, and I needed comfort. Other than a real need to be close to this filthy garment, I don't know what I got from it. There was theory bandied about that when my mother suffered a serious back injury and needed hospitalization for a month. I took to the blanket like a southern matriarch takes to bourbon in a Tennessee Williams play.

There is a vague memory I have of running to a neighbor's house to get help for my mom when she had a spell with her back. I think paramedics came, and I stayed with the Kiley's until my dad could get back home from the city. There wasn't a lot of talk about it, and in the interest of keeping it from meaning more than it does, I don't ask about it now. I don't have a burning need to have this memory corroborated. I'm fairly certain it's not made up. There must have been some trauma associated with having to get help for a parent, but it seems like I processed it quickly and turned to my blanket. I do remember brief conversations on the phone with my mom as she lay in traction—a torture device she strapped to for nineteen days. This may be what people would call a shaping experience. It might be a compartment that I have locked away.

The only people who have a real grasp of what your childhood was like are your parents. They know when you started crawling, then walking, what percentile you were size-wise, what your first word was. That's their job—to live your early years with you, every waking hour. They have to break the monotony by reading into how you reacted to events which you barely remember. That's the prism through which you see your childhood unless you are some freak spawn who can remember how much you hated the vegetable flavored baby food. Salvador Dali recounts memories of the womb in his autobiography between memories of specific farts and bowel movements.

People talk about early childhood memories and I wonder whom they're trying to impress—themselves or me? I suppose it becomes clearer when you start school, you can remember your first grade teacher. Mrs. Aldio was mine, and I thought she was pretty, and I had a crush on her. From there on you start to use your memory for what it is, storage of your life's events. That's when I think childhood starts its decline. So maybe you do get everything before the age of five without even knowing it. This reverses an early opinion. I do that a lot—change my mind about things I thought were important. I thought ELO was the greatest band of all time, but now I know Barry White occupies that space. I also thought I'd spend my life with every girl I messed with in high school, so you reserve the right to change your mind.

Grade school is where you begin to stack up with the rest of the world, and I was a shut down kid as far as I can remember. Some of the teachers were old enough and tenured enough to remember my brothers and sister. This was good and bad. I didn't know them that well, but I knew they were smart. I was feeling the pressure to keep up with their scholarly specters. One teacher was always using figures of speech, like "don't throw the baby out with the bath water." She always had me explain it for the class in my own words as if it were my job. I should have been flattered that she thought enough of my smarts to be sure I'd be able to translate, but it just wound up bugging me.

"Why don't you ask the kid picking his nose in the corner?" I would think to myself.

I was expressive with my own words, but wasn't a great reader when asked to read aloud. It might have been the early stages of perfectionism showing up. That's not a good thing. People interviewing for jobs say that they're perfectionists as if that would be an asset. It really is a way to ensure nothing will get done. I'd be worried about reading well. I knew the words, and I read well on my own, but I wanted to sound like a newscaster when I read, and if I miffed a word, it would start a domino effect. This would also be the early on-set of what I'll coin as frustration syndrome, or the De Gregorio effect. This is better than a perfectionist streak because if you fight through the frustration, you will learn to master the thing that flummoxes you. It's murder on the people close to you. They don't understand your process and just see you losing your shit over simple tasks and bellowing at inanimate objects. As you get older and goals slip by, frustration syndrome turns into dour monologue syndrome where you talk 'til four AM about what's wrong with your life. OK, now I'm starting to see how it does really start in childhood.

12

I SING THE BODY ELECTRIC

If there truly is a moment when you come out of your shell, it happened to me in fifth grade. How old are you in fifth grade? Maybe ten years old, that sounds young, but I think that's right.

Mrs. Beckenstaff was my fifth grade teacher and she was a gifted person. She made school something to look forward to, but there was another fifth grade teacher, Mrs. Fackerty, who was the short straw choice. I was lucky to be in the right class. This is when I found a passion for all the things that I still do today; unfortunately math and practical courses of study never took for me.

The moment where I knew I had turned a corner or shed my cocoon was a rather simple project that Mrs. Beckenstaff had assigned. The project was to create a motorcycle, draw it, and describe its features. The motorcycle was to then be sold to the police department. This was during the phenomenon of *Chips*, the TV show about motorcycle cops. I would have killed to meet Erik Estrada, and the idea of drawing a motorcycle for school almost seemed like a trick. Nothing offered by a public school in New Jersey could be fun, inspiring, and worth a grade. Could it?

It's the first time I went to work on my homework with any intensity. My motorcycle would run on air. It had a refrigerator on the back for soft drinks, and it had a cool helmet. The artwork was pedestrian, but it was fun work. The real purpose of the assignment was to combine all these elements and culminate the effort with a presentation for the class. The class was to play the role of the police department. They would decide which motorcycle to buy. I wasn't the first one to present, and I barely remember anyone else's presentation except my friend Ronny had a couch for a seat. He wasn't big on spatial relations, and his idea of police work entailed a lot of reclining. Other students could draw better, and their designs might have had some basis in the reality of mechanics, but they didn't sell their motorcycles.

It was my time to present my sales pitch to the class. I stood before them and held up my picture and described the motorcycle and its features.

"This motorcycle was once owned by a little old lady from Pasadena." I opened.

It made no sense as far as a sales feature, but it got a laugh. This was a common phrase you heard on TV, and it just sounded like a good thing to say. My confidence was starting to bubble, and I was telling the class why they had to have my motorcycle. After the initial presentation the class had to ask questions, and this is where things really took off for me.

"Does your motorcycle have a kick stand?" a classmate asked.

"Does it have a kick stand? Does a devil have horns?" I said.

The class laughed at my improvisation and I was looking for new ways to boast about my invention. The class erupted in applause as much as 30 fifth graders can erupt into anything. I sat at my desk feeling as good about myself as I ever had. There were a few other presentations, and all in all, it took a couple of days. A vote followed to see whose motorcycle the class/police department had chosen to purchase. It was the first time I was sure of a positive result. All but one of my classmates voted for my motorcycle. Like I said, my drawing wasn't the best, and my ideas weren't the best, but my sales pitch and presentation were the best by far.

My father told me a few years later when I ran for president of the eighth grade that I should vote for myself because if you didn't think you deserved your own vote, how could you convince anyone else to vote for you? I won the election, but by his logic, the motorcycle vote should have been a 30-way tie. I had super-ceded people's instinct for self-interest. My path from that day on was set in a new direction for better or worse.

Do other people have that feeling of coming from nowhere to somewhere? I literally felt like I was parting a curtain and walking into a new room, a room that wasn't as cold and cramped as the one I left behind. It's not an original observation that teachers can save lives or at least change lives. I didn't need saving I was fairly normal if a little shut down, but I didn't have disabilities, I just needed to break through this film that surrounded me like the albumen of an egg. Mrs. Beckenstaff had a way to make you feel special without showing favoritism. I spent time hanging around the classroom after school, because I wanted more time with this special teacher. Other kids did too. It wasn't a constant love fest. When I showed frustration with certain tasks and handled it poorly or pouted, Mrs. Beckenstaff would quickly tell me to cut it out. It was when I realized that pouting is not attractive, which is a good lesson to learn before your dating life begins. I'm not always able to keep the pouting at bay, but I try thanks to Mrs. Beckenstaff.

It was during this year of my burgeoning confidence and awakening that I first had a noticeable fear of losing a parent. It wasn't that stomachache of insecurity that all kids feel, but it was something I discovered being nosy.

Being a family of readers, our kitchen table was covered with multiple newspapers and magazines and of course books. I got in trouble for squirreling away the *Sports Illustrated* Swimsuit Issue, "What?

It comes every week. There's a story about Tony Dorsett." I said in meager defense.

I noticed a hard back book with the cover turned inside out under a pile of papers and took no time in flipping it around to see what was up. It was a book about how to manage diabetes. I knew a girl in grade school who had it and how she had to take insulin, but that seemed like something else, like a childhood disease that made the girl seem different, like Leukemia or something that scared the shit out of everybody. What did this have to do with us? In what I'm sure was an overdramatic gesture, I dropped the book (with the cover now righted) on the table and asked what this was about.

My dad had developed adult on-set diabetes, which his father had, and they didn't want to worry me. I was upset that they thought I couldn't handle the news, that they were treating me like a baby, but I was also worried about what it might mean for my dad. I was assured it wasn't fatal, that it could be managed with diet and all would be OK. I don't know how they brought it up with my siblings or if they even mentioned it. I was actually very angry about it all. I was a kid, and I had no one to talk to, like a wife or a drinking buddy. I knew I was being sheltered, and I didn't like it. I felt alone. My parents were keeping secrets. I suppose all parents do, and all kids react poorly when they find out they were lied to—I was no different. It seemed to me that just as things were starting to look good, there was something to balance the ledger. I may be gleaning too much from this incident and how it impacted me down the line. The other shoe was about to drop has been a pervasive thought for me ever since, but that could be a by-product of being from New Jersey—if pessimism where a living thing, it would be the state bird.

13

BORN TO RUN

I like dance music, specifically a type of dance music called free-style. This must be a closeted interest because in high school it was the heartbeat of the Guido culture. It's actually a Latin style started out of New York and Miami and it was actually the original beat to break-dancing. It is the musical equivalent of polyester. The music is made with synthesizers and drum machines. The vocals are often reed thin and monotonous, and the lyrics would have you think it's a simple task to party one's body, but it speaks to me. Stevie B. is the artist who made the classic track "Party Your Body," and it is in heavy rotation on my iPod to this day. When you start to come into your own, and let the influence of what you react to organically replace what your brother thinks is cool, you find yourself turning away from music snob tendencies and rock out to whatever gets you going. This got me going or the poetry of Lisa Lisa.

This is when I learned you could enjoy atonal Springsteen demos *and* dance music. I hid Madonna's first album in a more secure place than my pornography. What I think it also signified was an attempt to keep my mood positive. As I fought through a depressive nature, it dawned on me that you choose the soundtrack of your life, and once in a while, a mindless track that got you moving was something I needed more.

I balanced out my taste in dance music with heavy stuff like The Clash. They were writing real lyrics about civil unrest in tough neighborhoods in England that I knew nothing about.

After my two summers away from my hometown, I really thought I was hot shit and my impatience with high school was at an all time high. The one through line in all the training I had with acting was discipline and work ethic were important; I was starting to pull away the lazy skin that covered my academic onion. I found myself knocking out my homework at my desk, and I started getting organized. The problem was my new attitude toward my studies came too late. I needed the three previous years on my transcripts to be as good as that first semester of my senior year. I had a bunch of colleges in mind, but no guarantee I'd be accepted. My mind would drift to the still photo of the back window of our old car, college decals from good schools taunting my mediocre G.P.A. I had a real panic that I'd have to go to community college and try to transfer into a decent school. My worries were also compounded by my confusion as to what course of study to take. Was I going all in as an actor or was I going to study liberal arts and dabble?

My work habits improved, but my dissatisfaction with the social aspects of high school were dragging me down. I hit the road almost every weekend to visit people from the Governor's School. I especially looked forward to seeing Tori because it usually meant a chance for sex. Back in Rutherford, we were lucky that Jimmy Carver's mother had a boyfriend who lived in south Jersey, which gave us an empty house to party in almost every weekend. Jimmy also worked at a video store, so we had free movies and he had a creepy twenty-something boss who bought us beer and let us drink in the store's back office. Every Friday we would fill all the sinks in Jimmy's house with ice and cool the beers.

Years later, his mother was cleaning out the eaves in the attic. Jimmy's room was on the third floor. She was astounded at the volume of cans and bottles she pulled out of the rafters. As I matured and grew to a legal age to drink, it never occurred to me to pay that favor forward. I can't imagine hooking up a teenager with beer. While we owe that guy a debt of gratitude for making our high school partying easier, it's never crossed my mind to do the same. I just had a kid ask me to buy him cigarettes the other day and I told him "no way" with a haughty attitude and plenty of judgment. What an ingrate I am.

This book of admissions continues as we approach the first campus visit that my father and I made. Northwestern is outside of Chicago and was one of the places that I really wanted to go. My chances were slim, and considering it was two plane tickets away, it was mighty kind of my folks to consider the trip worth it. I was breaking in a pair of penny loafers and shredded my feet on the way to the car back in New Jersey. I wish I remembered more about the trip with my father.

The campus was great, but it was cold and my feet were bleeding. I had an interview with someone in the admissions office, and I thought that a good showing there would weigh more heavily than my grades. I'm sure I was pontificating and talking shit. The lady was nice and told me there was no audition to get into the drama program. The degree would be a Bachelor of Science in Speech; grades and scores were the predominant means of acceptance. It would be a reach. We came out of her office, and she told my dad that I was an articulate young man, which was probably code for "he should have talked less and studied more."

My dad and I spent a night in Chicago and wound up seeing a movie written and directed by Chicagoan David Mamet. It was called *House of Games*, and it was a double cross crime flick with the patented, halting, and profane language that you would expect from Mamet. I came home with a purple hoodie and more worry than before. I still had NYU and Carnegie Mellon to go, and I was avoiding a visit to Rutgers because then I'd have to eat the words I wrote in my yearbook blurb—staying in state after quoting "Thunder Road" seemed like more than I could bear. As if going away to college was some grand gesture of independence, I was full of pretense and self-narrative, but seriously, I had to get out of New Jersey, I'd go into the Merchant Marines if I had to.

Digging through a box in my folk's garage, I found a bunch of my journals. Men have to call their diaries "journals," even if they don't have key locks on them, and they're written in tattered spiral notebooks. You just don't call it a diary if you're a guy unless you're a 70-year-old head of state, and even then, maybe you shouldn't. I say this not to preface me transcribing many pages of my seventeen-year-old self into this text, although I might, but to recount part of that trip as it came up in that time and space. It's in dialogue form and that only makes it a little better, but it's a recounting of the cab ride back to the airport after our trip. The cabby's name was Calvin Johnson, and he and my dad were having a great conversation. He said that he was a lawyer trying to avoid debt by driving a cab, that he had a son who was an actor, and that he was once a boxer. They talked about Joe Louis and lesser-known fighters that they both remembered.

December 10, 1988:

DAD: We're going to O'Hare – United. (pause) Is this the main drag into the city?

CABBIE: Well, you could take Rolliver on the south end, but I like to take this route.

DAD: I'm not from this area, myself.

CABBIE: That right – where you from?

DAD: New York area, actually New Jersey – I work in the City.

CABBIE: That's what they need out here, a tunnel or a causeway or something.

DAD: It takes a lot to get that done.

CABBIE: They put a bridge across San Francisco Bay, didn't they?

DAD: Yeah, marvelous thing. Great world we live in. Where you from?

CABBIE: I was born in Iowa.

That's where the dialogue stops, I wrote that I would finish it later—I wish I had. I also wrote that it was "really something and that if you study life you'll find the most amazing things." This might be an odd recollection, but it really has to do with my dad and how he would always look for ways to connect with people. Sometimes he'd force me to connect with people and it would embarrass me.

On our way to Pittsburgh, we were going to do a round trip in one day. Carnegie Mellon is closer than Northwestern, and in an effort for me not to miss school and my father not to miss work, we jet-setted our way to Pittsburgh. The weather was bleak and those penny loafers were still killing me. I was wearing grey slacks, a blue blazer, and a yellow power tie. I looked like a young Republican. We had a tour of the campus and met a woman in admissions, and I went into my routine. She told me what she knew about the program and that auditions would be a big part of the admissions process. Grades were important, but the professors at the auditions would be essentially trying to build a company with the actors whom they would be seeing across the country. I was pumped about having that opportunity.

My father and I went to grab something to eat, in a campus eatery, and he pushed me to try to ask some of the students some questions about the school. We had learned that drama students were called "dramats" at CMU. My dad badgered me to approach a table of what were clearly drama students; they were dressed a bit more fashionably than the other students and were more animated. I approached the table looking like a Michael J. Fox on *Family Ties*.

"Excuse me, are you guys dramats?" I asked.

"Yeah." A scruffy guy replied.

"I was wondering if I could ask you about the program?"

"It's hard. It's twelve hours a day. That's before you have to rehearse or do crew, and then you have your academics." A girl said.

"What about social life?" I asked.

"There is no social life. It's all about work." A stunning black woman said.

"Well, thanks for talking to me, I'll see you next year." I said, and skulked back to the table with my dad.

"What'd you find out?" he asked.

This is before the advent of being able to tell someone to "talk to the hand" but that was the gist of my reaction; I was mortified. That had not gone well. I looked like I was working for Joseph McCarthy and was trying to find commies on campus. The students barely held back their disdain, and they made it sound like it was voluntary torture to go to school at CMU. What happened to reading a brochure? It wasn't my dad's fault. I'm the one who said, "I'll see you next year," before I had even put a stamp on an envelope. Those kids seemed so much more mature than regular college kids. They looked like men and women; they had scarves. All I was missing was an "I Like Ike" pin.

We got on the plane and made it back to the house and I jumped out of my clothes and put on some torn jeans and a concert tee. The next few months were spent digging through pages of applications and trying to make myself look better on paper. We also had to schedule auditions and thankfully that was easy being so close to New York.

This is where you get to use the benefit of hindsight. When a child shows a desire for a life in the arts, you need to think long and hard about allowing that to happen. This is not to say I regret being supported and indulged. Ultimately you wind up doing what you want with your life even if your parents disagree, which my parents didn't. I'm also not saying I wish someone had stepped in and saved me from myself and insisted that I major in business and act on the side.

Showing early promise in theatre or acting might be a bit of a misinterpreted early discovery. When you are verbal and bright, and when you read well and understand a bit about how to use your voice, you will be ahead of average teenagers who'd rather carve into their own arms than talk and learn lines and do anything that would make them feel self-conscious. Most kids operate on the "leave me alone" mode of expression. Young actors want to be noticed. I wanted attention, and I was smart. I took the study of acting seriously. When I got further along, I found the confidence, and the study skills made me a better student, a better athlete. All this was good. What I've found out since is that intellectual curiosity is not a common trait shared by all actors or people for that matter. It took all my study in acting to open up my mind, and I would have been able to apply that to anything. I was seduced by the instant gratification and the status that being on stage gave me at an early age. The fact that I was radicalized didn't mean I only had one way to go. My mother told me that she voiced concern to her mother about what I had chosen as a path. My grandmother said, "He didn't choose it, it chose him." She was a soulful, tough woman, and I'm sure that allayed some of my mother's fears.

I've joked before that having a junky in the family is similar to having an actor in the family. With a junky, they always promise that this is the "last time." With an actor it's always "this one is the one." The callback is the relapse. You ask for money for headshots not heroin. The only major difference is that the family doesn't lose appliances and electronic equipment in their support of an actor. There is, however, a shared heartbreak when things don't work out. But, this is the upside part of the story. All I mean to say is be as sure as you can be, and be ready to work harder than you thought you'd have to work. If any of that sounds good, go for it. You can always change course. That's what I keep telling myself, anyway.

14

THOU NATURE, ART MY GODDESS

Until I made these discoveries, I was determined to get into Carnegie Mellon where I thought I had a fighting chance. Preparing monologues was the most pressing thing for me. Monologues can be the bane of an actor's early life. You have to find two contrasting monologues, one dramatic, one comedic, unless one has to be Shakespeare. There is nothing more difficult than trying to encapsulate your entire being into three minutes of words that you didn't write. It means you have to comb shelves of plays; you might have to edit lines together. You have to find obscure plays because everyone does the same thing. The comedic ones are really hard because you think it should get laughs when all it really needs to be is lighter than the other. You're also seventeen years old, and there are not a lot of plays about seventeen year olds, so you wind up doing a speech by Abraham Lincoln. You can't blow it off and risk writing one of your own although that's probably the best idea. You have to show savvy and cast yourself appropriately. You could use something from a movie, but that looks lazy. It's the only thing you have control over, and it seems so hard. I still know the monologues that I worked on twenty years ago. If anyone needed me to do one, I could stop on a dime and bust one out; I might even be able to pull off some verse. All this gets me barely employed and annoyed with myself.

I was lucky my senior year of high school because my schedule after lunch was too good to be true. I had Theatre, Speech III, and an eighth period study hall, which meant I could leave school early. Most of the time I would hang out in the halls flaunting my freedom to my friends. A buddy of mine let me practice my driving in his Plymouth Volaré. The upshot of this schedule was that I could try out monologues with all this rehearsal time. Most students stuck to the bare minimum, but I was up almost every day doing something new.

My other asset in preparing for auditions was Pete and Curtis who worked in the theatre and could suggest some more serious stuff that I wanted to present.

There was a competition that was based out of Miami where you had to send in a video of those dreaded contrasting monologues. It was a good chance to have a dress rehearsal and a high stakes run-through before the CMU audition. If they liked it, you'd get a free trip to Miami. A teacher helped me shoot it with a borrowed videotape recorder. I ran through the pieces, one from *King Lear* and one from *Buried Child* by Sam Shepard. These were on the edge of over-used, but I was really tuned into the material. My friend Alicia from Governor's School was also sending a tape, and we watched them at her house. It's no surprise that I don't remember her pieces. Self-involvement develops early. We cued up my tape, and my first monologue was my Shakespearean piece. It was the famous bastard speech by Edmund in *King Lear*. My dad always liked the way I said the final line:

"*Now God's stand up for bastards.*"

The tape was wobbly, at first, and my head was cut off. We watched and waited for my head to come into frame, and it never fucking happened. The second piece had me sitting, so my whole body made the frame. If I weren't at someone else's house, furniture would have been thrown across the room. Instead, I fumed, as stifled laughter excused itself to other parts of the house with the laughing out of my immediate earshot. It could not be worse. We were watching copies. The originals were already in the mail on their way to Miami before the deadline. I'm sure my rants are still being talked about.

"Fuckin' New Jersey does it again, these motherfuckers, I can't wait to get the fuck out of here." I cursed.

Months later, I went through the mail and found out that I received an honorable mention in the National Endowment for the Advancement of the Arts nationwide competition. There was a brochure with all the names and pictures of kids partying in Miami. I had something else to put on my transcript, but I was pissed. Maybe if my fucking head was in the fucking shot, I would have been getting my "drama on" in sunny South Florida. This is where you have a choice to see things *half empty* or *half full* and this is also where you see the meaning in *honorable mention*. I was an *alternate* for student senate and that didn't include a trip to Washington D.C. either. These mild disappointments should have helped inure me to the times to come. Maybe I was too good at taking lumps at an early age. This is a bit of self-analysis that won't cost me the ninety bucks an hour.

February 12, 1988, was a Friday and it was a slushy, windy, crappy winter day. My dad and I *both* wore galoshes. Normally, I would wear work boots and jeans, but this day I was auditioning for Carnegie Mellon University, and boots weren't part of my outfit. I donned the oft-mocked shoe condoms my dad would wear as he braved the elements on his way to the *New York Times* everyday. Those penny loafers were starting to loosen up and I could walk without a limp. The convenience of living close to the bus route was lost as freezing rain came down on us, and we waited uncovered from the elements. My nerves did not arrive as we boarded the bus; I was shaking off the snow and worried about my hair.

We were headed to the Minskoff Studios which were well known to people of the theatre but seemed off limits to passers-by. The studios were near the Marriott Marquis Hotel, in Times Square, and were walking distance from Port Authority (although nothing is walk-able in that kind of weather). Entering the door and not being turned away was a thrill. This is where Broadway productions rehearsed, and I was treading along the same floors. We were wrangled into a waiting area where a professor from the university spoke and assured us that CMU was boot camp for the actor and that the odds of getting in were not great. He showed a video with several well-known alumni and took some questions. This is where the nerves started kicking in; kids were stretching and warming up. They were in dance clothes, and some were mouthing their monologues, which is the worst habit of many bad habits some actors exhibit.

My dad tried to keep me loose, and I'm sure I waved off his efforts, even though I needed his calming presence. I suppose I could have gone alone; I was a seasoned traveler to the city, but it was neither discussed nor thought of as an option. Even in the midst of your excruciatingly self-conscious teen years, there are moments when both parent and child agree that this is something that we do together. My father was a writer and an English major so he knew his way around Shakespeare and many playwrights. He had a latent desire to perform and certainly showed the ability to hold the center of attention. He often talked about working as a character actor when he retired, and while my fear was seeing my dad develop a career before I did, it was a shared interest without the stage-father or mother trappings.

We were going to be serious—and this school seemed as serious as cell therapy. Some of my Governor's School friends were turned off by the workload before they even applied. Some of the rhetoric coming from faculty members was almost discouraging. It had to do with rooting out the casual student, the talent show crowd. They wanted it to be clear that this was going to be a challenge and that hard work was the only guarantee. It made me think of Debbie Allen's speech in *Fame*, in which she tells her students that their dreams came with dues that had to be paid in sweat.

Of course, I had to bury that reference because it wasn't serious enough. There was an option to audition in the musical theatre track, and although much of my experience was in musicals I passed up that option thinking it was not the serious choice. Also, you would have to subject yourself to a dance audition, and while I was one of the few dudes in high school who would venture onto the dance floor, I didn't think my love of Lisa Lisa and the Cult Jam would carry me over the hurdle.

We waited in the bullpen and saw kids come and go. Some looked shell-shocked upon their return; others were beaming as if they knew something that we didn't. A few kids came out in tears as if they had botched the audition badly enough to secure a negative outcome. My name was called, and my dad shook my hand and told me to, "go get 'em." I walked down a long corridor with wide plank wood floors and noticed how enormous the doors were. My escort opened one of those behemoths after we winded down several hallways, and there was a large studio that may have once housed some famous cast.

The woman at the desk was an elegant English woman. I introduced myself and went into my material. We spoke a bit, and she said she wanted me to audition for another professor. I waited outside another room and tried to listen to the person auditioning through the door. I was kind of skipping the line because I was going to meet another person; this would account for a longer wait back in the bullpen. In the future, you realize that waiting means someone else is kicking ass in their session. I remember wanting to tell my dad that I was getting another crack at it, and that had to be a good sign, but I didn't want to move from my post.

There was a rugged looking man at the front of this next room. He introduced himself and asked me what I had prepared. I told him I had Edmund from *King Lear* and something from *Buried Child*. I did not try to loosen up the mood with a joke this time. This was serious. I ran through both of the pieces and felt a wave of adrenaline course through me. I really belted out the last line of my Shakespearean piece.

My dad told me later that he snuck down the hall and heard me bellow the big finish. The auditor said, "Good audition, that was a good audition." I knew that much, so I didn't take much from it. He then had me try one of the pieces while pulling a bucket from a well. Not actually, but in the space like air guitar, I can't bring myself to say that he had me pantomime pulling water out of a well because I don't say mime in any context if I can avoid it. I had had enough training thus far to know that he was trying to see how adaptable I was and how the activity would change the monologue. He also may have been some kind of mime sadist who just wanted to put actors through odd, but chaste, motions. He then said he wanted me to meet someone else.

The next meeting was with a school administrator; he might have been the Ombudsman. He asked me if I had some idea of how I might pay for school. I don't remember if my father was with me. The school representative told me not to read into the fact that we were talking, but what was I supposed to think? You don't have to time travel to *American Idol* to know my audition went well. Still, I kept the feeling of assurance at bay and thanked the man for his time. Of course, my father was reading into the whole thing as we made our way out of the city.

As we made our way out of the studio, I noticed that a few of the other schools, with ranked departments, were also holding auditions. I tensed as if maybe I didn't cover all my bases as far as auditioning for other programs. I returned to the high school for the second half of the day and retold the events to Mrs. Becker, my theatre teacher. There was both a sense of excitement and disbelief as I replayed what was a positive day. People intend to support you, but sometimes when you reach for something, they tend to temper their enthusiasm in an effort to hold you up if you fail. My hopes were high.

15

THE WEIGHT

It's a very subtle form of torture, waiting for news that you think houses the key to your future. Trying to recall the order of things, I think I received my rejection from Northwestern earlier than any other news. By that time, I had re-established my first choice, both as a true desire and as a way to save face in the event the Wildcats didn't come through for me. This did, however, ratchet-up the stress of waiting for mail from Pittsburgh. My fall back school was Rutgers, and I still had an audition scheduled. I was getting a bit nervous.

There was a mix-up that my mother noticed. Southern Methodist University had held its auditions at the same time and at the same place as CMU. I had missed it. I was only slightly interested in going to Texas and hadn't read the application carefully. Like Carnegie Mellon, SMU held auditions in several major cities to accommodate a national pool of applicants. I called the school and could have caught up with the caravan in Dallas, but that was not an option financially as the application fees were piling up. My mother, the genius, told me to mention the honorable mention in Miami and see if that tape could suffice as an audition. The head of the department agreed to take a look. I was mortified that I had to use the headless actor tape to secure a shot at what I thought of as a fall back school, and now my options were dwindling, and all hopes were fixated on my first choice. I also didn't want anyone to see it. I can't imagine trying to live down a sex tape.

The standard wisdom when deciphering mail before it's opened, in regards to college acceptance, is that a thin envelope is a "no," and a thick envelope, filled with brochures, is a "yes." The day a letter arrived from Carnegie Mellon, it was thin. It was just the paper and the envelope. It appeared to be a "no," but I had rocked it at the Minskoff Studios. The dude told me not to read into meeting three different people, but come on—they practically begged me to come to the school. What was with this thin fucking envelope? I rocked it. How could it be a "no"? I was never an early riser, so the mail was on the kitchen table for a few hours before I approached the stack. My poor parents should have poured a glass of cold water on me to wake me up, or at least steamed open the letter. I was left to myself as I approached the pile of mail on the cluttered kitchen table. This was movie of the week territory. My folks were on the other side of the wall listening to the tear of the paper. If they were cast, they would have been over-acting in the dinning room—close-ups of their anticipation.

I used a wooden letter opener that my sister brought back from Peru and sliced a clean line through the seam. I pulled out the paper and took the nanosecond to read the letterhead. Mercifully, the first word was congratulations.

"Yes!" I shouted.

My parents came into the kitchen, and we had a moment. It's funny that they were so happy about the news; the financial burden they were about to assume would be crippling although I'd never hear about it. It felt like a start. It felt like breaking through. It felt like I was about to step into life and that I wouldn't wind up on the scrap heap. I would put a good sticker on the window of my parent's car. I wouldn't be a fuck-up. There are, hopefully, several moments like this in life, but not a ton, and they feel good. I've had some since and hope to have more, but just in case, you savor what you can and write about it. I thank whatever power above for this one and try not to feel too put upon when things go south. That's not true. I get low often and need to climb out of deep ravines, but I do try. That I shared that moment with my folks is something for which I will always be grateful.

Mail of a proper weight and thickness started to arrive. There were decisions to make and an accepted students' weekend to sign-up for. My parents were pouring over the fees and the loan applications. During this number crunching and, I'm sure, hand wringing and temple rubbing, I also received a call from the guy at SMU. He wanted to accept me based on the tape. That negative turned positive as he also offered some scholarship money. He also said he heard a slight lisp in my speech that would need correcting, and I almost went to school in Dallas just to confront him. I'd never heard this lisp-talk again. It was maybe his way of knocking me down a peg since he accepted me off a tape with a missing head and such bad audio that it sounded lispy. Years later, I thought about how I would have faired at SMU, which is a bastion of southern gentility. I would have been an exotic bird, the Italian-American from New Jersey, wreaking havoc on the southern debutants.

My mother found some small print in the Carnegie Mellon paperwork that said the school would match another school's offer of money. I eventually told the guy thank you, but no thank you, and I even withdrew my audition at Rutgers. I would be able to live up to the Springsteen quote in the yearbook at least for four years. I should also thank that guy for helping me get money out of CMU.

There are few times in your life where you orbit in a sweet holding pattern, when you are in between a transition and the happy anticipation actually puts a lift in your step. That's the time I had left at school with my good news in my pocket.

I became obnoxious with my constant reminding people of the

alumni from Carnegie Mellon. Holly Hunter was making a big splash in *Broadcast News* and my brother took me into the city to see it at the Ziegfeld on 54th Street. Turns out Albert Brooks went there too (real name Albert Einstein). Ted Danson, another alumnus, was at the top of the television ratings on *Cheers*. It was a time when CMU was number one in a lot of the rankings, and I got in. You almost couldn't turn on the TV without a CMU graduate being involved. My choir teacher, Mr. Garibaldi, stopped a performance to let the audience know that one of his students had been accepted to a very select program. It was overkill considering a classmate and friend was accepted at West Point, but I didn't mind the plug.

I had a job as a gate guard at a pool that summer, and my sister left me her Mustang to use since she was out of the country. I was itchy to get out of New Jersey, but there was a little room to have some fun. It was the last time I had a tan and the last time I was debt free. I'm a worrier by nature, so I can't cop to being care free, but I was on an even keel, and that's been a challenge for me ever since.

With Jimmy Carver's boss and beer connection at the ready, my crew and I had to prepare for graduation night. We pooled our funds and might have splurged on Lowenbrau or Molson Golden, something classy. We also procured some wine coolers for the ladies. We filled the trunk of our buddy's car with all manner of alcoholic beverages, and ice, and hit the town. I'm not advising this, but just telling you how we went about it.

There were a couple of parties to hit and of course drinking on the bleachers of a local baseball diamond at the end of the night. That's one thing coming of age movies get right young men like to drink in public parks. Older gay men like to congregate in public parks too, but this is something different. It's just that when you're drinking with the boys, it's fun to throw cans on the diamond, and the bleachers give you some levels to work with. You also get to practice your batting stance in an effort to avoid real emotion and real conversation. I remember that a couple of unlikely suspects were with us and a buddy drunkenly telling everyone I was the next Tom Hanks.

That night, a friend from another high school, who was prodigiously funny, cornered me and rambled about how he wanted to do what I was setting out to do. His parents thought he would get in less trouble at a Catholic school a few towns over. It turned out that he got into more trouble and barely graduated. It was at a party at Laura Petruccio's. We pulled up with our four-wheeled cooler and popped the trunk. People came out and gawked at the trunk 'o beer. It was a good party. It was the officially sanctioned party after graduation, like the *Vanity Fair* party after the Oscar's, minus the stature, beauty, money, or anyone giving a shit.

Tim Ritchey was drunk and I was on my way, and he kept asking me for help. He wanted to act, and he didn't know where to start. I didn't know what to tell him. Had he gone to the public school and kept his shit together, he would have been a shoe-in for class clown. In grade school, he did voices and was fearless. He was more than merely extroverted and attention-starved. He was funny, a natural. We both got to sing at Lincoln Center in an opera and had that bond from childhood. He just got caught up with drugs and a dirt bag crowd. I felt bad, and I wish I had something to tell him. I kept telling him that he could do anything that he wanted; I tried to encourage him. There was desperation in his voice – he was almost begging me for answers. It felt like I was talking to a fifty year old. It made me sad that he felt his time was already up.

Our time was up as a group. It floored me and came out of nowhere when I hung out with Jimmy Carver and the guys the night before I left for school. I knew I would see them again, but I realized our childhood was over. It seems like a luxury to think of your childhood lasting 'til seventeen. I'm still in adolescence as it stands, (so much for developing at a normal rate). I have my parents to thank for keeping me in that bubble so long, not that the hallowed grounds of college was really jumping into the real world. That came later.

16

A REAL KICK IN THE DICK

pril 2010: What do you do when you get devastating news? Does anyone take a jog or go to the gym? Do you hit the heavy bag in your basement? Do you go to your local church and pray? I am sure certain people handle bad news in some productive way. But, that's not what I did when I got off the phone with my sister and then my brother, the doctor, who looked at the imaging of my father's MRI and saw the bad news. I was lucky to be able to fall into my girlfriend's arms and sob. I made hazy calls home and made the insipid comments about beating this thing and beating the odds. My girlfriend asked me what I felt like doing, and at first I said, "Let's go to the beach. I want to be near the water."

My girlfriend and I got in her car and headed west to the beach, which is fourteen blocks away from my studio apartment in Santa Monica, California. Sometimes you behave like you have a judgmental audience watching you. Your better nature says, "Go to the beach and shed a tear at sunset." That was my first instinct, which wasn't instinctual at all. I wanted credit for reacting in a meaningful way, and

I didn't want to be a cliché.

Of course, I wound up at a bar a block from the beach and got drunk, not the most mature way to deal with it and by no means original. It is what I did. A few friends arrived to comfort me. I was on the phone for much of the time, and as the sun set outside the walls of the Irish pub, I felt farther from home than I ever had.

My father had a cancerous tumor in his gall bladder, and it spread to his liver. The prognosis had him living four to six months. He could choose chemotherapy, and in the short term, it would abate the march of the cancer, but we were not talking cure. That's when the clock started, and when I found some reserve strength, which I didn't know I had. This is not to say I was anything but a slobbering mess for most of the time. It just meant that I had been living in fear of my parents' mortality since I can remember, and I truly felt I would crumble under the strain. Now, I had a quantifiable timeline, and I didn't know if I could get through it. I wasn't particularly happy in my own life, and this only compounded the feelings of inadequacy that I was trying to repress.

My brothers and sister were able to mobilize faster than I could, based on geography and finances. I was trying to figure out what the fuck to do. I knew I needed to get home. I didn't want to play the guessing game of how long my father would survive and how I would afford multiple trips home and covering my job in LA. It made me feel weak and angry. I had been in Los Angeles for ten years and was now wondering what the hell I was doing. If I had stayed in New York, I would be twenty minutes away. I could live my life and still be there for my family. That wasn't an option, and it didn't serve any purpose to think that way.

I had held onto an apartment in Manhattan for eight years and had finally been caught by the management company for illegally subletting it. I was feeling that loss acutely, considering I no longer had the option of moving back and re-inhabiting my New York home. It felt like a vise or that trash compactor thing in *Star Wars* the walls, floor, and ceiling converging to crush me. I didn't have a plan to move back to New York, but when you're looking for something else to think about other than your father's illness and your own life, you grasp at scenarios to distract you.

I thought about chucking everything and heading home for as long as it took. That didn't take much hold when I thought it through. It was grandstanding; as meager a life as I had cobbled together in LA, I wasn't going to blow it up. Do other people feel guilty for leaving to another coast? I guess it makes sense if you have a family or a practice, but what was I doing other than preferring the weather and being three thousand miles away?

At my weekly comedy show in Santa Monica, I would corner a friend and work him over with my woes. People were patient. Eventually, I worked out two weeks to be home and help my mom and dad. A generous friend threw me some frequent flyer miles to get me home, which revealed my true age and ongoing lie. I hadn't been home for two weeks for almost twenty years.

17

THE YANKEE CLIPPER

Thankfully, my brother, the doctor, was already home and could ease me into what my responsibilities would be. In a harrowing scene, the week before my arrival, my dad headed up the stairs to bed and found out midway that he wasn't going to make it. His mobility had been dwindling over the years as spinal stenosis continued its march. Now fighting cancer and chemotherapy, he couldn't power his way any longer. My sister, and brother from Florida were on the scene, and my brother had to carry my two hundred pound father the rest of the way up and get him to bed. My brother has that supernatural strength that comes from some place other than the gym. He carried me up the stairs when I blew my knee out playing in the street, when I was thirteen. I've been told that my grandfather, on my mother's side, was a physical specimen, and maybe my brother got it from him. Thank God he did.

When I mention I found an inner strength, I never had it tested to the degree to which my brother's and sister's were. There was palpable heartbreak; a moment when my father knew that he would not see his marriage bed again, when he could feel the lens narrowing. It makes me emotional at this very moment, and I wasn't even there. I suppose that's what true love is, when you hurt for someone else, when empathy and breathing combine. The moment I heard the story of the stairs, I felt the pangs of devastation that must have coursed through my family members on the scene. I also ached for my father who must have felt like a frightened child as he found himself stuck between floors.

The next day the decision was made to get a hospital bed and set up an area in the dining room. My father would not make it up the stairs again. His favorite chair was brought downstairs to the side of his bed. This is what preceded my arrival. All the doctor's even toned delivery of bad news, all the x-rays or charts, and all of the grief settling in.

Part of my egomania derives from my birth order and the gap of time between my siblings. While a lot of heavy lifting had been done before my arrival, it wasn't an officially handled crisis until I got home. I'm not saying I brought any extra comfort or skill set, but it's just that when you bring up the rear, your entrance is noticed. Part of being the youngest was also evident—I was the baby—and I was not sure I could handle this. And by now, we know that ego doesn't always equal confidence.

I was worried about messing up. I was also stressed out to be the only sibling on the scene. I was also stressing out about the fact that my nocturnal existence was about to be flipped in a different time zone, and now I would have to handle this responsibility without sleep.

What made this ordeal difficult was that we are not a direct communicating family. While we knew what was before us, we weren't talking about it. It wasn't our way. It may be a group denial mechanism or just a way of bracing for the fall. I never heard the phrase "stage four" or any other specifics. My brother was keeping us aware of the ramifications, but we weren't talking. I would step outside, on the back porch, to talk to my girlfriend, Sadie. I was strung out emotionally, and I would pour my woe into the phone.

"I don't know if I can do this."

"You're doing it." She said.

"I don't know what I'll do if something bad happens."

"You'll do what you have to do. I'm proud of you."

"For what?"

"For being there for your family."

"I'm barely holding on." I said.

"You're there."

I would head back into the house and try to regain my composure. I didn't want anyone feeling bad about me feeling bad.

A routine was in place, and I felt like a novice water skier, trying to hold on as the speedboat towing me raced in every direction. My father would wake up at six in the morning. This was after three or four trips to the bathroom during the night, which required my escort. We would make breakfast and check with my dad to see if he wanted to bathe and dress for the day. My mother would head out for the papers, and my father would fire up the television and find a news station and a volume level that would jar my skull and psyche in equal doses.

The tent poles to the day were the meals, and they brought much needed distraction and purpose. My father's sugar scores were all over the place with his diabetes, and it was a fine line of worrying about his scores and depriving him of hankerings for food that could give him pleasure. My dad was a prodigious eater in his day, and food was a constant in our lives. It still matters to me with whom I will or won't break bread, and it's rooted in the important meals of my life.

Lunch would come and go, and I would distract myself with the crosswords, which is a habit I picked up after my dad. I would throw a few clues at him thinking it would be good to keep his mind active, and he would pretend to be impressed if I finished a Tuesday puzzle.

The movies make these times seem packed with meaningful dialogue, and I would like to say we said beautiful things to each other all day, but mostly, it was waiting for the next meal. I don't want to diminish this time by my previous statement; it was just so many hours, and sometimes fatigue would weigh us down. I held my father's hands a lot and checked in with his comfort.

When I would suggest we put on the Yankee game, I noticed my father was not showing much interest. It troubled me a bit because I thought it would help us keep our minds off of my father's illness. My father took me out of school for my first Yankee game when I was a kid, and I remember us getting lost on the way home, my dad trying not to blow his stack, as we drove through the South Bronx. He managed tickets to the '96 World Series and we watched the Yanks get smoked 12-1. Balls were flying over the fence near our seats in left field. He told me he was making up for "parental neglect," because he hadn't taken me to a World Series before. When the Yankees wound up winning, I raced to a pay phone on the streets of Manhattan to call my dad.

"They did it!"

"How about that."

"Lost the first two."

"Back on top."

"I love you, dad."

"I love you too, son."

I know that it's starting to sound like a Mitch Albom story, but fathers, sons, and baseball always move the needle. This is why I was curious about his lack of interest. He preferred old movies and cable news, oh and Rachel Ray, which sent my mother batty.

It wasn't until I got back to LA that I understood why my father wasn't interested in the Yankees, and it hit me hard – he wasn't sure he would make it through the season.

He could get to the end of a movie, but the season is long, and he would have to beat the odds to see the playoffs. It scared me that my dad, the eternal optimist, was seeing the glass half empty.

18

GERMAN POTATO SALAD

My father took pride in his appearance, as did my mom; perhaps she also took pride in making sure my dad took pride. He had the distinction of being the best-dressed guy in the sports department, which was like having the prettiest track marks on your arms, in a room full of heroin addicts. With only a powder room on the first floor of our house, we had to find a way for my father to get clean. We found these microwavable disposable medicated towels that he could use to bathe. We would set up a dressing screen and pull some shades for his privacy, and we would hand him a towel for each body part or region. At first, I wasn't sure I would handle this task well; this was nurse stuff, and I was squeamish, but as time went on, it was a routine and a very tactile way to take care of my father. When my mother would do it, watching her take that care, put me on an emotional ledge—seeing her love, and her absence of hesitation, would floor me—this was her dude, and she would do what had to be done.

It was also a time when I got to see the heart of a man who wanted to keep trying, a man who would comb his hair and still squirt some cologne. It made me proud to be his son, and gave me a hint into my attachment to store-bought fragrances.

One day before the bath, the phone rang and I answered. A lifelong nosy neighbor was on the phone and was digging for information. My folks are private people, and they wanted to control the way information was disseminated. Of course, I crumbled under direct questioning and spilled the beans. When I returned to my father, he asked me who was on the phone. When I told him, his old temper reared up.

"I don't want people knowing my business, least of all her, of all people, God damnit ..." He shouted.

"I'm sorry, I don't know what I'm supposed to say."

"You don't say anything."

I was sick to my stomach. I had broken a rule. I felt like a little boy. I was dressed down. I had disappointed my father. I called my brother and told him I had fucked-up. He told me it was the least of the worries at hand, and after about three days, I didn't have a knot in my stomach. It was a flash of the sometimes-blustering man my father was.

Looking back, the stress of spilling the beans is meaningless. What remains is the power our parents hold over us, even when we grow to twice their size and live three thousand miles away.

We didn't leave my father alone, but my mother had to shop and take care of things when one of he kids couldn't be there. While I would jump at a chance to go to the store, my presence was also a break for my mom. What I could do was get out for a walk after dinner, and I figured if I was back before dark, it wouldn't be too much strain. I'm sure some people would have jogged for the exercise or walked to the old high school and shot hoops or sat in the park and poured their woes into a journal. I, on the other hand, race-walked to the Park Tavern in East Rutherford, which is literally across the railroad tracks. Rutherford is a dry town, and it wasn't more than a mile walk to the tavern. I would sit at the bar and drink two or three of the coldest draft beers in the states. I could have stayed all night, but had to get back. In an effort to make the trip seem productive, I would stop at Forest Dairy and get a half pint of German potato salad, which is the vinegar-based kind. When I got home, I would offer it around and dig in the fridge for another beer.

We were a couple of hours away from sleep, and I would call my girlfriend or check-in with my brother, the doctor. My father would check his scores and take his meds. Once a week, we would organize his pills, and then we would get him ready for bed. My mother would kiss him goodnight, tell him she loved him, and head upstairs. I will never regret being able to sleep on the couch next to my father and to be able to say goodnight and tell him I love him, as I tried to make him comfortable.

My father would say his prayers aloud, and I would put in my earphones to give him some privacy. At the time there was a wireless network I could jump on, and I would watch shows on my laptop. I was still a night owl and would get to sleep right on time for my dad's first bathroom trip.

On the way back to bed, my dad would stop at the kitchen table and have something to drink or a snack, like peanut butter and crackers or some cheese. These were moments when we could talk or just sit at the table, like so many nights before. Most of the time I was too tired to make these moments meaningful. I wish I had been more alert or less hazy, but I did get to get him back in bed and kiss him and try to sleep for a couple more hours.

Six AM would arrive in a blink, and my mother would head downstairs and get her day started. The TV would erupt and we would get breakfast started and think about what we would eat for the rest of the day. To know some people struggle for basic nutrition makes you feel lucky to plan a day of meals. As raw a deal as you think you are dealt, it could always be worse. We were doing the best we could, and part of me was starting to be proud—proud of us as a family, doing the right thing by the guy who put us on the map.

I was starting to deal better with the routine and was doing a pretty decent job as a caregiver. The test was about to come, with a trip to the hospital for another dose of chemotherapy. Things had gotten rough for my brother and sister with an early round, and my anxiety was rising. What if we had to use the bedside commode? What if he were vomiting? It's what people have been dealing with for years when this disease knocks on their door. It's a club you don't want to join, but far too many of us will.

19

CATHETER IN THE RYE

Taking this show on the road was giving me anxiety. I didn't want a slip and fall on my watch or a typical DeGregorio shouting match in the car. I wanted everything to go off without a hitch, as if my dutiful student approach would be able to affect the outcome of the chemo or reverse the diagnosis.

My dad could get down the steps in front of the house and to the car with a little help, but we had a wheelchair for the journey at the hospital.

We took the long way to the hospital, using surface streets to avoid highway traffic. I think it was also a less stressful way for the folks. The hospital had valet parking, which is the first merciful and useful employment of this service. The transfer to the wheelchair was easy enough, and we entered the hospital and headed for the bank of elevators.

I was a bit stressed because as we wheeled through hallways, my mother was a bit slow to tell me which way to go and would walk ahead and not hold open doors. I think it was stress and fear getting to her. Usually organized and ahead of things with her research, she was using my presence as a way to shut down. It worried me when I thought about how she would deal if she were alone with my father, but it was mostly me, projecting my own powerlessness over the situation. I was here for now, but soon would be gone, but my mother had a 24/7 situation on her hands and would wind up dealing with situations that I would not have handled well. After a labyrinth of hallways, we made our way to the cancer wing and started to wait.

The waiting room had more amenities than most. It had a coffee bar with flavor options and a selection of teas. I tried not to scan the room and, of course, people-watched with a vengeance. I wondered how dismal people's situations were. I also wanted everyone to know how special this guy was sitting next to me. I didn't want to wait, and I wanted it all to be a nightmare and not the reality before us.

As we waited, my father thought he might need to use the restroom. This was a bit tricky since he used a catheter to urinate for as long as I can remember. I think it was a symptom of his diabetes. My father had adapted quite well, and after a circumcision in his fifties, barely made mention of the situation. The problem this day was he left his kit at home and didn't have a catheter with him. I flipped out.

"Fuck. How the hell could we miss that, goddamn it."

"I'll be alright. I didn't have one the whole weekend Grandma died." My dad said.

"Jesus Christ. Why didn't you go to a drug store?"

"You need a prescription." He said.

"Seriously? I wasn't aware there was a lot of recreational catheter use out there." I said.

"That's funny, you should use that."

"They have to have one in a goddamn hospital, and you can get your doctor to fucking prescribe it."

"I'll be ok." He said.

"Jesus Christ."

I called my brother and ranted about how I fucking forgot the catheter and what to do, and he told me to calm down. I was reacting in stress and emotion and, in some twisted way, in competition. I might not be a doctor, but as long as I did everything right, I was winning the game.

I hit every nurse station, and asked if an exception could be made, and they tried to chase down a piss tube while I paced the halls. I started telling parts of this story on stage and every male in the audience grabs his piece in phantom pain. Can you imagine? That's a tough guy—tougher than I am.

While every nurse in the building was trying to help, we made it to the chemo ward. He was hooked up, and we sat with him as the poison emptied out of the bag. He had a couple of bad days with my brother standing by, so as I watched the evil fluid pour out, I wondered how rough a night we had ahead of us. Funny how I was worried, he was the one who might be sick, and all this while he had to take a piss like a racehorse.

Trying to rush and not rush on the way home took some doing. As we waited for the only necessary valet stand in the world, my dad was shivering and I was trying not to panic.

"This happened last time." He said.

"Do you feel ok?"

"Yeah, so far, I'm just cold."

"Hang in there, pop."

"Doesn't help that I have to pee."

That night he was tired but not sick. We used a bedside bucket for him to urinate and he tried to rest. I was spared a tough night, but it was a seventy-two hour window we had to get through.

We were spared a tough couple of days, and my dad's energy spiked a bit. We had to wait for blood work to see if my father would face another dose of chemo while I was home. We were spared that second trip. The doctors wanted him to gather strength for a later session. I was given a gift of having my father be closer to his usual self while I was home. If only he could have slept eight hours, we would have had a blast.

My sister arrived from Philadelphia to stay the weekend and gave me a chance to get out of the house at night. I reached out to my friend Jimmy Carver, and we made a plan for the following evening. That first night, I went to Park Tavern by myself. I found a seat and listened to a horrible cover band playing extended versions of Grand Funk Railroad songs.

I spoke to no one and saw no one I knew, except for an old buddy who didn't resemble his younger version. He sang "Born in the U.S.A" to the back of my head, thinking I would understand he was referencing my annual performance of "Santa Clause is Coming to Town" back in high school when I would dress like Springsteen and sing at the Christmas assembly. I didn't bother to correct him.

"You had some balls back then." He said.

"Thanks, man."

"What are you doing with yourself, you producing or something?"

"Nah, I'm doing stand-up and some acting, you know." I said.

"You had some balls back then."

"Yeah."

"Let me buy you a beer."

"Thanks."

He walked back to his wife and played air guitar along with the band. I sent a beer his way, and he nodded. It had been a long time since high school, and I've been in and out of town, but in a pathetic "Glory Days" way, I was flattered that he remembered my performance from back in the day. It was hilarious that he asked if I was a producer because he hadn't seen me in anything. You can be complimented and brought down to earth in one sentence. I had to get my shit together.

The next night I went out with Jimmy and brought him up to speed on my father. Jimmy's father left his family to start a new one when we were kids, and Jimmy spent a lot of time with my folks. Jimmy loved my dad and was a great support. My dad represented a father figure to a few of my friends. My childhood friend and his family across the street, the Testarosas, were an extended family to me growing up. When the father left that home, my dad became a symbol for my friend and his sister. Anna Testarosa was pregnant and visited my father with her husband. I heard my dad rubbed her stomach the whole time.

The real relief of having my sister home was that I could go upstairs and sleep through the night. She would take the pullout sofa and escort my father to the bathroom. I should have capitalized on the chance to get some rest, but stayed out late, and cried in my beer with my high school friend.

There was a familiar tug of New York at my heart, but I was home to be of use. I was pulled back to my childhood before I ventured into the city. It was the first of two weeks and nine miles from Manhattan and a lifetime passing before my eyes in my old room, which was now the office where my father wrote his poetry, sleeping off a night of drinking in my thicker, older body, and wondering how I was going to deal with the second week.

20

WHAT I DID FOR LOVE

I was settling in to a routine, but with no sibling on hand for the next seven days, I was starting to crack under the strain of little sleep and a lot of sorrow. I was also starting to feel guilty about looking forward to getting back to my life. This scared me and made me feel inhuman when I thought these thoughts while my father's time on earth was being curtailed. As the week dragged on, I was starting to feel relief that I was getting to the end of my tour of duty. I don't know if that's normal, and shame on me if it's not, but it was a grind and my father was not feeling well, and I just wanted to be with my girlfriend and not have to hear the drone of cable news television. It was like rehab where beer was available. I had to get up early and do chores; it's just that once I helped with the meal, I could crack a cold one, which was a relief I leaned on too much.

It felt like before the dawn of modern living when nightfall literally meant the day was over and not much could get done in the dark. When we settled in after dinner, a small anxiety would come over me. I would call my girlfriend and try to keep it short.

I wanted to have some conscious down time before I fell into that half-waking-one-eye-open slumber.

I still had night owl instincts, and my father was staying up a little later, but we had to shut things down and take medications, and it wasn't simply turning out the lights and hitting the hay. Once you lay down, it would be a couple of hours before my dad was up. A few times he tried to get up and go to the bathroom without me. I would always come to in time to help him, and it would remind me what I was really here to do. He was trying to let me sleep and be thoughtful, and it made me smile inside that he was still trying to take care of me. It made me grateful to be woken-up and grateful for the time that I had to be helpful for my dad.

"I don't care if you get up fifty times. I'm getting up with you."

"I'll never forget what you kids did for me." My father said.

"We're not doing anything special. We just want to help." I said.

"I'm a lucky man."

We would head to the kitchen and then on through to the bathroom. On the way back I poured him some root beer and sliced some cheese. I was happy to be awake, happy to be tired, and happy to be eating cheese with my father. It really is the simple things we remember. It brought me back to the year after college when I moved back home. My dad and I would be vying for some quiet time. My dad would be getting home from work, and I would be getting ready for bed or coming in from a night out. He would have the Times crossword going and would ask me a couple of the pop culture clues, and I would ask him how this helped him unwind. It wasn't until years later, when I started doing them myself, that I understood the answer he gave me.

"I don't know; it just relaxes me."

For brief moments in the middle of the night, we were just hanging out, and eating cheese at the table I had known my entire life, and it occurred to me that I was a lucky man too.

As my departure neared, I was thrilled to see my girlfriend. We had not spent this long apart before. I was spiraling in and out of excitement and woe. I was worried for my mother, who would have to do all that I had done, alone. I was worried that there would be gaps in my visits and my siblings. I was worried something would go wrong, and I would be saying goodbye to my father for the last time. It was a thought that shuddered through me and brought me to my knees. I know that I am lucky to have had such constant support, but the thought of losing it was crushing.

My hands shook as I made the call to the cab company to take me to the airport. Our farewells were always filled with tears, and now I had no idea how I would hold up.

We sat and tried to make small talk.

"Here, take some money for the cab." My dad said.

"I'm OK."

"Take it."

There was no point in arguing.

"Thank you."

"Is Sadie picking you up in LA?"

"Yeah."

"You make up some time going west, so you'll still have some daylight left." My mother added.

"Yeah."

"I'm sure she'll be glad to have you back." My dad said.

"Let's hope so." I replied.

The local cab company has a bad habit of being fifteen minutes early. This only makes it harder to say goodbye as you sit and try to say inane things to keep from crumbling. While the Lincoln Town Car is idling outside, you realize you have to go. It's the emotional equivalent to a bungee jump. I hug my mother and thank her.

"I love you, mom." I say.

"I love you, too." She says. We hug better than before, my mother holds on, and I don't let go. It's time to say goodbye to my George, my dad, and I'm past the point of fighting off tears. I bend to wrap my arms around him as he sits in his chair. We're both crying.

"I love you."

"I love you."

"Thank you so much, Carl."

"You never have to thank me."

I hold my dad, and he squeezes hard. I kiss my father over and over, and he kisses me back. We're sobbing and kissing. We're so overwrought that we start laughing through our tears. I pull away and say, "You do whatever you have to do." I kiss him again, tell him I love him, and stare into his eyes. I hug and kiss my mother, tell her I love her, and head out of the house.

I can't pretend to keep my shit together in the cab; I lose it and sob my way down the New Jersey Turnpike, as glimpses of New York get farther away at my back. I'm devastated but have cried myself out by the time I get to the airport. I made my trip early in the diagnosis, and I have faith that I will see my man, again, but I can't be sure. As I cross through security I am tempted to turn around and scrap all my plans just to be with my family. All the stress and yearning to return to my California dream is gone, I want to be home. It's a moment when you feel the boot of life pressing down on you. Youthful invincibility is a distant memory and you feel the stakes that life places on all of us. This is big boy stuff and yet you have to keep moving, literally, because that business man on the security line is about to blow a gasket if I don't get my shoes off more quickly. Another human pulls me out of my emotional state, from sadness to anger in seconds. As I place my laptop in the plastic bin, I mutter aloud, "Calm the fuck down," and look back at the guy slipping off his loafers and sighing in frustration. I am, at least, at my balance point and am ready to find some overpriced food at the airport and maybe a couple of beers.

Los Angeles is different when I arrive, or more accurately, I am. They say that once you are glad to be back in LA, you know you really live there. It takes two years for you to decide to stay, and then you get into a routine, and finally, touching down makes you glad to be home.

This was not the case this trip, and how could it be? I was in a limbo, where my venal goals meant so little, and only my father's insistence that I keep trying kept me semi-positive.

My girlfriend was there to get me, and I was warmed to see her smile and to kiss her lips. She had been through the sudden loss of her mother, many years ago, and was as supportive as a scuba tank is to a diver during these times. I held her hand as we drove off looking for a place to eat. I was home in her arms but still felt the void of the Garden State. I would make it back soon, and she would come with me, and we would find a way to be happy. We would see our George, again.

21

BEGIN THE BEGUINE

The summer before I left for college, I was hell bent on getting out of New Jersey as soon as possible. Pittsburgh was calling my name. In an effort to speed up this process, I signed up for some ridiculous thing called freshmen camp. It was a week before orientation, and the setting was a summer camp somewhere in western Pennsylvania. As soon as I walked into the bunkhouse and saw a dude playing a mandolin on the edge of his bed, I knew things were going be different for me than for my friends who went to Rutgers or Delaware.

I introduced myself to the traveling troubadour and got a few monosyllabic responses. I was about to ask his major when I think he started juggling. I dropped my bag and headed out of the barracks, so much for this being the serious choice. Every step I took was costing my parents money. Maybe I should have skipped this extra week as I found out that most of the drama students had passed up this chance to swat at mosquitoes in the woods.

Sidestepping any chance of having a psycho roommate, I decided to room with a kid whom I met at the accepted students weekend. Pre-selecting a preference for roommate put you at the bottom of the list for actual lodging. Our dorm had fewer amenities than the prison in *Midnight Express* and had the same demographic: all male (minus the good heroin). My new *cellie* was from Texas, Longview, to be exact, and he seemed normal, albeit with a southern accent straight out of the Country Music Awards like Tim McGraw, but eighteen. His mother was concerned he'd be a hermit since he had a girlfriend back home, and she made me promise to get him out of the dorms and into some kind of social life. I did not have a high school sweetheart at home, and my plan was to get to work on the ladies. I swore to his mother that he would see plenty of good times.

The indoctrination starts right away at Carnegie Mellon. The first official meeting of the department took place in the main theatre. I later found out that it was called convocation. The Kresge theatre was a professional and venerated space with a ton of history. A classic proscenium, the wood was hand-carved and light brown, and the seats were lush. The freshmen sat in the front rows of the orchestra section; the sophomores sat in the back rows. Juniors sat in the right loge, and the left loge was empty. As we waited for teachers to make their remarks, there were chants going back and forth, inside jokes which we didn't yet get. The juniors would do some sort of rhyme, making fun of the sophomores and vice versa, and there was clapping and singing.

The head of the department made her way to center stage. She was the first person whom I met at the audition months ago; she was regal and assured as she spoke. She mentioned that the freshman class was 41 people, picked from thousands, and yet not all of us would make it to the back rows where the sophomores sat. She said the only thing to do was to be brave, take risks, and learn. She didn't mention that you should also shit your pants because if you got cut, you didn't get a refund, and that mortgage your parents took out to pay for this was also non-negotiable. She then introduced the senior class who came down the aisles and sang to us. They were stunning people. I sat there thinking, is this what I'm going to look like in four years time?

The group looked like a bunch of 36 year-old actors, hired to play seniors in college. They wrapped up their Broadway quality song from the stage, and the crowd erupted. They then took their rightful place in the left loge, and more chants followed. All I could think about was ensuring I get to be one of those seniors some day, to be able to take that seat in the loge. Nothing but this outcome would be acceptable. This is drama school employing these techniques; can you imagine what they feel like at West Point or Annapolis? Hearts and minds, hearts and minds.

One thing you figure out quickly at CMU is that no one is there to fuck around. Yes there are activities and parties, but there is a reverse peer pressure to work hard. The typical flaky drama student did not exist, just a bunch of hyper-intense people trying to ensure their futures. The schedule alone was daunting. They had you from eight AM, until six PM; after that, you were assigned to crew. Crew was building sets, costumes, or running the lights and sound for any given show that the juniors and seniors were presenting. Crew went from 7:30 PM 'til 11:00 PM. Oh, yeah, crew also needed to be attended on Saturdays at ten AM. If I wanted to party and flunk out, the schedule would not allow it. For that I am still grateful. That I was immersed in my chosen discipline so intensely was something from which I almost had to recover.

The drama department, unofficially but officially, insisted that joining a fraternity was not a good idea for a "dramat." Knowing that during rush week kept me loose and free. Fraternity parties at CMU were open to women but private for men. Carnegie's male to female ratio was three to one, so it was a matter of supply and demand. During rush week they were open to all. My drama crew and a couple of art majors hit the dance floor. I verbally committed myself to almost every frat on campus.

"Well, Chad, I think DTD is the place for me." I'd bellow over the music as I drank free tap beer.

It was fun to get these pledge guys all worked up; it wasn't a problem until I started getting mail inviting me to the next level of recruitment. I avoided people whom I barely remembered. I couldn't even tell who was from what fraternity. Most took the hint, but one dude got worked up and told me it wasn't cool to mess with this very coveted invitation to a brotherhood. I saw Spike Lee's *School Daze* and many other college movies, not to mention *20/20* specials about hazing, and I didn't have time to be left in the woods to find my way back to campus. I couldn't wear a dress unless the scene required it, and I didn't need to be coaxed to drink beer rapidly. Besides, the drama department was about the size of a frat. It was co-ed, and the preponderance of attractive girls on campus was in it. What did I care about the Greek alphabet? I had the phonetic alphabet to learn.

At an early Drama party off campus, I was floored by the hotness of the girls throwing the party. It was at a three-bedroom apartment, and the hostesses were juniors, two blondes, and a brunette. Freshmen had to live on campus. The girls had cool furniture and a wine rack. My crew and I were the few freshmen who were in attendance. It wasn't really a welcome party but more of a "how was your summer party." I met a sophomore who knocked me out; she was a stunning black woman with a Jessica Rabbit body, a short black dress, and a pin over her left breast that read, "Bronx Bitch." What are you supposed to do with that?

"Nice to meet you, bitch."

"What did you just call me?"

"I'm sorry, nice to meet you, *Bronx* bitch."

A slap is issued, and I try to recover.

"It practically says, hello my name is bitch—what am I supposed to think?"

Of course, none of that transpired, but I found out her name was Denise, and I moved to the other side of the room. There was another sophomore of Latin descent who oozed sex, and I fumbled over myself to make an impression and barely managed the handshake with any proficiency. Every nook of this top floor apartment was packed with a hot girl with classical features and a confident bearing. The dudes were all backslapping charisma machines, and it was hard to keep up. Never mind trying to find like-minded peers, this was a world of exceptional people. Not only did I have work to do, but I needed to grow some chest hair quickly.

22

RELAX

Classes were about to begin, and we went to the College of Fine Arts building, (known as CFA from here on out) to find out where we had to be. CFA is a stunning building; it has stone carvings on its façade, marble floors, and statues all through its grand first level. It has been featured in the films *Wonder Boys* and *Smart People*, among others. There is a bulletin board where all the important information is posted. Classes, cast lists, and messages would be tacked up from teachers or fellow students; it was the wall on Facebook before Facebook, only the analog version. Carnegie Mellon is usually top five in computer science, nationally, and there was an email system in place called *Andrew*, but the Drama Dept. was not yet wired or, at least, my crew wasn't wired. The board was also a place to meet, kill time, and post flyers for parties. I think that's how we found our way to the house party.

Since we didn't know how things worked yet, seeing who would be our teachers and in our groups, didn't mean much. Of course, down the line, these decisions would be important. If you didn't have chemistry with a teacher, you might not develop on pace, and with "The Cut" always looming, that could be trouble. Ignorance is bliss, and as people congregated, or met in the cafeteria, there was much to discuss.

"I'm in your acting class." I would say.

"Cool."

Maybe it wasn't the greatest icebreaker, but you get the idea. Credits were called units, and we had a lot of them. When you asked non-drama students how many units they were carrying, you found out we were holding double the amount of the average CMU under-grad. We had crew on Saturdays, but we didn't have to write computer languages or develop satellites.

I never had a subscription to *Playboy* magazine (too tame) and never saw the issue that had the polls that named the biggest party schools in the country. I also never saw the poll that listed the biggest geek schools in the country, but I never doubted the veracity of the source material. I would never argue with the ranking of University of Maryland or Arizona State as party schools. When it was revealed that Carnegie Mellon was listed as the number one geek school, there was no arguing. During the first two weeks of school, I could see why. One night, trying to sleep in the Stalag style all male dorm, I heard screams out the window.

"I got laid," shouted some lucky loser.

"Shut the fuck up," replied some angry sleeper.

It was like smart guy prison. The geeks, who had never learned to hold their booze in high school, were puking in every stairwell and entryway. There was a sleep walking "urinator" on our floor. The dude would walk into rooms and piss on the victim's laundry in the middle of the night. He would pee on the door if he found it locked. The dude entered our room, one night, weeks after the initial "waterings," and I told him to get the fuck out, not even considering whether or not it was dangerous to wake a sleepwalker. Who came up with that, anyway? If a dude is about to void his bladder in your laundry basket, you wake his ass. The kid kind of came to, and shook off sleep and apologized; as an acting major, I didn't buy his performance. He was just troubled, and was crumbling under the stress of the Architecture Department. He didn't make it a semester. Poor guy, but seriously, there are other ways to act out—ever heard of binge drinking, or graffiti?

There were some academic classes where the jump from high school to college was acute. There were big lectures with hundreds of students; we would then break off into groups another day to discuss the lecture with the teaching assistant. Most drama classes were physical; we would move or interact. In the classes where participation was more Socratic, my body would shut down and I would fight sleep for most of it. This put me in a panic. What if I flunked one of these classes? We had world history, a computer class, and writing. I thought I was OK with the writing class. I thought that was one skill with which I could compete on a high level. That was until the professor singled me out in class after our first assignment.

He waved a paper in the air like a prop.

"Now take, Carl, here, for example. Carl was a successful writer in high school. Am I correct?" he asked.

"Uh, yeah, shouldn't that be a good thing?" I replied.

"Yes, you would think, but this is *Strategies for Writing,* and you need to strip away all the things you've learned thus far." He said.

I was singled out for having written well but not according to his format. Now, I was slipping in the one class I thought I could handle. What was going to happen when I had to take a dance class? I did have a ballet class a year later and found out what a dance belt is – it's like a jock strap, for a male dancer. The glaring difference is it only has one strap that goes up the crack of your ass, like a skinny Sumo wrestler or a T-back bikini bottom. It was not comfortable but does for your equipment what a push-up bra does for breasts. I also bought the wrong tights and was told after three weeks that my ass was visible through the sheer fabric. From that point on, I wore a jock strap and bicycle shorts. I would rather look like Milli Vanilli than have my ass on display with a self inflicted power wedgy. This class was pass/fail, I think, but the writing class was the real thing.

Back on the home turf of the drama department, things weren't much better. Our first class was Voice and Speech, and the teacher was a silky voiced dandy who spoke every word as if it were to prove he taught proper speech for a living.

"My name is Lawrence. Please mill and seethe and warm up your voices with some sound." He said.

What the fuck is milling and seething—sounded like something a Bolshevik did, or maybe I'm thinking hammer and sickle. It actually means to wander around the space and randomly change direction. After we walked around the room, like characters in *One Flew Over the Cuckoo's Nest*, we were told to lie down on the floor. This was 8:30 in the morning. If you put me on the floor, two things are going to happen—I'm going to fall asleep, and I'm going to wake up with an erection.

Lawrence would then use his melodious voice to take us through visualization exercises and breathing techniques. His voice was like a human white noise machine; the only thing that would keep me awake, intermittently, was the fear that I wasn't *getting it*, that I wouldn't pass the test if asked what my quiet space looked like. After some of these exercises, Lawrence would ask students what they experienced.

"When you said we were resting on a hot pan, I actually felt the heat on the back of my legs." A student recounted.

I kept thinking, "Wait, there was a frying pan? I'm way behind here. I'm going to flunk lying down and breathing. How can you fail at lying on the floor? And by the way that kid is full of shit."

During what I can only term as a lucid dream, I heard Lawrence blathering, and then he said, "… and relax your sphincter." It took everything in me to not bolt up from the floor, and I tried squinting to see if anyone else heard the same thing. Lawrence moved onto something else, and I went back to sleep.

At lunch, I sat there uncharacteristically quiet, and waited for someone to mention Lawrence's directive to relax a muscle of which I had only recently become aware.

Finally, I spoke, "Did anyone else hear Lawrence tell us to relax our sphincter?"

"Yeah, I thought I heard that, too." My friend Paul said.

"Can the girls even do that?"

"Yeah, you dumb fuck, they can do it." I snapped. "What does that have to do with acting?"

"I don't know, but I won't be there tomorrow. Do you mind watering the plants in my quiet space?" Someone quipped.

"You have plants in your quiet space?" I asked.

I didn't even know what my quiet space looked like. It changed every day, and that's if I didn't sleep through the whole thing. It was getting so bad that Lawrence had to tell people to wake me up; I was definitely going to be the first student to flunk breathing.

23

GET READY 'CAUSE HERE I COME

There was an evening class early on where we all got to do monologues for each other. What this accomplished was uncertain. There was a looming assignment that had us sizing each other up, like college basketball coaches at a high school all-star game. It was called the Free Scene; basically, you pick a partner and work without any input or instruction. You were on your own to find a scene and on your own to rehearse and direct it. After the monologues, I approached one of the women in the class, Liz. I thought her monologue was great, and I noticed that as opposed to most of the classes in the department, ours was not heavy on the females. My thinking was that it would be easier to find scenes with a guy and a girl, and if you had to rehearse for months, and alone, it might be nice to have a girl by your side.

I had a plum partner, and I felt like my monologue put me in good stead with the rest of the class. Now we had to dig through the stacks in the library and try to find a good scene. There was a student who was repeating freshman year. He was an intense fellow who was cultivating a look that said, "I will play the bad guy whenever given the chance." He liked to share what he knew even though he didn't know enough to move forward. That's an unfair assessment. He was a living, embedded example of how serious "the Cut" was and how there were other fates to befall you at CMU. He did make a suggestion for a play for the free scene. Liz and I raced to the library to get there before another pair of actors found the scent.

Silly as it seems, there was a sense that this needed to be a covert act, and that it was important to find a scene that would, essentially, be the first big showcase to the faculty. The play we were hunting for was *Loose Ends*, by Michael Weller, and the scene we were hunting for was a barnburner. Of course, we were too young actually to play the roles in the real world, but we were sure it was a smoker, and we wanted to go on record that we had found our Free Scene and that we had dibs.

Liz was from Michigan and had steel blue eyes, like a Husky. She had dark hair and a lanky grace. She was goofy and intense and was a serious theatre geek without the crossover appeal that playing ball and being a wise ass had given me. I might have had a crush, but that was a few weeks away, and I was so wrapped up in my work that I was almost shunting the thought of romance.

Without boring you with all the details of the play, which is actually not boring in the least, I'll break down the scene as best I can; it's a wife's birthday. The husband has a gift. The wife opens the gift to see a beautiful urn shaped like a horse. The wife is stunned by the gift. She wonders how much the husband might have spent. He tells her it cost in the neighborhood of $100,000, once you added up all the accounts he emptied and the stocks he sold. The wife is curious if he's joking. The husband assures her that he is serious. He explains that it is an actual Ming Dynasty urn, meant to carry the ashes of the Emperor's son who died before he grew old enough to rule. The reason the urn is shaped like a horse is so the dead child could see the life he would have lived, had he survived. The wife is still in the dark, and the party is not going well. The husband finally lets her have it. He knows that his wife terminated a pregnancy and did not tell him; he sunk their shared assets into this urn to make a point and to torture his wife in this elaborate way. It was not Neil Simon.

The scene was heavy drama, and it gave me a chance to really "peacock" as an actor. It also gave Liz a chance to show her emotional range, meaning she could cry, almost on cue, which never fails to impress. We were going to crush it. We also had the horse prop that we found at Pier One Imports. We also worked harder than most. We never skipped a day to rehearse, and we tried it every way possible; we switched roles; we did it rapid speed; we did it while we walked to class; we did it with accents. What we didn't know about being a yuppie couple we made up for by spending an inordinate amount of time together and working on our scene. We almost had to give ourselves a vacation from rehearsal. Other students were working hard as well, but only a few were as obsessive as Liz and I were.

Much of the time was spent thinking about whether or not I should try to kiss Liz, thinking we were playing man and wife, and it would be good research. Ever the purist, I didn't want to mix business with pleasure, and I was sure the only way to keep the cut at bay was brute effort, work myself into a nub, and I'd be in the clear. I also had a real hot scene that I knew was going to blow the lid off the room.

The free scene was completely self-paced and was an outside responsibility. Classes were trudging along, and some were more harrowing than others. The sheer volume of work was crushing. I scoff at anyone who thinks my course of study was like play time. Sure, we had a class where we still played dodge ball, but we also had more work than time to get through every day. Memorization was pushed to the limit. We'd have our free scene, plus a scene for our main acting class. We'd have an assignment in Voice and Speech, which was usually a poem or speech. We would transcribe it into phonetics, and we'd have some Drama Literature stuff to get through, not to mention that World History class where we were 200 pages behind. The girl in the cafeteria was right a year ago when my dad encouraged me to approach the table when we were touring the campus, but I thought there would be some fun.

The problem with going into such a training program directly after high school, at least for me, was it was no place to mess around or to find yourself. In keeping with the rest of Carnegie Mellon, we were essentially in a trade school. There were not a lot of undeclared majors at CMU. You were there to learn your trade and go out in the world and ply it. I was as sure as I could be that this was the place for me. I just needed a little breathing room. I wasn't going to get it. No one was going to get that room, and that was a bonding element.

Some of the only time we got to ourselves was at the cafeteria. We would travel en masse and eat prodigious amounts of food, and I would hold court. Lunch was a short break, but dinner gave us almost two hours before crew. This was a chance to get to know students from other classes, and very rarely from other departments. Most people complained about the food, and it wasn't that I didn't agree. I just liked the sheer amount of choices. Where else could you have a salad bar, cereal station, and taco night?

While parents might worry about spending their money helping a kid get a degree that might lead to a life in the hospitality arts, they could take comfort in the fact that most of our social lives took place in an antiseptic cafeteria. It was really hard to get in trouble, which may have made it easier to make a mess later in life. Funny thing is, the girls rarely joined us in the cafeteria; there were other options to eat where you could opt to use your meal plan as a dollar equivalent and pay a la carte. The cafeteria was an all you could eat option. The girls were bonding over salads that they had to weigh and sometimes pay the balance. The fellas needed the trough. A few times we went to the glorified salad bar and came up short of our caloric needs, and short of cash that could have been spent on beer.

It was a place where I felt comfortable. We could simply sit, break bread, and break chops. It was where we would make plans for the one night we could really do any partying, which was Saturday.

Occasionally, a friend of mine from the playwriting program would sit in on our bull sessions. Zeke was an intense dude who had played college football at Duquesne University, which is also in Pittsburgh, and he found his way to CMU because he told the director of the program, " Yo, I wanna write plays." He was an African American guy, who grew up in the Hill District, which is a black neighborhood in Pittsburgh. He was funny and loud, and we always found things to debate and often had to be chased out of the cafeteria as the chairs were being stacked around us. It was during these jam sessions, with Zeke and whomever, that I started to see the limitations of our field of study and an expansion of my interests and a lurking desire to have more to do with the creation of art, rather than the interpretation of art.

Actors interpret a role. They are led to believe that they create the character, but really the writer did that. Richard III is deformed. The actor didn't invent that, but Bill Shakespeare, and history did. When it really works at a high level, the actor does bring something that makes them a vibrant collaborator. If you wanted to say something from your own point of view, you had to think of an outlet creatively.

There was no time with our workload to explore interests other than the curriculum, and I was not actively looking to create a piece. I was just percolating, and thinking about where I might put my creative energy.

Part of my burgeoning frustration was our lack of performance opportunities. The department in those days did not allow freshmen and sophomores to perform in plays; that was reserved for the upperclassmen. The idea was to break bad habits, if they existed, and strip the actor down to the bolts. The program would then build you back up and send you out on stage with a new turbocharged engine.

The other source of my frustration was my emotional state. I'm not sure if I was stunted or underdeveloped, but I had a hard time expressing myself without anger.

My mother was going through cancer treatment, which ultimately led to her having part of her stomach removed. This news came to my attention with a phone call from my father, during which I was assured everything was going to be OK. My parents didn't want me to worry or come home, and I was shielded from what must have been a difficult time. It brought me back to discovering my dad had diabetes, wondering if they were covering up bad news. I was appalled at my lack of emotion. Sure, I was worried, I wanted my mother to get well. I didn't want to think the worst; I couldn't even approach that type of thinking. I was miles away, and I was being protected from the real world drama on the ground, in New Jersey. I tried to spiral into hysterics but was forcing it. I just didn't get the whole picture; years later, I would be brought up to speed on how serious it actually had been for my mother. The scare and the surgery forced her to quit smoking which was some consolation. I felt emotionally stunted and was wondering if I was abnormal or a sociopath. I was also obsessed with my work and the program.

The day had come to present our scenes. I was champing at the bit. We were ready. It was the first time we would see the entire class' work. We were split into groups, so we didn't know who was up to what. I was relieved, mostly out of a desire to show what I could do in terms of result instead of process. I was having difficulty in a couple of classes, thinking it was because I had had too much training prior to entering the program. I was spinning my wheels and anticipating the desired effects of certain exercises, thinking I knew better, but on this day, I felt like a fighter entering the ring, knowing that I was bringing a world of hurt on my opponent.

24

SHOW AND TELL

There was a jamboree feel to the class as we prepared to perform our Free Scenes. We knew each other socially, and we knew whom we liked as people, but we were still waiting to see who would emerge as the strongest actors of the class. Why this was important is a question with which every society and sub-culture deals—it's just one of those things.

There was bulky and utilitarian furniture in the rehearsal studios, and we all had to secure our set pieces. Some people had costumes. Liz and I did our best to look like we were a married couple from the 1970s. There was an order handed down, and we finally got to set up. I remember bits of other scenes, but not much. I remember one duo did a scene lying on the ground because their scene was set on the side of a mountain, so they had to achieve some kind of vertical plane. It was disconcerting and hard to picture their situation without some kind of set piece.

All we needed was a couple of chairs, a table, and our horse prop. I think we were earlier in the line-up because I remember the joy of relief in watching more scenes after performing than before.

The adrenaline and rush of an audience that made me thrive, was back. Liz and I conferred and took our spots. She started onstage, and I made an entrance, and we were in the scene, and we were hitting our moments, the performance energy fueling us. There was a crescendo where I slammed a chair. It wouldn't be the last time I slammed a chair, but it was the most appropriate use of the technique, and it jarred the crowd. It was acting. It felt great to be working on a play that didn't have "Bye, Bye" or "Birdie" in the title. It was a moment where I was sure I was at the right place at the right time. There was a sense that preparation and performance had come together.

The scene spoke about the chasm some relationships have to traverse. It dealt with a relationship's demise and loss of innocence. It had a man performing an act of cruelty, which he felt was justified retaliation to an act of cruelty from his wife. It was good drama, and we nailed it.

Sometimes there is a moment in theatre much like the moment when a symphony ends, where the silence is a punctuation mark, ending the piece before the crowd reacts. In that silence, we could feel the impact of our performance—the message, and the vitality of the words and, yes, the vitality of the actors. It's a sweet spot for an actor and certainly for the writer, where the audience is absorbing the work, and then the applause comes. The silence is the better part, believe it or not, especially when you control the tempo of your scene. You know what the last line is and the last moment, and you drop it like an anvil, and the crowd has to regroup, if only it were in a proper space and time. For us, it was about 50 people in the middle of the day clapping against the perceived idea that everyone should get the same consideration.

Liz and I hugged and knew we had made good on our partnership. It would be the last time we were so close. We struck our set and thanked the well-wishers. It was a satisfying feeling, helping the next scene set up and hearing people mutter about how good we were. It may be a fantasy recollection, but I think I heard a teacher say "Wow, that was good." The rest of the day was a blast; we watched the rest of the scenes and glad-handed with our classmates. Liz and I were shot to a place of esteem in the eyes of our peers, and I would think the faculty had to notice too. It was a few days of not worrying about the cut and basking in a job well done. Can you imagine what an Academy Award nomination must feel like?

Much of the first year was frustrating for me. While I counted the Free Scene as a victory, it was short lived. It was a classic back to reality moment. Perhaps, there was some separation anxiety with the process that we had just experienced. Once the scene is performed, you don't get to walk around with the secret that you have a hot scene anymore.

The second half of the Free Scene assignment was now to work on the scene with a professor in our acting class. We had to reform our classes, because some partnerships were made in cross-class alliances. The problem for us was that we didn't need as much work as others. The point that they were trying to make was that on your own, without any guidance, you might find yourselves off course. You would need a teacher to get your scene up and running. This is where working so hard independently had backfired. There wasn't a lot of room to grow, and that made it seem like we weren't progressing with the instruction. We were literally burned out on our scene and had peaked with our presentation. Some of the other partnerships were so off the mark that after a half an hour, with a third eye watching and some directing the scene made sense and looked like two new actors were performing it.

The only direction our scene seemed to go was backwards. I was angry that I was having my work retrofitted, and it was not a good time in class for me. How could the best scene of the bunch wind up being a bad thing in the eyes of the faculty? Of course, there is always room for improvement. Of course, our scene wasn't perfect. Of course, the years of experience that the professors possessed, was a resource. Of course, this is a subjective recollection. But, this was the problem with the scene. I was Jonesing to do another performance, not continue with one I felt was at least a semi-finished product. You will never look good in the eyes of those whom you have to impress if you look like you don't need them. I learned this after the Free Scene. Perhaps, their method is actually fool proof. Maybe they knew there would be one duo that would implode after early success, and down the line, learn the lesson. I'm not sure. I was pissed and resentful that I had performed well and was now stymied with the teacher's input, and that a positive had turned negative.

Social life was at a standstill. There were weekend nights where we went to the computer lab. We were all sleep-deprived, and the few occasions that a class was cancelled sent us to the library to find a place to sleep.

A new me began to emerge as I found myself mirroring input I got from my classmates. While I came to school thinking I was the All-American boy, it soon became apparent to others that I was from the North East. I was also Italian-American. I began to hang out and form a clique with the guys in the class who were from New York. The great thing about going to a prestigious university is that it draws from all parts of the country. While some out of state students go to Montclair State, it's not likely you'd meet people from Iowa and California, at least at the undergraduate level.

Another aspect of a university like CMU is that the student body favors a certain socio-economic strata. We knew some diplomat's daughters and foreign students who were from wealthy families. I don't know if my bubble was burst in any kind of hurtful way, but there were distinctions being made based on the region you resided, and what your parents did. I've always been proud of my father having worked for *New York Times* and being an author. One of my professors thought I was a rich kid, which was a compliment I should have shared with my parents. I think she thought I was rich because I was well dressed and well mannered and maybe a little cocky. She was off on her assessment, and I don't know why it came up, but socially,

I began to cultivate a more street-smart persona than was actually accurate or earned. It began to flatter my ego that people thought I was tough, that I'd been around the block that they thought I looked like Robert DeNiro. The fact that we all owned tights seemed lost on most—how tough could I be if I was in the drama department?

While there was very little social life, there was still a desire to carve out an identity and find some stature in the group. We did this by being those New York guys who new how to dance, liked club music, and would crash upperclassmen's parties. What was a drama nerd going to do—kick us out? We would have cowered in apology if it ever came to that, but no one ever called our bluff. It was, and remains, a silly dance that nobody even noticed.

For a Halloween party freshman year, we shirked our work, and tried to come up with cool costumes for a senior party. We were blanking on ideas, until someone came up with the idea of going as the Village People. This was not the most original idea now, but back then, it was groundbreaking. I insisted on being the hardhat guy, and we tried to think of the rest. We had to shop and thought we might need to do some costume research. We went to a used record store to look for a Village People album. We found two. One was *Live and Sleazy* and I forget the other. *Live and Sleazy* had all the good songs but the album art wasn't great. We switched the records, and took the better album cover. I was the construction worker. My friend Paul was the Indian, and Kevin, was the Leather guy. We got to the party, and the whole place went bananas. We looked good, and the fact that the straight guys, amidst a fair amount of gay guys, decided to come dressed as gay icons, was not lost.

When it came time for the door prize, we were announced as the winners. The prize was the *other* Village People album from the same used record store. The guy behind the counter was alarmed that two separate groups bought his entire Village People inventory. We performed a victory dance to "Macho Man," and wound up at an *Eat N Park* restaurant late at night and dateless. I wonder how that happened? It was also at this party, in one of the more lucid moments, that a discovery was made.

I was chopping it up with one of the juniors, and something dawned on me.

"You were a dick to me last year." I said.

"What are you talking about? You weren't even here last year." He replied.

"At the cafeteria, I asked you about the program, when I visited the campus."

"That was you?" he said.

"Yeah."

"Holy shit, we laughed about you for a month. I can't believe that was you. We thought you were a narc." He said.

"Yeah, I was dressed a little stiff."

"You looked like a Mormon." He said.

"I bet you didn't think I'd get in, did you?"

"Not a chance, we gave you no chance, I can't fuckin' believe that was you." He said as he went to find someone from the table a year back.

"No fuckin' way," was heard across the party, over the music, and we raised our plastic cups in a toast. We laughed at the solved mystery, and the irony of me wearing another ridiculous costume. It was a compliment that he could barely reconcile the old image with the present image.

The narrative you try to write about yourself had me thinking there might be more to me than trying to brush up my Shakespeare. It never dawned on me during this time that I might write about the experience. I was a gung-ho actor and was trying to make it through the program to join the ranks of other famous alumni.

The Thanksgiving break was close, and it was the first time I'd felt a need to get home. I'm trying to avoid saying that I was homesick. It wasn't like my previous studies in the summer; this was a long haul, and it wasn't all fun and discovery. I remember my flight home and remember my buddies and Jimmy Carver picking me up at the airport. We went to the Candlewyck Diner, which was a constant haunt of ours. I remember the house felt smaller, and I remember not knowing what to do with myself. It took a few days for me to decompress.

25

THE POSSE'S IN EFFECT

I was going through a dry spell with the ladies. My friend, Jordan, who was outside of the New York crew, and I had a reverse bet. We would lose the bet if one of us broke out of our slump. The thinking was it would give us incentive to "go out and get some" because who would mind coughing up a couple of bucks if you just got laid? Putting a reverse jinx on it seemed like a good tactic. Jordan was toying with this thing called straight edge, which I'm not sure I understand to this day, so my competition was a guy who was pledging to not drink or fuck. This guy was from California and was the dude with the mandolin at freshmen camp. He was also a fellow music-head, and we often tripped out to tunes and picked apart the songs and the mix.

"Listen to the ride cymbal. He's really cracking the bell." I would say.

"The bass is playing a chromatic scale." He'd add.

We had to blow steam somehow, and Jordan was a different kind of kid. He was soulful and sloppy. We were constantly breaking each other's chops about our perceived differences. We'd pretend we were cops, one from New York and one from California, the New York guy eating hot dogs, and the California kid eating sprouts. It was almost as if hanging out with him was a respite from the other version of myself. He was mellow and sedate, and I was volatile and antsy, yet we got along. Once I got over his messed up fashion sense and the way we met, we became friends, but it was not helping me get some ass. He was not a good wingman, so most weekends it would be me and the recently named Posse. We were becoming obnoxious. We even had a chant worked out.

"Posse's in effect, y'all. And that's a fact y'all. And if you don't like that, then step back y'all."

There's not a lot to say after that. We had issues. We were in drama school, and we had no women. Man, it was a long year.

At the end of each semester of freshman and sophomore year, the faculty holds a conference with each student. You had to sign up for fifteen minute time slots and sometimes you had to switch with people to accommodate someone else's flight home. These were serious meetings. You sat at a round table with all of your teachers, and they broke down your work as they saw it. The conference before the Christmas break was meant to give you something to think about and bring back for the next semester. The luxury was the one-on-one attention every student got. The hard part was the critical tone.

There is the legend of the student who gets a B in acting, freshman year; they are rare like the white whale. The rumors swirl, and people whisper, but it's not a common event. Somehow, Liz, my old scene partner, would be that rare bird who achieved that mythic status. She had weathered the storm of our Free Scene, and her work must have been steadier in her acting class. None of this stopped me from seething. It appeared I'd have to learn that the process was more important than the result, at least in drama school.

I had scholarships that wouldn't look well on me getting a C in my chosen major. A professor had to send a letter to one of my scholarships to let the administrators of the scholarship know that, in the

Drama Department, a C was the standard grade, and that unlike the rest of the university, the drama department worked on the plus and minus system. I guess this pacified the people at the Newspaper Guild because I didn't lose the scholarship.

I went home for the holidays and relished in the time off. That's the true gift of college, down time is down time. You can really enjoy your holidays because when they're over you get to go back to school, and that's not as bad as getting back to your life when you're a bona fide adult. There wasn't much to prepare for over the break, just a needed bit of rest. Talking to my friends from other schools, they could tell that I was in a different kind of program. I was a rapid-fire-talking-machine, and there was a shift in my personality.

I was used to the pace at CMU. I wasn't used to down time, and I felt as if I was slipping without a million things to do. I reached out to the classmates who were nearby in the city, and set up time to get together. They would understand the antsy feeling that I couldn't shake.

26

COULDN'T STAND THE WEATHER

I got through my freshman year without getting laid. If I had been kicked out of the program that wouldn't have been the ultimate failure. Freshman year in a normal kid's life should have at least yielded a couple of turns in the sack, but not for me. I was supposed to be one step up from a gypsy and banging all the emotional wrecks I could find in the orchestra pit, but I was worried about my studies. My friend Jordan was also holding on to his five dollars and his celibacy.

Toward the end of our freshman year, there were several examples of stress taking a toll on the class. For much of the second semester, I found myself battling fatigue and thought I was depressed. I went to the doctor and found out that I had mononucleosis but was on my way to recovery. He said that I was already through the worst part. I was walking around like a zombie and sleeping whenever I had a down moment. I thought the grey weather and hard work was beating me down. Turns out, I was undiagnosed and somehow got to a place where I could function. This is one of the last times I had health coverage, and I still didn't go to the doctor. That kind of medical stoicism is not recommended. If I had known about having mono and was told by the doctor to rest, I would have defied that advice. There was no way to miss class in the drama department; assignments couldn't be worked on from bed. I might have had to leave school and come back with a different class. In the end, I did what needed to be done, and it was a relief to know I wasn't crazy.

My friend Paul suffered a freak accident in his acting class. The doors to the studios in our main building were old. They looked like the doors a detective would have in the old movies—the glass with the stencil of the detective's name. We were preparing for our final scenes; Paul was in a different class, and they were working on *Fool For Love*, by Sam Shepard. It was a volatile scene and Paul was dating his scene partner, which was a volatile relationship. Rather than use the weird fake doors that were available in the rehearsal studios, some of us took to using the actual doors to the room. The staging has Paul's partner exiting the room and Paul stopping her, slamming the door with two hands. Instead of shutting the door using the frame, Paul shut the door by pushing the glass area. We had done this a million times, but Paul was really worked up in his scene and went through the glass. A jagged shard caught him under the arm, and he was nearly impaled, not to mention decapitated. It was bad. I was in the class next door and ran to the scene but was barred from the classroom. The medics were working on Paul, and my buddies didn't want me to flip out and compound what were already serious issues.

It was a serious accident; Paul's family came out to Pittsburgh. He had lost a lot of blood and had a punctured lung; he was lucky the glass didn't stab his heart. He was laid up in the hospital while we had our final scene presentations. Another guy in our class coughed up blood in a rehearsal and had to be hospitalized. We were banged up, but we got through it. I had a small technical difficulty in my final scene and was telling Paul about it in the hospital. It was painful for him to laugh, but I was telling my story in as much vivid detail as I could. This involved a fair amount of profanity. Paul's roommate in the hospital did not take well to my colorful language and yelled at me through the curtain, which only got Paul laughing more.

There wasn't a lot of talk about what happened to Paul in our classes. This was before grief counselors, or trauma counselors, were in fashion. It was a rare moment in our invincible years where we had pause. We had a chance to think about something other than our desires and ambitions. It hit me that this was just a glorified circus; all the pressure we were putting on ourselves, or that was imposed by the structure of the program, was absurd and ultimately not the only way to embark on an acting career. Of course, those thoughts lasted a few days, and then we had to worry about our conferences and our futures at CMU. Paul and I joked that he really went to the extreme to ensure that he'd be back, who cuts a guy who almost died for his art?

The year-end conference was a bit more fraught with tension. While I was as certain as you can be in these situations, I went in there listening for the magic words, "we'll see you next year." You hoped to hear those words early in the conference, so you could relax and talk about what you needed to work on. The gist of my meeting was that I would continue next year, but there was work to do. I needed to show more consistency. News of people who had been cut didn't spread as rapidly as you might think. People were literally leaving their luggage in the hallway as they went in for their conferences and then headed to the airport or piled into a car after they were done. News came in trickles if you stayed in touch with a classmate, but it would really hit home when you got back to campus for sophomore year. Of course, some people pulled the plug on their own volition. Some might have been wise to do so. Others who were cut would have to find a new path with a bunch of credits that wouldn't transfer, or at least which left them to catch up academically. Some were gone to work on major motion pictures and become stars.

27

SUMMER BREEZE

That summer I carried an air of confidence that I had made it through the year. I had to find a job, and that started out badly. Jimmy Carver and my friend John had found a job in a warehouse unloading automotive parts, and they could get me on the crew. It was a disaster. The job consisted of emptying boxes, taking out smaller boxes, and finding a shelf to put the smaller box on. There were multi-digit numbers and codes on the small boxes, and I never found the same number on any shelf that matched a box the entire time I was working. I would try to get close, but it never worked out. I apologize to the car owners of the early 1990s for the wrong part arriving at your mechanic's garage. This drone work was not as easy as it looked.

The worst part of the job was the bullhorn on the ceiling that announced breaks, lunch hour, and quitting time. There was some sadistic nasal-voiced dispatcher or foreman who enjoyed reminding us that, "BREAK TIME IS OVAH, OVAH. BREAK IS OVAH." He would use the same cadence and perverse sense of pleasure as he announced the end of the half hour lunch break. I remember having a hard time putting a sandwich down in that short amount of time. I would be washing down the bread with a Yoo-Hoo and hustling back to the warehouse, all the while being berated by the voice from the sky.

"LUNCH TIME IS OVAH, OVAH."

The job was also undependable. Every other week we would be laid off for a day or two. While that was like getting a conjugal visit in prison, it didn't help the paycheck add up to more than beer money. When those days would come, we would pile into our buddy's car and head to the Jersey Shore, which was new to me because I prided myself on summering on Nantucket as a child, as if two weeks in a rental house can be called summering.

Eventually, I decided that I wasn't going to work at the warehouse anymore. My college friend Paul, had found an employment agency in Manhattan that had gotten him a job at a Beefsteak Charlie's, and I wanted that life. I went in and told a buddy who had recently graduated about the agency. We both interviewed and lied about our experience and got a job at Tequila Willie's. I was hoping for Beefsteak Charlie to give me the call, but Tequila Willie had the offer.

Tequila Willie's was somewhere near 49th Street and Broadway, maybe 47th Street. I'm not exactly sure. It wasn't the kind of place for locals, not a neighborhood spot. It was the kind of place that, once you became a New Yorker, you would avoid like much of the touristy areas of the city. I had zero experience, and the training waiter was kind enough to pretend he didn't notice. My friend who had just graduated was in the same boat. I was glad to have a friend to train with; my friend was probably feeling something else as he learned that a quesadilla is like a Mexican pizza and how to pronounce pico de gallo.

We showed up for our training and, eventually, we were allowed on the floor to take tables for real. It was a panic situation for me. I was not adept at handling the drink tray and once the shit hit the fan I would get overwhelmed. I would screw up often, but I suppose I was so earnest I rarely got yelled at. There was a young manager who was a sometime boxer, who also had a few neurological tics that were either fight-related or a mild version of Tourette's syndrome. He liked to show off his quick hands and would do dips and leg raises between chairs in the dining room.

When I would have a problem and had to get him to appease a table I had messed up, he would say the same thing.

"Remember, the customer is always wrong."

"Got it, but I forgot to put their food into the computer and it's been an hour." I said.

"Doesn't matter, they're always wrong and full of shit. I'll take care of it."

He would make his approach to the table, and something that didn't quite resemble customer relations would ensue. Usually, a round of frozen margaritas would smooth the way toward a solution, but, sometimes he let the table stew in anger if he felt they were being jerks or if he thought my screw-up wasn't that colossal.

The kitchen was upstairs as well as the bar and lounge. The dining room was downstairs. This was a painful bit of architecture, especially when you had a tray loaded down with four sizzling skillets of fajitas, inches from your face. My friend came to work with what looked like a knife wound on his cheekbone.

"What happened?" I asked.

"I was going down the stairs and slipped. I didn't want to drop the tray with the fajitas, and one of the skillets slid against my face."

"That's a burn?" I asked.

"Yeah."

"Jesus Christ, you should have just dropped the tray". I said.

"Vinnie would have gone ballistic." He replied.

Vinnie was the other manager who took the gig seriously and didn't like that he had two novices on his staff. He had a lot of clichés to impart.

"Make every trip a business trip." He would say.

"What?"

"Don't walk around empty-handed; either bring something or take something away, capeesh?"

I would walk away carrying a napkin thinking to myself, "Did he really just say capeesh and mean it?"

The job sucked, but I was just trying to pile up some cash before heading back to school, so the true dismal nature of the ordeal was lost on me. My friend Rick was seeing it differently, I'm sure.

Vinnie was actually a decent guy, and the fact that I wasn't fired for incompetence was always appreciated. Rick was late to work once, and Vinnie told me I'd have to pick up some slack. I asked him what was wrong with Rick.

Vinnie said, "He calls me and says he walked out of his house and that a flock of pigeons dropped a bomb raid worth of shit on his head and clothes and that he had to go back upstairs and shower and change."

"Wow, that's crazy."

"I don't even give a shit if it's true or not, just coming up with that story is worth it." He said. "Make sure to set up Rick's station, would you?"

Vinnie was partial to Rick, figuring he might have a full time employee. With me he knew I was a goner and didn't want to invest too much. That was OK with me. This job went a long way toward teaching me a few things about keeping your shit together and not getting bulldozed by people. It wasn't uncommon for the more seasoned waiters to steal your food and take it to their tables, making it seem like they were superstars while you had to fetch a manager. These guys were mercenary, and they made better money than I did because of their ability to sell, turn tables, and steal. I was just trying not to fuck up.

28

MANSION ON THE HILL

Sophomore year, we decided to move off campus into a house on Fair Oaks Street. We almost rented a place that was forty feet from train tracks because it had a wet bar in the basement. If you are like me and didn't know what a wet bar refers to, let me tell you. A wet bar simply means it has a working sink. The idea that we could have a basement with a bar almost made us forget the rattling of the house as the trains came by. The house was also just outside of the route of the campus shuttle bus. Thankfully, we came to our senses and figured we could build a bar.

We rented a house that had been in the drama "family" for many years. It was the top two floors of a large brick house about a mile up hill from campus. It had six bedrooms and two bathrooms and was dubbed the "Dramat Frat." We basically took it over from the previous group of students. It didn't get the makeover that a place will get when new tenants take possession. It was cheap, and it was familiar, so the adjustment would be muted. We might not have our wet bar, but we had a small piece of history. Roberto Clemente's accountant once lived on Fair Oaks Street.

The crew, which had named itself the Posse, now had a clubhouse. We had to furnish our rooms, but the common areas had rummage sale furnishings that we inherited from many years of drama students past, not to mention odd canned goods in the cupboards.

The posse included Paul from Riverdale, New York. Of course when asked he would say he was from the Bronx. Kevin was from Bushwick, Brooklyn and was a fellow graduate of the High School for the Performing Arts (the *Fame* school) with Paul. The last member of the Posse was an art major, Tommy J., who was from Philadelphia.

Our residency of 432 Fair Oaks gave us all a feeling of growing up, our first pad, our first place to call our own; the first place to destroy by having a party to end all parties.

We needed to advertise and we wanted to build the anticipation. We used a three-prong attack. The first sign we posted on the drama board read, "Da Posse." The second sign, with a day in between read, "Da Party." The third sign on Friday read, "DaRections" and included a map to the house. Tommy J. had a great idea, and we went to Radio Shack to buy a strobe light. If you haven't played around with a strobe light, you haven't lived. We had a friend who was a DJ, and we set him up in one of the bedrooms. We ordered two kegs, and we locked the doors to our rooms. That night, we blew out the DJ speakers, which put us in the hole for about two hundred bucks. We were also shut down by the cops, which made it official and an unmitigated success.

Time constraints made it hard to meet people who weren't in the drama department. More to the point, it was hard to meet girls. The lack of a female population was another difficulty. The University of Pittsburgh had the opposite student ratio of three females to every one male, but we had no time to get down the road to cruise the campus. I had to break out of my slump. Now that I had gotten through my first year, I felt I could breath a bit and might be able to handle the work and a girlfriend, or several.

By the time sophomore year had rolled around, our class was

whittled down to having only four women, and after our first year together, they were more like sisters than dateable entities. The lucky thing for our class was that the class above us was predominately gay, and the girls in the other classes were looking for attention from our class, which was predominately straight. I had my head up my ass freshmen year and didn't play these favorable odds.

At a second party at 432 Fair Oaks, I was dancing with a girl named Nancy, who was a senior. I was working with some privy information that she was interested in me. While she might not have been on my radar before, she was now. I didn't push it too far at the party, I was trying to keep options open, and she was actually on her way to another party. I forgot that girls have more options for social life; I was stunned she was leaving. We were so insulated from the rest of the world that it didn't dawn on me that there was someplace else to go.

I spent the rest of the party threatening anyone who looked like they might be about to get sick.

"I'll kill you if you puke in my house, take it outside, you lightweight." I bellowed.

Eventually, I made inroads with Nancy. By inroads, I mean there must have been some kind of date, and some period before we became more than acquaintances. I'm not trying to be coy or polite, but it's just that we went from strangers to lovers in that condensed college percolator, and I was now in a relationship after much time alone.

Nancy was slim, had dark wavy hair and was a yoga practitioner. I think that's what you call it. She was an advanced student, maybe even a yogi. She had a portfolio of herself in poses that looked impossible to get into with a skeletal system. She was limber shall we say, and this was a good thing. She was different, in that she had interests outside of acting, and that wasn't the case for everyone. She gave me facials, walked on my back, and was into the zodiac. I found out what my rising sign was, but don't remember, and I'm not sure I had the right information for her to come to that conclusion in the first place. She was now a senior, so she had made it through the rigors that now enveloped me, which caused some friction. She had time on her hands, and I did not. Our schedules were incompatible and I still tried to mix in my time with the boys.

One night, I was hanging out at her well-appointed apartment, and a buddy of mine knocked on the door. I'm not sure how, but he was in possession of a large van, and wanted to go to Mt. Washington, which overlooks the city, and cruise around. I thought it was a great idea, and we both tried to get our girlfriends to pile into the van with us. Nancy was not game, and she said. "I forget how young you are, and how you still want to play with the boys."

"Does that mean I can go?"

As my buddy and I reveled in a few hours with wheels, it dawned on me that Nancy was only 20 or 21 to my 18 or 19, and where did she come off telling me that I was immature, as I screamed "nice ass" at a gaggle of girls out of the window of the van. Nancy had money and a nice car; she didn't see it as a novel thing to be able to drive around.

I don't think there were any class issues between us, but there were starting to be some glaring differences. While I wouldn't put myself in the type casting of a Jersey Boy, the fact that Nancy was a new age hippie was a bit of a culture clash. It also dawned on me that I hadn't selected Nancy. It was brought to my attention by a well-meaning friend, that she was interested. This put the relationship out of balance from the start. My lack of female attention over the last year had me looking for any port in a storm. My guilt and inability to be honest had me saddled with a relationship when maybe what I wanted was something casual, if not short-lived.

Another well-meaning dude, from another class, asked me if I was seeing someone, and I wanted to know what cards he was holding before I said anything. I told him I was, in fact, seeing someone and asked him why he was curious. When he revealed the card and told me for whom he was inquiring, I tried not to let on that I would have jumped ship if I thought I could.

It's a lesson that the ladies won't be glad I'm sharing. I didn't do anything wrong, but the idea of taking it slow would have given me some wiggle room if I had feelings for someone else. It wasn't virtue that kept me from not moving on to someone else—it was a lack of confidence to be an asshole and to do whatever I wanted. It could always get sticky, but at that age, options are all you have.

The Christmas break was on its way, and I was glad for the break from my relationship. Nancy was heading home to North Carolina a few days before I was leaving, and I was looking forward to a couple of days with friends and no schedule. I got a call form Nancy from the airport, telling me she left something back at her apartment that she needed before her flight—maybe a confirmation number. I was irked, thinking that she had roommates, who couldn't all be gone for the break, already and why did I have to go over to her place? I'm not saying it was nice, but it was how I felt. I made my way to her apartment, on my almost-attached-to-my-body- mountain-bike, and let myself in, only to see one of her roommates, a classmate of mine, sitting, on the couch. Nancy was going to call her apartment and tell me where to look.

"Bob, do you know what she needs me to find?" I asked.

"I think she left you a present, on her bed, and wanted to hear you open it," he said.

"I'm a dick." I thought. "She's doing something nice and I'm grumbling about it."

I made my way up the stairs to Nancy's bedroom and saw a life-like stuffed toy dog at the foot of the bed. It was a companion to the one I had gotten Nancy. I was hoping for something electronic, but it was a nice thought. I reached down to pick up the card and the gift, as Nancy jumped out the closet and scared the living shit out of me.

"Surprise, I changed my flight." She said as she jumped on me.

Now, under normal circumstances, and with a nice person receiving this kind of surprise, you would think I would say, "Great, what a great surprise."

Instead, I said, "What the hell are you doing? You scared the shit out of me."

"I was just trying to surprise you."

"Yeah, well, you did, but I thought you were out of town, and I have plans and now I have to change them and ..." I replied.

This brought on tears and maybe a deserved punch in the arm. It really just slipped; I let my inner-monologue come out of my mouth. Now I had to do damage control and try to stop her from going to the airport. I felt like a dirt bag, and probably was. I'm not sure what kind of weekend we had after that. I was driving back home with Paul, so I had more flexibility in my departure. Nancy's plan really only gave us one more day, and I was sorry I reacted poorly. I had some thinking to do over the break.

I had my mid-semester conference, where I was told to work hard on the scene we were carrying-over to the next semester, which was from *Romeo and Juliet*. The faculty wanted me to dig deeper, find a working technique that would keep my work consistent, and not rely only on spontaneous reactions that would fluctuate from day to day. I was heading home to figure out what I was going to do about Nancy.

29

SOUTHERN MAN

That break, Tommy J. came up from Philly and we caught up with Paul in New York City for New Year's Eve. This would be the first in a long line of insane New Year's Eves in New York. Tommy's dad had a beautiful Oldsmobile '98, which was a boat with wheels; it had beautiful spoke rims, and the backseat was a leather couch; it was in mint condition. Public Enemy had a song about the '98, and we were playing it as we crossed the George Washington Bridge. He parked near Paul's house, and we took Paul's beater into the city. We managed a couple of stops and went to an NYU party; we finally wound up at a nightclub with unisex bathrooms, balconies, and cage dancers.

We hit the dance floor, and two girls started dancing with Paul and me, their backs to us the whole time. I never saw a face; as we danced for fifteen minutes, there was no talking, and by minute five I was pitching a tent in my pants. I thought this was a good start toward getting to know someone better and hoped it wasn't embarrassing the girl. I guess it would have, but she hung in there for ten more minutes, which is like 7,000 songs in a club. My big mistake in this whole situation was trying to scream a question into the girl's ear. As soon as I tore my vocal chord saying, "Where are you from," she turned, touched my face, and disappeared into the crowd with her friend. Paul looked at me wondering how I ruined a good thing. I shrugged and tried to let the bulge in my pants subside as I danced solo for the rest of the night.

We made it back to Paul's apartment at dawn and slept past noon. We woke up and headed to Tommy J's car. As soon as we hit the cold New Years Day air, I knew his car was gone. Tommy kept walking down the street, past all reasonable distance from where he had parked the night before. He didn't want to believe it.

"No. No. NO. NO. FUCK NO. FUCK. FUCK."

Tommy stalked back in our direction and started kicking cars on his way back. He put a good dent in someone's quarter panel. He got back to where we were standing.

"They fuckin' took my car. My dad's going to lose his shit."

"I'm sorry, bro" was all I could manage.

We headed back into the apartment building and into the elevator. Paul and I had a horrible problem in class freshman year; we couldn't stop our laughing fits. We'd shudder and blow snot trying not to get caught laughing, while everyone else was learning how to be an egg. Now, stuck in an elevator with Tommy, and possibly the owner of one of the dented cars, Paul started breathing funny, and I started clamping down on my laughter. I felt like a bad person, but I was shocked by the theft and Tommy's reaction, I guess I was nervous, and that's how it was working itself out, laughing at my friend's pain. Tommy had to call his father and was told to get on the first train to Philly. We took him to Penn Station and finally laughed about the boot he put to the station wagon on Paul's street. We later found out from Paul's dad that Riverdale is the worst place for car theft on the East Coast—probably not the best place to park a collectible Olds.

Christmas was upon us, and Nancy had sent me a mix tape, which is rare for a girl. We talked on the phone a few times, and she told me she was coming to New York for a couple of days with her father, who was big in real estate, and was speaking at a book signing or seminar. She had sent a gift, after the mix tape, and all had I managed to send was a mix tape in return, albeit, with better music, if you ask me. Nancy sent me a nice watch and some silver champagne flutes. Actually, the watch was hidden in one of the flutes, and she had me open it on the phone, so she could hear my reaction. This time I managed to be gracious, but part of me was worried about the extravagance of the gift and the impending meeting with her father.

Somehow, a meeting at my house was arranged, and Nancy was gracious and charming. She had made a reservation at an Indian restaurant in the city, and I tried to be enthusiastic. We boarded the bus, which was a new experience for Nancy, and made our way to the restaurant. Her father had some business and didn't join us for the meal, but we were to meet him for a drink at a midtown hotel bar. The food was new to me and not in a good way. I consider myself an adventurous eater, even back then, but this cuisine has never meshed with my palette.

I don't know if I ordered a beer or a Perrier when I sat in the plush, dark, lounge that overlooked Times Square. I was uncomfortable with the food as it settled in my system. I was also uncomfortable meeting Nancy's father, considering how I was in a quandary about whether I wanted to stay with his daughter. Normally, I would try my best to dominate the meeting, to charm the parents, in an attempt to assure them their daughter was in good hands. I enjoyed these meetings in most cases. Perhaps, there was bad chemistry with Nancy's dad. He was in town to speak and sign his books. He had a copy for me, which was nice. It was one of those, *Real Estate With No Money Down* type of books—a big grinning picture of the author on the cover and a blurb about how successful he had been in his field. He was a natural storyteller, and he liked to command the room. I don't remember much of what I had to say about myself. I do remember him telling a story about one of his employee's, a Guy-Friday who had worked with Nancy's dad for years, and in the telling of the story, he dropped an N-word. I was totally pulled out of the conversation. I felt heat rising to my face, and I had to ask myself if I heard what I heard. There was a debate with myself about whether I would confront him. I wasn't going to, and maybe we both knew it. It was a major turn-off. My mom heard that word once while some friends and I were playing ping-pong in the basement, and let me have it.

"I don't want hear that word in my house!" She yelled down the stairs. This rebuke coming from a woman who joined the N.A.A.C.P. in the 1950s, well before the Civil Rights Movement engendered support on mostly white college campuses. It was a moment of shame, not to be repeated.

There was an option to go somewhere else or to share a cab, and I decided I would walk back to Port Authority. I thanked her father and shook his hand. On my way back to New Jersey, I replayed the night. We had some weird scrip money for the dinner, so, essentially, her dad had paid. He refused my money for the drinks and was pleasant if a little pompous, but when he crossed the line with his word choice, I went cold. I had his book and contemplated chucking it, but I knew my dad would be curious to see it.

I never mentioned Nancy's dad using the N-word because I didn't want it to reflect badly on Nancy, but mostly I didn't want it to reflect badly on me. We made it back to school. I think Nancy rode with my dad and me, and it wasn't soon after, that Nancy and I broke up. I would like to say it was the racist slur that pushed me over the edge, but that wouldn't be true. I was just not as invested as she was and had to make the break. It would be hard to avoid awkwardness in the hallways when you are in a department that has less than 200 people. Seeing her would occur on a daily basis. There was no anger or arguing, but these things are never fun.

While I might have told Nancy that I was not in the right place for a relationship, it didn't stop me from trying to get involved, soon after. It didn't stop her. The ego is a funny thing, while you might have been the catalyst to break up, you don't want to see the person get over it too soon. Nancy found a guy, and that should have been a good thing, but my ego was hoping she'd be a heaping mess for years to come. When you're immature you see these things in terms of wins and losses. Nancy getting on the board before me was a loss. I wasn't interested in getting back together or messing with the dude she took up with, I just wanted to move on sooner than she did. Guys just don't have as many options.

It should also be said that at this point in our lives, time is kept in smaller increments. Two months is an eternity, and relationships that last six months are considered serious. I was enjoying the time with the fellas, and I suppose I was putting in better effort in the classroom. It was just after winter break that Nancy and I split up, and maybe a month or so before she surfaced with a new guy. It's funny how she was now more likely to say hello in the hallways. She knew she was on the record as the first to move along. Man, I have issues even to notice this stuff.

30

SMOOTH OPERATOR

Before we secured fake IDs from a design student, who was so good that he was able to make them with their holograms, we had a few places to go where they served us underage. Bar 4 was a place that had been a drama spot for a while. I think the drama kids had affectations that made them seem more mature. Some didn't drink beer, and a lot of them smoked. Of course my group changed that when we became regulars at Bar 4. They had great wings and pitchers of Iron City Light, the greatest local beer in the states. The older students had paved the way, and the waitress knew them and took care of them. I think we had to sit interspersed with the older students until we were familiar to the staff. We were also schooled to the fact that we better not be cheap and to tip appropriately for the privilege of being served. Part of the deal was to sit in the booths in the back; we never sidled up to the bar. They also had a fridge to buy beer to go, but we needed ID for that because the bartenders were not going to sell beer out the door to punk kids.

During this time of wings and things, there was a production mounted by the senior girls that was outside the purview of the department. This happened from time to time but was rare because you would had to squeeze-in rehearsals between class work and other productions, had to be motivated, and probably had to get it done in two weeks. The senior girls were putting up *Steel Magnolias*, and this was not the typical fare at Carnegie Mellon. It was too commercial and not heavyweight enough to be presented as a drama production.

It wound up being very well attended and was fun and well presented. Of course, like many of the plays we did in college, no one was old enough to play most of the parts. It was a party atmosphere in the studio theatre, which was a black box theatre that supplemented the main stage at CMU. That the senior class was replete with comely ladies might have had something to do with the attendance. There also wasn't a lot of comedy at CMU, so maybe we needed some escapism. My friends and I were doing a little front-loading before the show, and I remember having to find an alternate bathroom in an academic building at intermission. Knowing where bathrooms are on campus lets you know that you're home; having mastery of the map of your school is a nice thing to notice.

Clearing out the beer in my bladder made me late getting back from intermission, but at least I could uncross my legs and enjoy the rest of the show. I found myself drawn to one of the women on stage. Kiera Lyle was a raven-haired beauty if raven hair means dark brown hair. She had blue eyes and was what I think they refer to as black Irish if that term applies to women equally. She was tall and full figured and was playing the sharp-tongued sassy broad in the play. She had all the laugh lines, and it was a side of her I had never seen. Kiera was the reason we could drink at Bar 4. At least, that's what I thought. She drank scotch and was very cool with the waitress. She spoke in a clipped almost Catherine Hepburn kind of way, at least compared to me. She was from Manhattan, and I thought she was a bit unapproachable. She also might have had a reputation as a man-eater but not in the Hall and Oates kind of way.

That night, after the play, I was hanging out with the boys and tried to hatch a plan to take Kiera down. My buddy Jack told me that coming right out with it was the best play. That was easier said than done. I liked to meander.

Figuring the chances were good that Kiera would be at Bar 4 after the show, we descended on the spot, and I had a mission to attempt to enact. Jack and I made our way to Kiera's table, and I tried to be charming, which entailed me bumming her cigarettes and doing my Robert DeNiro impersonation. As last call arrived, I was at the end of my time line and had to do something. I had calmed down and put the smokes down enough to have had a decent conversation with Kiera, and I asked her if she wanted to keep talking.

"Uh, yeah that would be nice." She said.

"You want to get some coffee?"

"We could just go back to my place. I have some wine." She replied.

"Great."

We got in her car, which was a Toyota Cressida if anyone knows what a Cressida is. It might be that annoying bug that makes noise all summer long and sheds its skin, leaving its bug shell all over the place —wait, that's a cicada.

We made it to her apartment, which was the same place from the year before where I attended my first drama party. There had been a few since. It was the top floor of another large brick house. I know now that smart people buy a place and convert attics or guesthouses into rental property, and this helps pay the mortgage. She had two roommates who weren't home that night, or maybe they were, and we had to be quiet.

I might have nursed some wine as I sat on the couch, and Kiera sat on the armchair next to me. The couch was covered with a sheet that was only slightly better fitting, than the sheets draped over furniture in a haunted house. We talked about art; I told her I was a closet art nerd. I referenced the prints she had on the wall. Part of the conversation involved me making a case against what I thought was a persona that belied who I really was. Kiera was also shaping up to be different in person than she was from afar. I was becoming aware of her intellect as much as her physicality. She was razor smart.

It was getting late. There were two armrests separating us, so making a move would not be easy. Actually I had no move. I had spent half the time telling myself that I needed to make a move, but how? I tried an old technique that I had long abandoned and didn't think would work on someone as sophisticated as Kiera.

"I wonder if what I'm thinking is a bad idea?" I said.

"What are you thinking?"

"I'm thinking about how much I want to kiss you." I replied.

"I think it would be a bad idea. I'm flattered, but I'm friends with Nancy and…"

"I understand."

I knew it wouldn't work. I excused myself to the bathroom and berated myself behind the door. I returned and told Kiera I had a great time and had to go.

She said, "Before you go, I'd like you to kiss me. That is, if you still want to."

We kissed, and tried to make out in the chair, which led to the floor, which led to the bedroom. The whole time I'm thinking, theatre is awesome, and I can't believe I'm making out with Kiera Lyle.

31

DON'T GIVE UP

The next day Kiera let me borrow her car, and I drove to my place and parked it in front of the house on Fair Oaks. My roommate Kevin was home, which was rare. He kept a room in our place, but lived, most of the time, with his girlfriend who was a grad student at Pitt. We caught up for a bit, and he asked me what I was up to. I told him that I hadn't been home.

"Oh, yeah, what'd you get into?" He asked.

"Look out the window."

"What am I looking at?" he asked.

"You see that car?" I replied.

"The Cressida?"

"Yeah, guess whose car that is?"

"I don't know." Kevin replied.

"Kiera Lyle's." I announced.

"No shit?"

"Yeah, man." I said.

"What are you doing with her…oh, wow, really, Kiera Lyle?"

"Yeah." I said.

He was impressed, and I was giddy. It was a bit embarrassing, but Kevin was someone I could be giddy around.

His girlfriend was a beautiful Jamaican girl, and Kevin was from Trinidad. He was closed off about himself, but easy to be around. His girl was very sweet, and was almost like an older sister we could talk to about affairs of the heart. He was duly impressed at my conquest. I was, at first, simply excited that I put a target before me and went out and made it happen. You don't get giddy from a one-night stand—you do, but in a different kind of way. This was a walking-on-air kind of giddy, and I'm more than a little certain that giddy was the word in my head. I think we can see where this was going—I was in trouble, and I liked it.

I spent the little free time I had with Kiera. I loaded my bicycle in the trunk of her car when we went to her house. Sometimes, I raced her, but this left me sweaty and winded, so we opted for the bike in the trunk.

Keira, like Nancy, was a debutante, albeit a New York version and not the Southern kind. I didn't really know what a debutante was and still don't. I think it involves a big dance that is not the prom, and you have to have a lot of money. Being from New Jersey, I was aware of sweet sixteen parties and the like, which usually occurred in an Elks Club. I thought these kinds of balls had become a thing of the past like *Gone With the Wind*.

I would often be on my way to the cafeteria and Kiera would ask me if I wanted to go out to eat. I would tell her I liked the cafeteria, and that I couldn't roll over my meals to the next week, and this was wasteful, and my parents had paid for me to eat the institutional food. I didn't mention I was broke or cash poor. She would wave off my objections and we would go out to eat, at her whim and on her dime, most of the time. I was trying to be chivalrous, but that was difficult on a bike and with no cash.

As I fell deeper and deeper into Kiera's snare, I found out or was forced to remember that she had a long distance boyfriend. I think he lived in New York and was older, of course. The relationship was seldom mentioned, and I initially was trying to keep things casual, so I thought I could handle it. I couldn't, as I began to think of Kiera as a serious contender for my heart.

In the spring at CMU, there is an event called Carnival, which is about what it sounds like. There are game booths that are designed by the fraternities and sororities, and there are rides from creepy county affairs. Most of the campus shuts down for a few days, not usually the drama department, and there is a weird thing called buggy that races on the Saturday of Carnival. Buggy is a tradition of building a man powered, push powered vehicle that is sort of like an urban bobsled mixed with a relay race. Frats and special interest houses compete, and it is rumored that the design and development budgets can be in the $10,000 range. Most of this stuff went over the dramat's heads. We were busy with productions most of the weekend. This year we had a bit of down time. This is when I knew I was getting under Kiera's skin in a good way. She liked to play tough and above it all, and she kept herself from being too exuberant. Somehow, I managed to convince Kiera to get on one of those rickety rides, and she admitted that she never would have done that before or with anyone else. She said I made her happy.

Back in the classroom, I had a breakthrough that semester. We were working on our Shakespeare scenes. I had been sent home over the mid-semester break with a mandate to whip my scene into shape. I had gone to the library in Rutherford, and poured over my text. I photocopied the scene and pasted it onto loose-leaf paper, using the additional surface area to make notes. While you would think working without your partner is a futile exercise, you actually have a lot to do on your own, with certain texts.

My first class back, I insisted on working first. We were doing the famous balcony scene from *Romeo and Juliet*. This was tough because it is so well known and has been lampooned in so many ways. We had to play it straight, and I had to show off my efforts over the break. I pushed a lot of furniture around the room. We had cubes and platforms and flats. We made a balcony for Juliet, and we were set to go. My take on the scene was to break up the famous words with actions. I made an obstacle course, and my main objective in the scene was to get as close to Juliet, without being caught, as I could. I literally climbed and ducked and said my lines in bursts. It worked. It was funny without being a spoof. It made the character come to life as the impetuous teen he was. The class got to critique each other, and their praise was universal. The professor was in agreement. One of my classmates had a lot to say.

"That's the first time I saw you be as good as you are when you're in the cafeteria, and I'd pay to watch you be that good." He said.

I don't recount this to boost my ego, but to illuminate the key to what ailed me in drama school, and what can plague artists until they find a way to be more like themselves in their work. That doesn't mean you can only play your exact type, but it means becoming a conduit for your personality in the work. It was hard for me to bring my own dynamism to my work, and this was a time that I had succeeded. I hate to say dynamism, but it is the word that fits. I don't say it immodestly (we all have it) but to better understand where my blocks were.

As an artist you have to bring *that thing* to your work, and it may not be as easy as you think. The people who can harness *that thing*, tend to be more interesting to watch. Certain actors are hired for *that thing* more than any other skill or trait. Charles S. Dutton comes to mind—his speech in *Rudy* is an example of that thing he does—that quiet intensity, he almost boils, and you are mesmerized. James Woods is cast to do that thing he does, when he's hyper-verbal and bouncy with a hint of menace. When you watch Daniel Day Lewis, you are waiting for that moment when he erupts and makes you forget you have popcorn in your lap or are sitting on the couch, "Stay alive, I will find you," or when he has an outburst, in *My Left Foot*, where you, along with the characters, forget he can barely speak and hear him shout. That's what actors have to figure out and exploit to their benefit. That day in class, I was doing *my thing*, and that is a moment to try to bottle.

There was one opportunity to perform this year. It was a student produced talent show, and it would be on the main stage but was really an outside endeavor. It was just a chance to get up there and do something. The musical theatre students had the advantage in that they had a repertoire of songs to perform. I knew that I wanted to be involved but didn't have an act in mind. Doing stand-up was not an option. This would be well attended, and I was trying to be serious, almost shunning a natural leaning toward comedy.

I came up with an idea, and it was bold in the sense that anything that doesn't involve fighting, loss of money, or nudity can be considered bold. Peter Gabriel's album *So* was a must have for the thoughtful, sensitive, students of the era. The song "In Your Eyes" was a cliché by the time the album was two years old. The song that got me was "Don't Give Up," the duet with Kate Bush. It had a stark, almost Springsteen vibe to it, and I thought it could be an interesting stage piece. My idea was to perform it as a two-person scene, the words telling the story. I needed a setting, and a milieu—I think that word choice applies here. I had an image of a table overturned in a kitchen; a blue-collar guy comes home after a domestic argument. He rights the table and straightens out the chairs. The first words of the song are his text.

I sang the first words. They speak about being proud and strong and wanted and being taught to fight and win. Where he grew up there was never a thought of failure.

The background I constructed had a young married couple, going through a hard time. The husband's promise to get them out of their dead-end town has fallen short. They have a fight. He destroys the kitchen. The scene starts with him alone in the kitchen. When the female vocal begins, his wife, in a nightgown, enters from the bedroom and starts her text.

She sings simpler words. She tells her man to stop his worrying, to rest his head and that he could fall back on their love and most importantly she tells him to never give up.

The song crescendos, and I have a high note to hit, and we come together in the middle of the stage and embrace. It was a nice scene. I had boldly asked Terri Buford to be my scene partner. Terri is now an opera singer and has been on Broadway. She's a real singer, and I was trying to sing along with her. The problem was that the music had to be transcribed, and the instruments on the actual recording were not going to be available. We had a piano and a bongo player. The rhythm was atypical, and during the performance, I missed my cue on the second verse. I stayed in the scene, and stayed with the acting, but I was close to losing it. I didn't know how to get back in on time. I finally managed to jump back in and we got to the end.

Off stage, I went ballistic; I was beside myself and felt humiliated. I took off and didn't talk to anyone for hours. I was being dramatic, but my threshold for embarrassment was not at an all-time high. It was the first time the whole department would see me do anything, most notably, Kiera. It wasn't for a grade, and it couldn't work against me, but I put a lot of pressure on myself, not the least of which was singing along side a world-class voice.

Once I calmed down, and came off the ledge, Kiera was there, both to comfort me, and tell me I was being a baby about it. She said we looked beautiful up there, and no one noticed the foul-up. Another person, from the junior class, said it was like the *Grapes of Wrath* and that I had balls singing with Terri. Terri knew that I had messed up, but thought the piece had worked.

The most interesting reaction came from the guy I was going to see for therapy, I have a hard time saying my therapist, but he had an interesting take. The fact that he saw the performance and had been listening to my problems, gave him a perspective I was very interested to hear. He told me that he was a trained opera singer. He knew he was finished as a performer when he became affected by the music and couldn't sing well when he got emotional. He said the performer has to make the audience feel and had to be able to control his own emotions. He said that he knew it didn't go as well as I had hoped, from a technical stand-point, but the fact that I was, literally, telling myself not to give up, that I was encouraging myself, in some way, coupled with the setting, was powerful to watch. It didn't dawn on me that I might have been trying to quell my own fears and worries. I thought I just liked the song and thought it would be fun. He was clear that it wasn't even a subtle cue from the psychological point of view and that I needed to see it as a step in a good direction. I was in therapy, partly because of my work, and as an artist you find out that the work and the psyche, are at very least, dovetailed and so is every facet of your life, especially your love life.

Therapy was free, so I made an appointment. I remember looking both ways as I entered the office. I remember trying to avoid eye contact with people walking out of the office before me. I don't remember the exact catalyst to get me to go, but I knew I felt like shit. Emotionally, I learned some vocabulary, and started to see some patterns. I was always looking for external approval, and it put a lot of pressure on my relationships. I was obsessed with losing my virginity and was still obsessed with sex. It seemed to me that you couldn't get more approval than when you are having sex with someone. I suppose I could trace a lot of this back to childhood, but I got a lot of attention. Maybe I was greedy and needy. I suppose I put too much emphasis on it, and it was distracting me from my work.

32

THE HOUSE OF BERNARDA ALBA

The specter of Kiera's graduation and a campus visit from her boyfriend were looming. What was I doing to myself? I got caught out there and made a play at a girl thinking I could keep it casual. I forgot that I was a drama king and would start having feelings. That I knew about this situation and still hung in there embarrassed me. It made me crazy, and I think I liked being crazy. I thought that was how you were supposed to act. It was a quadruple trap; Kiera was an ice queen, with a boyfriend, who was a senior, with a lot on her mind about the rest of her life. It was the perfect challenge, and what better way to test the limits of your charm and loveableness?

Kiera and I would play music to mask the noise we might make in an effort not to annoy her roommates. She had a tape that had the great classical guitarist, Segovia, on it. She had another tape of the greatest hits of The Band. It was country rock, or roots rock, or whatever you want to call it, but it was good. I'm a kid from New Jersey, and "The Night They Drove Old Dixie Down" was speaking to me. Of course, I forced Kiera to listen to the softer side of Springsteen.

We were getting along on all fronts—all the fronts, but the fronts of practicality and fidelity.

The schedule of plays for the main stage listed a production of the Lorca play, *The House of Bernarda Alba*. I was to be on the run crew, running sound. The play is heavy, not a lot of laughs. It's about a woman whose second husband has died, and as is custom in her family, the mourning period is eight years. She has four daughters, and the oldest has an inheritance that makes her attractive to suitors, most notably, one Pepe El Romano. The youngest daughter sneaks around and has an affair with Pepe in the stables, always the stables. When the shit hits the fan, the mother shoots Pepe and drives him out of town, driving the youngest to suicide, and leaving the heiress without a husband. Nancy was playing the oldest daughter, and Kiera was playing the youngest. It was method acting at its best. I was Pepe El Romano. Pepe doesn't appear in the play; his presence is off-stage, just like my presence, sitting up in the sound booth, watching two actresses, feeding off the awkward situation, which I helped to create—only in drama school.

Of course, it was a bit of a problem in the dressing room. The play was intense, and the actors needed to prepare. Kiera had to make the emotional arc, whereby she would hang herself, or at least her character would, at the end of the play. That would have been tough to do every night.

Being on the run crew meant that our job started during tech week, which starts the day the production moves from the rehearsal space to the actual stage and set. This is also culminated with the 12 to 12, which is the final technical rehearsal, where lights, sound, and sets get on the same page as the actors. It is exactly what it sounds like: you get to the theatre at 12 noon and you leave at 12 midnight. You do the play from cue to cue, and you attempt to run the show after the cues are worked out. It should be enough time to iron out problems, but it's not a guarantee. There is still a dress rehearsal and a preview or two. Thank God, I was holed up in the sound booth, behind glass, and not backstage where I would have gotten between Nancy and Kiera. Nancy had moved on, and was happy in her relationship, but since the play called for tension between the characters, there was now more tension between the actors. I might have had a perverse enjoyment in all this, but I was concerned for my girl and wanted her show to go off well.

Opening night I knew I had to come up with a good gift. Flowers in the dressing room are customary, but I wanted something to make a statement. I had it delivered to the dressing room with a card that read, "You're a trucker's dream if I ever did see one." It was a line from "Up on Cripple Creek" by The Band. After the show, Kiera was smiling but punched my arm.

"What was that for?" I asked.

"I have to get ready for a show where my character has to kill herself, and you have me smiling all over the dressing room."

"Sorry, about that." I replied.

"We're getting ready and everyone's saying 'I got flowers, I got candy,' and I'm smiling and say, 'I got a Bonsai tree.'" She said.

"That kicked their ass, didn't it?" I said.

"Thank you." Kiera said and gave me a kiss.

That night, there was an opening night party, and Kiera and I had a great time, it was probably the beginning of the end of our smooth sailing. Her boyfriend would, at some point during the run of the show, descend on the campus. This would not be a good development. We tried not to talk about it. Actually, I stopped any attempt to talk about it. I was in this position again, and I was flashing back to Oberlin, but this was higher stakes for me. In my mind, she should have sent the Dear John letter by now. I was not taking it well.

The weekend he came, I was up in the sound booth. My buddy, Paul, was an usher and made sure to step on the guy's foot. That was some comfort, to have a friend's loyalty lead to a stubbed toe, but there was little else for me to do but simmer. I could have fucked up her world and made a scene. I could have stepped to the dude and fought for her, but I was cool and tried to get through the weekend by drinking my weight in Iron City Light.

Days later, Paul let me borrow his car, and I picked up Kiera and drove the winding roads of Schenley Park. Schenley Park borders the campus and was a place to get away from the bustling of the day; at night, it was desolate and quiet, full of trees. I was driving in silence and maybe taking the corners a bit too fast. I drove to a plateau and parked the car. Kiera sat on a picnic table and lit a cigarette, and I paced and ranted and tried to communicate a message I hadn't really worked out in my head. I suppose I was just going out of my way to make her feel bad, and when she had little to say, the more my anger rose.

I've heard it said that your issues in relationships are the issues with yourself. I was reeling on a few different fronts. Looking back at it now, I have no idea why I was such a mess. Actually, I had a few ideas; they were just so jumbled up in my mind. I tried to figure out who I was trying to be, and what would be most important to me. It was a battle between my artful aspirations and my natural cynicism. I was feeling unsure of my place in the world.

Having a girlfriend, who had a boyfriend, was pushing me over the edge. From a debating point of view, Kiera was correct that I had gone into this whole thing with that knowledge in hand. That was true, and it felt like a hot poker to the calf to hear her say it. In my mind, I was losing her approval, her affection. I was losing. I was unable to stear her out of her own dysfunctional path.

We came to a lull in the conversation and got back in the car. We made it back to my place where we seldom stayed. The bathroom situation was substandard, by any accounting, and Kiera wouldn't shower at Fair Oaks. She did have class, and a lot more sense than we did at the time. I had tired myself out, with my rapid angry speech, and we settled in for sleep. The lights were out, and we might have mumbled our *goodnights*.

In the darkness Kiera spoke.

"I didn't think you would want to see me so soon after he …"

It was all she could say before I threw a candle I stole from a restaurant across the room. It was instantly regretted. She broke down.

"You're not the only one with feelings, you know. This is a messed up situation for me too. I'm graduating, and I don't know what my future is, and your screaming at me for three hours is not my idea of a good time." She said.

She finally had something to say, and it made me feel like a raving lunatic. I apologized, and we found a way to approximate sleep for the rest of the night.

Kiera and I settled back into what was sort of normal for our situation, and we both had work to do as the year wound down. In my acting class, we were working on our final project, which was a classroom production of *The Lower Depths* by Gorky. It was a play about a group of Russians who live in a shelter and try to get through their lives at the bottom of society. It was a bleak story. I was playing an old actor who winds up killing himself at the end of the play. It didn't dawn on me, until now, that Kiera and I, were both closing out the year by playing characters that took their own lives. I probably buried the inference at the time, knowing it couldn't be a good omen.

In an attempt to mimic the kind of preparation for which the Moscow Art Theatre was famous, we took some time, outside of class, to improvise in character. We found an industrial space in the basement of a building that we didn't frequent. We dressed in our period clothes, and we tried to behave as if we were in the lower depths. It sounded like a good idea, but the flaw in our plan was to have actual wine and vodka to stoke our creativity. There were no teachers around, and the value of the exercise was debatable. Some actors use these moments to excise some demon that lurks within them. They can blame their character for bad actions. Ten minutes into our exercise, I knew it was a bad idea. Someone started a fight, in character, and all hell broke loose. Bottles got broken and I walked out in character. A few of the "more committed" actors stayed to continue their exercise, and I went home.

That Monday there was a teacher asking if we knew anything about a bunch of students acting crazy and leaving a mess in the basement of an academic building, and I played dumb.

33

WORKING ON A DREAM

Kiera and the rest of the seniors were working toward their "League Presentation," which even at that time was a misnomer. The League was once a consortium of theatre schools that bound together, and brought their graduating classes to New York, to perform for casting directors and agents. The schools still did their presentations, but were now more loosely affiliated. Carnegie Mellon, SUNY Purchase, Boston University, and North Carolina School of The Arts were some of the schools that were part of the League and still converged on New York, same for Julliard, NYU Grad, and Yale. For some time now, CMU presents its graduating classes in both New York and Los Angeles. This would have been nice in my time, but things have to evolve.

Leagues were a big deal; other than the great training, they were one of the main reasons why so many people wanted to go to Carnegie Mellon. The hope was that you would get your agent at Leagues, and your career would start. Recent graduates were already getting work. When I was still in high school, I remember reading an article in

Rolling Stone magazine about the drama schools and the presentations and the stress and excitement of the showcases—the article was written by Aaron Sorkin, who is now the mega-successful writer and creator of *The West Wing*, *The Newsroom*, and Oscar winner for *The Social Network*. Turns out he was a theatre major at Syracuse.

While I was trying to act like an emaciated Russian actor at the turn of 20th Century, Kiera and her pals were getting ready to show their wares to the world. She had a lot on her mind, and she was pulling away.

At the end of the year, the seniors perform their presentation for the entire department, at the year-end convocation. We were sophomores, and we sat in the back of the theatre. We were not organized enough to have good chants and rhymes to shout. The seniors ran through their forty-minute showcase. They looked great and the piece moved like lightning. At the end, the actors get a moment at center stage and a moment to state their name. When the students are done, someone says, "Ladies and Gentlemen, Carnegie Mellon University Class of 1990" and the theatre erupts into applause and the chant of "Let's Go Seniors" starts. It is the Department's way of celebrating the efforts of the class and preparing the class to take on the world. It has a rally feel that is hard to beat. The seniors take their place in the left loge, and the chants go flying around the space. I sat there all fired up for the seniors but sad that Kiera would soon be released into the world, without me.

For my class, the last act was not filled with as much fanfare. We were to present our final performance in a classroom with ragged costumes and with the audience sitting on folding chairs. The audience was full of professors, the other acting class, and a sparse group of curious upperclassmen. Kiera was there, and I wanted to have a good showing. We trudged through our performance, and I had a final moment where I run off stage in despair, the play ending with someone yelling that my character has taken his life. It was one of the flashy parts, I suppose. I had a big arc to traverse, and I was glad to have an audience. I needed the performance energy, the nerves, and adrenaline to get my performance over the top.

Seeing the look of admiration in Kiera's eyes after the performance was a relief. She told me that her classmates were teasing her, but in a good way, saying that she was robbing the cradle but had her claws in the hot actor of his class. That was the real consensus I craved. It was irrational, but I thought if she thought I was talented and got to see it, it might be enough to keep us together.

That night, my friend Jack, who was a junior, was throwing a party at his house. The house had a good backyard, and we were all there. The next day Kiera and her class were boarding a train for New York City, and I was on my way to my brother's medical school graduation after my conference with the faculty. If Kiera and I were struggling, at least that night, we were content. We were both being congratulated. For her, it was for making it to the end, and for me it was for a good performance. I was looking forward to my conference, feeling like I would finally get the pat on the back I deserved. Kiera was feeling optimistic about her chances at her showcase, and for the rest of the night, we could bask in our good fortune. We could push the next day away and just be happy.

34

THE NIGHT THEY DROVE OLD DIXIE DOWN

My roommate Paul was making a little extra money, taking people to the airport after their conferences. I had a flight a few days later, but there were a couple of days of his makeshift shuttle service for him to make a couple of bucks. I woke up a little late the day after the party, and Paul had a fare, so I rode to campus with him. He would pick up the student coming out of the conference before mine, take him to the airport, and swing back for his conference or another fare. You had to admire his entrepreneurial spirit. A couple hundred bucks in college was a princely sum. Paul knew how to hustle.

I made it to the drama office on time. I spoke with the department secretary and waited for the conference in progress to wrap-up. I shook my classmates hand as he came out, and we agreed to talk over the summer.

I walked into my conference a bit hung-over but feeling pretty good about the feedback to come. The final performance was well received, and I was ready to hear my teachers tell me so. The faculty sat around the wood table, and I took my seat and said it was good to see everyone. The head of the department spoke first.

"How do you think you are progressing?" She asked.

"I felt really good about my final performance, thought things really came together for me."

"It's true your last performance was a big leap from rehearsal." A professor added.

"Thanks." I said.

"We think, as a faculty, that you are certainly one of the most talented students in the class, and you are clearly very cast-able so this is no reflection on your ability in the marketplace, but we see you not taking the instruction to heart and don't see enough consistency in your work. We don't think you should continue with the program." The department head said.

How do I avoid saying that I couldn't believe it if that's what I felt? Shock rose up my shirt like a fire. I looked at the faces of the professors but didn't say anything. In that pause, some professors said they liked some of my work, and others said things that were new to me about my lack of performance in their class, and part of me wanted to refute that revisionist history of my work. I couldn't speak, and I didn't want to lose it in front of my firing squad, so I nodded and left the room.

In the hallway some of my classmates were milling and seething by the callboard. I walked by, still not speaking, and my friend Kevin asked me if everything was OK.

"No." I said, and walked out the side door of the College of Fine Arts. Kevin ran after me, and I was finally falling apart.

"What happened?" Kevin asked.

"They cut me."

"What, no way." he said.

"Yeah."

Kevin didn't show a lot of emotion, but this really stirred something up. He kicked over a garbage can. He tried to comfort me by the Studio Theatre but was ranting himself. "We'll fuckin' hate them for this." He said.

He had a car and asked me where I wanted to go. I said I wanted to go to Kiera's house. By the time we got there, Kiera was on her way to meet her class to leave for New York. I told her the news and she said, "That can't be right." It was an excruciating scene because she had to leave; we only had a few moments. She said she would call as soon as she got to New York, and she said to stay at her house if I wanted. That was all I could think to do, walk up the stairs into her room and fall onto the bed.

News spread fast. Paul was taking my freshman year roommate to the airport. Samuel was running late, but Paul brought him to Kiera's house to see me. It was brutal; Sam was a great friend, and I didn't know what to say. It couldn't be possible that I wouldn't be seeing him next year. Paul was checking the time, and they had to go if they stood a chance of getting Sam on his plane. Sam and I hugged and cried, and he told me I was one of the most talented people he knew, and that he loved me. He left for the airport, and I fell onto Kiera's many-thou-sand-thread-count sheets.

My friend Jack came by, and people started coming over to the house. It was like a wake where the dead guy can still talk. Zeke, my playwright friend, came over with a case of beer and proceeded to tell me that I was the last person that he pitied, as we drank. He was giving me a tough love pep talk as we sat in the kitchen, and people started to come over. Seriously, all I was missing was the casket.

One of my classmates relayed the story of what happened the rest of the day at the conferences. I had an early appointment, so every-thing after was tainted with the news of my being cut. Jordan, my mandolin-strumming buddy, took it hard and punched the callboard; people were hugging like a plane went down. The story that got to me was a classmate telling me that the class put together a petition and that a friend, with the last conference of the day, presented it to the faculty.

"Before we talk about me, I want to talk about Carl." He said.

He placed the petition on the wood table, and spoke about its contents—that I was a leader in the class, and how this must not stand. This is as heartwarming now as it was then. Funny thing is, the petition would have been pretty light on signatures, being as how we were a class of less than twenty. Of course, they weren't going to discuss a student with another student. I have always felt a debt of gratitude for that classmate. He had brass balls that could get the best of him at times, but he was not afraid to speak his mind, and I have always respected that about him.

A day later Kiera called from New York and told me that her class was thinking about me and couldn't believe it. She told me she thought I should fight it and offered what support she could. She was on a threshold, herself, so there was only so much she could give.

There was an article a few years before in *Theater Week*. It was titled "Black Monday" or "Red Tuesday," and it was about the brutal cut system in place at many of the theatre schools across the country, Carnegie Mellon being the most brutal. There was a story of a cut in the early 1980s that was protested with a bucket of red paint being splashed on the callboard. There was talk of my classmates doing the same. I think I was thankful that they didn't take it that far.

Part of my shock was the feeling of disbelief that I was to be one of those casualties. Also, having two years in the university felt even more acute. The other basis for my shock was not seeing it coming, based on where I thought I stacked up with the rest of the class. There was another cut made that year, and the reaction was not the same. It was tough to hear but not as tough. I felt bad for the other student, but it was an apples and oranges thing. That sounds arrogant, but that's how I felt.

There are real hardships out there, and this wasn't life and death, but it was a bad thing in my little world. I was essentially placed on the outside, in the cold, and I didn't know where to go. Where I *had* to go only made the whole ordeal more painful. On the heels of being kicked out of college, I had to go celebrate my brother finishing medical school. What the fuck was I going to do? What I did for days was remain mute and tried to look happy for my brother, which I was. I was just more messed up from my recent development.

I'm not sure when I came clean, but my mother knew something was wrong. She thought I didn't want to be an actor anymore and couldn't admit it. She was close, so her powers of perception must be noted. I was sitting in a diner with my folks and told them what happened. They were shocked to hear it and wanted to know what the next step needed to be. I wasn't sure.

My brother's ceremony was cool. The new doctors raised their right hands and repeated the Hippocratic oath, and even in my stupor, I was proud of my brother, and happy for my parents. A doctor in the family is good bragging material even though my parents weren't the type to gloat.

There was a party at my brother and his wife's house, and my dad asked me to take a walk. It was warm in North Carolina that day, and we headed down a quiet tree lined street, not really paying attention to where we were going. My dad wanted me to know that I was smart, and that this had no reflection on that. He even told me my IQ as if this would make me feel better. All that did was make me mad at myself for the lack of money in my bank account all these years. He asked me if I wanted to fight the decision. I said I did, and he said he would go to the head of the department and see what could be done. He told me I was special, and not to let this derail me. He said we would meet at the hotel, with everyone else, and come up with a plan, and then we took a few wrong turns trying to get back to my brother's house. A sense of direction was never a strong suit of ours.

We made it back to the party, and I suppose I was feeling better. My dad told everyone we were having a family meeting and that everyone was required to attend. My brother had to interrupt his revelry because his kid brother got himself in a jam. We were in my folk's room, and I had to tell my brothers and my sister that I got the boot. I told them that I was having trouble with my anger, and my dad famously yelled, "WHERE DOES THE ANGER COME FROM?" It was one of my first jokes in stand-up recounting my hollering dad, wondering how his son had become a *holler-er*. It was decided that I would go back to Pittsburgh and arrange a meeting with the head of the department, and that my dad would demand an audience. We also crafted a letter to the department. I had a finite time line because I had a commitment to a season of Summer Stock, which was starting to feel like a date to report to prison.

I had an ally on the faculty who was good enough to talk to me when I got back to campus. I asked him if it made any sense that I was out when I thought of myself as one of the stronger actors in the class. He said it wasn't a matter of talent; it was whether I was getting anything out of the program, but he cautiously agreed that it didn't make sense. He told me that I should count myself lucky to have the friends I had, and that their reaction was something to behold and had an effect on the faculty. He told me that a teacher that I thought of as a nemesis was not in agreement about the decision. It was mighty kind of him to let me vent. I was doing well in his class, which was Voice and Speech. I had long been on probation for my regional dialect but had almost reversed the issue, and I now sounded like a robot, even in my daily speech. He knew I was working hard and wanted to help.

I had my meeting with the head of the department after I had sent my first letter. She really just repeated her company line, and I was left feeling less than hopeful. My father came to town and had a meeting with the head; he wore a sharp grey suit, and I was hoping he might make some headway. It was really a courtesy meeting. A parent who spent two years of tuition to find out the program was no longer a fit for his kid, was going to get his say. The next step was unclear. I just knew that I had to write another letter, and this one had to spill its guts. I spent the next five days constructing a letter that wound up coming in at close to fifteen pages.

Paul and Tommy J. were staying in Pittsburgh that summer, so our house was bustling, and we didn't have to vacate it like they did at the dorms. Tommy was particularly helpful in keeping me on schedule and helping me come up with a strategy for my plea.

"This has to be the most honest thing I've ever written," I said.

"No, it has to be the most manipulative letter you can write, it has to get you back into school." He said.

He elaborated on his idea. It would be both honest and pointed. It had to make a case that there were issues holding me back, but play up the fact that I was CMU material. It also had to have a bit of drama. It had to move the people who were on the fence and convert the people who were staunch.

My idea was to pull the faculty into my life, let them know I was struggling away from class, and how they were both intertwined.

… As human beings we don't have total control over how strongly we respond to relationships. I was wrapped up in poorly timed romances that took over my time. A simple step in maturity says to me: at this age, at this school, what I want to achieve has to be my motivator …

I understand your concern for my ability to work consistently … for a few days I was concerned myself, but with all the self-re-evaluation, I know that if I change my lifestyle, manage my time, prioritize, and bear down, I will, with your help, be able to move forward with my work. I hope this letter made that clear…

I put it in the mail and had to go home. I had a few days before reporting to New London, New Hampshire, for a gig in a barn, for 25 bucks a week. The theatre was living off the fact that Barbra Streisand performed there in her youth and kept the pay scale the same ever since.

35

DON'T CRY FOR ME ARGENTINA

If you don't know what summer stock is, let me explain—it's a work camp set to music. The idea is you perform a play at night and rehearse the next play during the day. We also had chores and ate in a mess hall. The plays are from the American musical theatre cannon, and they are probably brutal to watch. Actors do this to themselves because it is considered a rite of passage. I was an actor who sang a bit, and I don't know what possessed me to try to sing and dance for three months in a barn. What made it especially hard was we had to sleep in a bunkhouse with beds that were five feet by eleven inches; I am six two and couldn't stretch out. I slept in the fetal position for the rest of my bid. The other difficulty was I was in limbo about whether I was going make it back to school or if I had to figure out another life plan. I was also nursing some emotional wounds.

My heart wasn't into it. I wanted to be the next Robert DeNiro not the next Nathan Lane, but I actually thought this would help my résumé to have some musical experience. The problem was if you didn't get one of the lead roles, then you were part of the chorus, and *all* you did was sing and dance. There were New York actors of the appropriate age who were "jobbed in" for the larger roles, so it was slim pickings. Thank God, there were no flip cameras and camera phones in those days—the footage would have buried me. It was a time that has no real record, other than the program my mother still keeps, and for that I'm grateful. I wound up singing quite well. I found out I have a pretty good ear, but I just never got my steps down. People paid to watch me butcher choreography. My reputation as a tough guy would never stand if any one of my friends saw me. A classmate of mine was also in the company, and he was in the same boat. It was a relief to have someone there, and to have someone with whom to share the humiliation.

It was a partial distraction from everything I was encountering. We had a phone in the main house that we shared. The main house was shut down around 11pm, and it was hard to stay in touch with people. It was like a halfway house with a lot of singing. The main role I got that summer was still pretty small, and I still had to do double duty in the chorus because the play was *Evita*, and the crowd scenes could not afford to be sparse as a nation looked on; it had to be more than four people waving at the palace balcony. I was playing a lounge singer who meets the future Evita in a nightclub. I had a song and a little interaction with the lead actress and was not seen for the rest of the play.

Without television or telecommunications, I would take long walks down the dark country roads of New Hampshire. It is true that, without the city lights, the stars are brighter in the sky. It is also true that it was dark as hell on the streets, and that headlights from oncoming cars cut through the dark and scared the living shit out of me as I would try to avoid being abducted by crazy Pineys. I was definitely a city slicker and would cut these walks short as my paranoia got the better of me.

On one of these walks, I found a payphone along the road, and I would take a folding chair from the theatre, and walk a mile to make my phone calls with some privacy, and by phone calls, I mean I called Kiera and ranted and raved about what I felt was her indifference and lack of feeling. How these calls lasted more than three minutes is still a mystery. There was a bone of contention I couldn't shake off. As I was finishing the touches on my letter to the department, and Kiera made her return to Pittsburgh to pack up, I made a stop by her house after she had left for New York for good. Her last roommate was there, and I wished her well as I walked around the apartment absorbing the fact that I would never see it again. It was during this maudlin stroll that I saw the Bonsai tree I bought for Kiera left behind in the kitchen. I was angered and that's the macho way of saying that I was hurt, but of course sitting on a folding chair on a dark country road, I was yelling and taking the indignant route with Kiera. I mention this now to show how out of sorts I was. It really isn't a burning memory that I carry. It occurs in this time frame, and I think it makes it clear how dramatically I was behaving. Somehow, we would finish these calls with some civility and promises to catch up in New York. I would lug the folding chair back to the barracks and get what little sleep was left in the night before I had to say hello to Dolly or say "all aboard" on a fake luxury liner bound for London.

Calls during the day would come into the main house, and you would be summoned. I was trying not to think about it, but I was waiting for a call all summer. When a call came, even from Kiera, I would be disappointed. This day, it was my mom, and the call I had been waiting for was at hand.

"I have some mail from CMU. Do you want me to open it?" she said.

"Yes."

She read through the letter, and I had my second chance. I was relieved, and still a bit angry. I still didn't think I deserved this treatment. My mother was relieved, and I had to make plans to leave the barn early. I didn't want to start my comeback a week late. The problem was I would be the third company member to inform the boss I was leaving. At $25 a week it should have been easy to tell him, but the Stockholm syndrome might have been in play. My dad drove all night after work to pick me up, and I said a few goodbyes. My summer in limbo was over.

36

BOUNCIN' BACK

Back in my room in Pittsburgh I knew I had to make a change. Even if I disagreed with the grief I was given, I had to accept that it was my doing. I had a choice, review the feedback as constructive and move on, or stay pissed and spiral out of control and blow it again. I think I was on probation, and it made me a bit tense, but I was getting myself organized, and my mind was clear.

My professor confessor was glad to see me back, and I was grateful for his concern. He said that classmates sent letters and that some teachers changed their tunes. It was nice to hear, but I wanted to distance myself from the not so distant past.

While I had not lost time and didn't have to get used to life away from Carnegie Mellon, I was seeing things with new eyes. Later, I wondered what my life would have looked like if I didn't succeed in getting back into the program. I thought about if I would have rebuilt at a different school or if I would have tried to act without a degree. While I fought back, it might have been braver to seek a new path. Stubbornness wasn't a trait that I thought I possessed at the time, but now I find myself twenty years down the line and realize it might be a defining trait.

Seeing classmates and being welcomed back by faculty was cool, but it was the first convocation that got me emotional, not outwardly, but inside. I took my seat in the loge, as a junior, and would have fought to the death if anyone tried to grab my seat. This year we had chants, and I shouted to the skies. Sitting there I suppose I was grateful, but not for the chance to be back. I was grateful my cage got rattled, and I would not let that happen again. While I was, technically, subject to review, I gave it no more thought. A mistake had been made, and it had been corrected. I would be sure of that. Losing control of my situation could be seen as a blessing but never a repeatable offense.

A supportive classmate asked me how I had made such a change in my attitude, and I told her, "I don't always feel positive or up-beat, but I pretend I do, and eventually, my mood falls in line with my actions." It was the old adage of faking it 'till you make it. It actually worked, and it's been hard to duplicate since, but I need to remember it's possible.

Junior year was the most fun I had at CMU. We were doing plays; we had a couple of days when classes didn't start until eleven. The first play out of the box was a coup for me. A professor came up to me in the cafeteria after the opening, and said, "I never knew there was so much humor in that role, nice work." I thanked him but wanted to tell him off. "See that, asshole, that's what I do. I act well, and you should sit down and watch." I was still bitter about the "D" I got in acting. It was as if they needed a paper trail to back up their decision. All it did was plummet my GPA, which could hurt me if I ever wised up and went to law school.

That's the beauty of the program, they kill you for two years; and then you make it to the third year, and you come out like a freight train. The underclassmen are on your crews, and they look up to you and marvel at your work. I know it was true when I was new at CMU. The first play I saw was a production of *Hurlyburly* by David Rabe. It was in the studio theatre, and it was part of a phased out series known as Junior Rep, which was six plays in six weeks, and this was one of the six. Everyone in the play was great if, as always, a few years away from being the right age. There was one actor who stood out to me, and I was thinking that if I were half as good by the time I was a junior, I could be proud. When I was dating Kiera, she critiqued his work in a senior play by saying, "That's just Guy doing the same Guy thing he always does."

"'That thing' that Guy does, is better than anything the rest of us do." I said. It might have been overstated, and I might have had a man-crush, but I wasn't inaccurate. He was *watch-able* and that was more important than having the supposed range to play an Irish feudal Lord, if that even exists. I was not prone toward this kind of humility all the time, but I had to give it up.

He found some early success after graduating but abandoned the business. To this day, I know that guy had something on me, and yet it wasn't enough to keep him at it. It's the first time that I learned that talent alone is not the only ingredient to success.

Now, he was long gone, and it was my time to soak up some underclassmen adulation. I steered clear of any serious romantic involvement, keeping my word with myself and in my sentiments to the faculty. I was glad to meet new people. I was very protective of my time and was focused on each new project. It was my plan to pour it on to be the actor I knew that I already was. It was also a chance for my family to see me do more heavyweight stuff than the musicals of the past.

My father started a streak that I know was an attempt to make up for the games and things he missed when I was growing up. He would sometimes leave work in the city, drive straight through the night, crash, see a play, and leave right after in a twenty-four-hour turnaround. My mother had to pick and choose the shows since car travel was hard on her back. She would fly in, and my dad would drive the Pennsylvania Turnpike, saving the airfare, and maybe enjoying the open road. I never thought about what my dad was thinking, or how those trips were tough or enjoyable. It was a good time having him around, and I liked to show him off when he came to town. He had helped me through a tough spot and wanted to see it all the way through.

On that winding walk in North Carolina, my dad said, "I'm not done with you yet." Hearing that then didn't embarrass me or make me feel like a child. It made me feel less alone and sewed up a wound that might have needed some attention from childhood. Today, it is a golden memory.

This was the year I also became a gym rat. In an effort to look better in a t-shirt, I became obsessed with working out. It also helped that I was cast as a boxer, in a Harold Pinter play and wanted to look the part. I was jumping rope, and even hit the heavy bag in a friend's basement back in New Jersey over the break. I learned why it's important to wrap your hands. You can't wail on a bag without messing up your wrist. I stuck with the jump rope and shadowboxing. My transformation would be mostly cosmetic, and I was OK with that. It was drama school, and I looked like I knew how to throw a punch. Who was going to check my references? I was in good shape and got the credit for making a physical transformation. I was the DeNiro of the drama department.

The play was also set in the 1960s, so we tried to grow sideburns to pull off the look. I needed to supplement my follicles with mascara, and so did Paul. We were playing brothers in a twisted play where our other brother stands idly by as we pass his wife between the two of us. The scene was tough; we had to make out with the actress, and not break the furniture that got in the way. It is truly uncomfortable to start making out with someone on a set because the script says so. Sure, you're kissing a girl, but it's not like she wants you to, she's just being a good actress and you're trying not to make her feel uncomfortable. The other problem with this creepy bit of blocking was the two dudes in the scene were wearing mascara—on the side of their faces. When the actress got off the couch and resumed the dialogue, Paul and I convulsed in laughter as we noticed that our make-up had bled all over our cast mate's face. She looked like a chimney sweep, covered with soot.

Now that I was a survivor of the cut, I could take some pride in where I was. Our class started with forty-one students, and we were now sixteen. This was how we would remain. Only a few years later and today, at CMU, there is less turn over, and the cut is not as powerful a threat. It may have had something to do with the way it went down for me. I would be silly to think so, but I know that there was a shift in the department with our regime. While keeping its top five stature, it is a kinder, gentler, program with less crew, less cuts, and more security. They also have new facilities, and this is all good, and they have a presence on both coasts. This year, The School of Drama celebrated 100 years of existence, and I am proud to be a small part of it.

Perhaps this is true for a lot of people at this stage of their lives, but things were good in my family. My mother had made it through her cancer surgery, and my older siblings were fairly settled. Being able to perform might have made it easier to have something to celebrate. There was always a show, and it felt like getting through the rough patch had put me back on a good track. I felt that I was carrying the support of my family with me. My priorities were back to making good on the second chance I was given, and you do carry your people with you. You are the product of a union, and you need to honor it. I was growing up and learning life lessons. It sounds corny, but this is the story of a drama nerd, not an outlaw biker.

37

JAILBREAK

In late November of 1994, I was trying to sleep in a new bed in my brother's house in Florida. I had made an escape from New York and was bailed out by my brother and his wife. It sounds dramatic, but I was bottoming out in a bad relationship with, at the very least, a compulsive liar. I took the branch that I needed to pull me out of the quicksand and got myself out of the city I never wanted to leave. Some would say letting a woman run you out of town is a terrible move. They might be right, but my brother said I could stay with him, and it was better than moving in with my folks or having a domestic squabble take on a more negative turn than it already had. I took the suggestion and eventually made peace with the decision. By eventually, I mean a couple of weeks ago. You have to let things roll off your back. I am varying the time line a bit in this story because I am truly uncomfortable talking about this period of my life. It is not a good habit to avoid things you don't want to confront. I'm not trying to describe me going on the lam after a crime spree. I'm describing a situation that got so untenable I chose to flee the scene. I wish I had a fugitive story to tell. Instead, I have a story about a troubled young person in the pits of a bad relationship. Mostly, I want to impart the advice that a friend shared with me—more on that later. Until I learned that lesson, I was making a mess.

It's a tough transition to go from the pampered walls of college to the work force and the real world. It's even more acute when you have no marketable skills other than the ability to learn lines and say them with feeling. Many of these complications had their roots back in Pittsburgh.

As good as my junior year was, my senior year was even better as far as how things were lining up for my future and entry into the real world of acting. When our senior year convocation started, we had to do a musical number to welcome the incoming freshmen. When we got through our little ditty and took our seats in the left loge, I tried to slow down the moment as I sat in my chair and looked over the theatre and heard the cheering and chanting. While it was probably a forgone conclusion that I would make it through my junior year, it still felt good. I suppose they wouldn't have taken me back, only to boot me again; they were dicks, not sadists. There was even some scuttlebutt that the faculty had run out of ways to motivate me, and their tactic was to see if I would bounce back and fight my way back to the program. I doubt that was the case; it would be a tough process to explain to your fellow faculty members, not to mention university officials: "We're going to kick him out to see if he really wants back in. If he fights his way back, we'll know we really made our point."

The beauty of junior year was you could focus strictly on the work. You were a year away from having to go out there and sing for your supper, but you were a big dog in the department. It was their way of building you back up. They had known you for a few years, and it was about bringing out the most in each of the actors. Thinking about this now, it sounds like such an extravagance, such a luxury. This might also have made the re-entry into the Earth's atmosphere all the more traumatic. I felt like I had the bends as I was trying to figure out what to do with my life after drama school.

Senior year was the year of building the perfect beast or the ultimate actor. Back in the 'Burgh this year, we split up the posse, and I had a different apartment with a different roommate. There were a lot of visiting professionals: casting directors and alumni. Hopefully, they were people we would meet after we graduated. One drawback to CMU is that it's in Pittsburgh. This is not a slight to the great city; it's just that the marketplace for actors is New York and Los Angeles. If we were going to get to know some important people, they would have to come to us.

Now that I was in Florida, it seemed like I was a long way from even the foot of the mountain that I needed to climb. I was in a remote base camp far from the summit, and it might snow, and I'd have to put off the expedition. I didn't know anyone. I had two daily goals—don't smoke, and workout, oh, yeah, and wake up before noon.

I had left most of what I owned in an apartment in the Chelsea neighborhood of Manhattan. It was on 15th St. between Seventh and Eighth Avenues and was a long time before Chelsea got its makeover. We might have had a drug dealer for a neighbor, but I kept my head down whenever I entered or exited the building, trying to avoid being able to identify any participants in a drug deal. I left behind that chopped-up, glorified one-bedroom apartment, and quit a decent bartending job. I also left a hysterical, chronically unemployed, and borderline sociopath girlfriend, whom I'd been supporting since my senior year in college.

One might wonder why a seemingly smart guy would fall into such a bad circumstance. I thought she was dying of cancer, and who breaks up with a girl who's dying of cancer. Movies are made about guys who *stay* with girls who are dying of cancer, not the other way around. I don't know if this assuages any of my poor decision-making or gullibility, but that's part of the reason I was tip toeing around my brother's house, and sneaking smokes in the night.

The summer between my junior and senior year, I decided to

stay in Pittsburgh. I had no slave labor dance troupe to join and no desire to hang out with Tequila Willie. Looking back, I think I was subconsciously afraid to leave the city after the trauma of being cut. Even though I didn't suffer that ultimate consequence, I didn't want to stray too far. My friends Paul and Tommy seemed to have had a good time when they stayed the year before. I tried to convince them to stay another summer, but they had other plans. I was now fretting about my decision to stay. Who was I going to hang out with, and what would I do for work? I started filling out applications. I got real close to gig at the Crab House downtown. This was relayed on an answering machine from a manager named Dawn. It was also the perfect tape to learn or recoil from the Pittsburgh accent. I'll try to transcribe the message. First, here's what the message said, "Hi, Carl, this is Dawn, from the Crab House, Downtown. Wondering if you still want the job. Let me know. Again, this is Dawn from the Crab House Downtown." Here is the transcription in the dialect, *"Hi, Corl, this is Don, from the Crab Hoss, DonTon. Wondering if you still want the Jawb. Let me know. Again, this is Don, from the Crab Hoss, DonTon."* I think I lost the job by asking for a guy named Don and not following up with a gal named Dawn.

A buddy from a couple of classes below me had a demolition job, and he said he could use me, so we started working for this independent contractor. He had enough work to keep us busy most of the summer. My friend, Clancy, was a transfer student, so he was older even though he was behind me in school; he also knew what he was doing on a construction site. I was brute, unskilled labor. We cleaned up vacant apartments, dug postholes, and built a deck for our boss. It was physical work, and it was outdoors, and it got me through.

38

THE CROSSOVER

Carnegie Mellon had a single digit minority population, and my hometown was not ethnically diverse unless you count Irish and Italian as races—percentage wise the drama department had more minority students, but there were still few. My friend, Kevin, was one of two African Americans in our class when we started and was the only one by junior year. I used to walk around campus and noticed Kevin nod to other black students. I would ask, "Did you know that guy?"

"Not really." He said.

"Then why did you nod?"

"It's a black thing."

"Can I start nodding?"

"You can try." Kevin said.

While I did not grow up in a particularly integrated town, I was from New Jersey and compared to some of the lily-white areas of some of my classmates, I was well rounded. I had more in common with Kevin than someone from Oklahoma. We bonded as New York guys, and I know that I'm from New Jersey, but if you grew up watching Sue Simmons and Chuck Scarborough on the news, you get to say New York as long as everybody who claims Chicago when he's from Wisconsin, and everybody who claims Boston who wouldn't even fit in the city, come clean. My point is that, at least from a mass media perspective we were from a similar place.

Knowing more about it, and knowing in what part of Brooklyn Kevin grew up, I know the similarities end there, but do they? People work hard in Bushwick, and Bed-Sty; they pay their bills and hang out with friends. Being predominately black is the only real difference. People refer to these areas as high crime areas, and that is true to some extent, but it is a minority of activities in these areas; most people are just trying to get through the week, like everywhere else. You might need to be on alert after 10PM or tuck in your chain, but that's urban living.

The real difference is in the flavor, the culture. If we stick with differences being cultural, then we might not get so wound up. Much of the celebrated culture of America is actually African American culture. Jazz is the prime example, so is Rock and Roll. Hip Hop is the most recent cultural phenomenon, other than that little thing called the internet, and in my college years, hip hop was making its initial inroads to the crossover market.

If you were like my crew and me and liked to dance and liked going to clubs, you would be influenced by the music of the day. If you didn't have cable and tuned to UHF on the top dial, you could find the Video Music Box, which played mostly rap videos. We had a black and white TV tuned to the Box at all hours of the day. The Box was a pay-to-play way of ordering a video that you wanted to see. Record companies, were said to have hired people off the books *to bang the box*, meaning to order up a song of a particular artist. You wound up seeing the same ten videos because the videos were requested over and over by covert music industry operatives, or so I've heard.

It was cool to be "down" which meant you were up to date with some of the things going on in black culture—or to know "what was up" or to be "down for the cause." It usually meant you had more than one black friend or only black friends. Maybe it wasn't cool to a certain segment, but it was cool to me. Trying to explain what "down" means is like trying to explain the essence of cool. Once you try to explain, it ceases to be. It also may have been impossible to be down at Carnegie Mellon, maybe even for the black students. This does not always mean it's cool to date black women. That can be a thorny issue, and one has to guard against it being on the line of fetishism. A penchant for dating black women with no involvement with black culture is not being "down."

What did I really know about anything? I had messed around with an African American girl toward the end of my junior year, but she was from a mostly white background. I certainly found black women attractive and didn't see any impediment other than the usual will-she-go-out-with-me-or-shoot-me-down dynamic.

Hanging out that summer in Pittsburgh in many cases, meant hanging out on the University of Pittsburgh's turf. This meant if you recognized a face from CMU out at a bar, you could introduce yourself. I met my friend, Dave, out at a club on Forbes Avenue down by the Pitt campus. I had noticed Dave around campus and didn't like him because he had a hot Asian girlfriend. He was a computer science major and was from Maryland. I joked with him about not liking him from afar because I liked his girlfriend from afar. He said they'd broken up, so I didn't have to hold it against him anymore. Dave moved into a special interest house called Spirit House. Spirit was essentially a fraternity and a sorority for black students. If you wanted a real Black Greek experience, you had to go to Pitt and pledge one of their chapters. CMU did not have the population to necessitate black sororities and fraternities. Spirit filled that void. They also had a winning streak in the Spring Carnival buggy competition where they competed against the frats. Spirit also had the best parties because they had the best DJs. Knowing Dave had given me some access, and I started hanging out at Spirit House. I'd been to a few parties on campus before but never made it to the house.

My good friend Tommy J. didn't finish with us at CMU because of financial reasons back home. He got his degree from CMU but wrapped up some classes back in Philadelphia. It was tough not to have such a good friend around to get through what was, the last hoorah for our college careers. This gave me some room in my social life, and I got to know a whole crew of people, who were not in the drama department. I wish I had gotten to know them sooner, but with our workload, it was probably difficult for any student to branch out more than across the hall.

That summer, I was probably a little lonely missing my core friends, and I didn't have the burdensome schedule to keep my mind off things. This is when I thought I might want a girl around. Young extroverts need to learn the joys of solitude, but I hadn't learned that yet. I made it a point to seek out a woman and made my way to the Metropole where I never had much luck. Occasionally, the Metropole would have a touring recording artist perform a song, or, more accurately, lip-synch it. This was an old-school way to break a dance artist. I think we saw Robin S. perform before her big hit, "Show Me Love." They also promoted fashion shows and it was during one of these shows that a girl caught my eye. My friend Kevin's girlfriend was also in the fashion show, so I asked Kevin's girlfriend if she knew the girl I was checking out. Kevin's girlfriend was from Jamaica, and Christine was also from the islands. She was pretty and mysterious, and I wanted to know her. I was introduced and was forward in my efforts to take her out. I knew my friends were leaving for the summer, and I guess I was trying to ensure my companionship for the next few months. We went to the Carnegie Museum and a couple of local spots. To be honest, she wasn't very friendly, but I thought she was cute and ignored her apparent lack of interest. We were seeing each other, regularly, and moved pretty quickly into a physical relationship. I was also trying to ensure my sexual needs were met for the summer.

One night, at Harris's, a CMU haunt, Christine told me something that should have sent me running. She said she was in Pittsburgh to be near the Falk Clinic, which was a renowned cancer treatment center. She said she had a form of cancer that was being treated, but if things didn't change, she might not be around much longer.

"So, if you want to end this now, I'd understand." She said.

I took a pause, and should have at least said, "Let me think about it," but instead, said, "No, I wouldn't do that."

I don't know what to say on that score. Would I have been a bad guy to let it go before it got too involved, or turned ugly? It wasn't my problem. I barely knew her, so what the fuck was I thinking? I'm not sure I even had the requisite feelings that would engender this kind of reaction. I didn't ask questions, and I didn't press for the percentages. I just continued. Was I hanging in there because I wanted a black girl-friend to bolster my being down? Did I care about her enough? Hadn't I had enough of complicated relationships? What was my deal? Was I breast-fed? Why was I clinging to such a situation? These questions would be in heavy rotation as I found myself in Florida writing in my journal on a beach in the middle of the winter, trying to avoid getting sand kicked in my face for writing in a journal.

That summer, in Pittsburgh, things fell into place, and it felt normal. I worked in the day, and we went out at night. My first clue that maybe Christine was not being honest was her propensity to want to party like someone without a terminal disease. I took it to mean her treatment was going well. She had roommates from West Virginia where she went to college who were nice and also happened to be gay, which would make George Carlin cringe as I used the phrase "happened to be gay." I say this only to lay a foundation for later reve-lations. When she wasn't with me, she was enmeshed in the gay scene of Pittsburgh, which is a big city compared to Morgantown, West Virginia. Being a bigger city meant a better gay scene.

When school started and Paul got back from summer break, he ran into a girl we knew from the Metropole who knew Christine. She said Christine was gay. Paul said, "You know Tanya, from Metropole, told me that Christine was gay when I told her my boy was messing with her." To which I replied, "Yeah I could see why she would say that, all her friends are gay."

"I was just telling you what I heard." Paul said.

I mentioned it to Christine, and she said she happened to have friends who happened to be gay, and she liked the gay bars and clubs better because she wouldn't get hit on all night, and the music was better. I was out of my depth but still insisted on proceeding.

That summer Christine moved into my apartment, by and large. I was cool with playing house, and my roommate wasn't stressed. Once school started we were back to our furious pace, and I was focused on making it the best year yet, leading up to the big presentation in New York City. I don't remember if she stayed every night, but it was fairly constant. I still ate my meals in the cafeteria and didn't really know what she did with her days. Naively, I thought her treatments were daily and about eight hours a day. Who asks these questions? Aren't they personal, and on a need to know basis? Why would I question someone trying to get through cancer treatment? It is hard for me to remember if there were good times. There must have been, but I was busy, and often there were odd fights and strange disagreements.

Senior year was full of some good fortune for me, as if the universe were replacing the grief of sophomore year with positive turns. A local professional theatre had broken ground on a new space on the South Side of the city. It was to produce its inaugural season with a play by a former CMU playwright. It was set in the Italian neighborhood of Oakland, and the playwright was a Pittsburgh native. The theatre had auditioned a few students, but I was somehow out of the loop. The professor, who had helped through my trouble sophomore year, stepped up for me once more. He was shocked I hadn't been thought of for the young Italian American role. He reached out to the artistic director, and I had an audition. I went in and nailed it, and a few days later I was offered the role. It was an Equity theatre, which meant it was under the guidelines of the stage actor's union. I would be paid and have a chance to join the union before I even graduated. It was my first professional show, and it was there for all to see.

I was in a lucky spot to be able to put all we had learned to practical use a few miles from my nesting ground. I felt better than vindicated. I felt bolstered and strong. I had to ask for permission and had to bow out of a production in the department. I also had to minimize my involvement in the television project that seniors got to do every year. I wanted to be involved, but I had tech week the same week we were to shoot the TV project. We auditioned for a director from the West Coast, and I had a small part. The director came up to me after the first read through.

"I would have given you a bigger part if you hadn't opted out. I think you're a really good actor." He said.

I thanked him and possibly regretted my decision, but I was a pro now and had to go where my bread was buttered.

Not only would my father continue his streak of seeing everything I did, but this time it was in the real world. I think everyone in the family came, and for some, it was the first time they were seeing me perform. The great thing was there was a lot of fanfare because the theatre was unveiling its new space. It was a feeling that I wish I could market in a pharmaceutical. It was more than gratitude in my getting the part; it was a feeling that my career had begun, that the tide had turned in my life. The problems of the past were a thing of the past. It was a reversal of fortune, and I was glad to be in it.

The play was rehearsing through Thanksgiving, and it was the first time I didn't make it home. I stayed with Christine, and it was fun to play house that day; Kevin and his girlfriend came over, and we cooked.

Another great thing was getting a paycheck every week. It wasn't a living wage for an adult, but for me, it was the first time I had a steady stream of cash. It felt good to be a working actor. The times I could say that in my life have been few and far between, but it always lifts your soul to make money plying your trade.

The play was called *Bricklayers* and it was about three generations of an Italian family of bricklayers and the push and pull from the old world and the new. I played Vincey, the youngest brother, who was a bit slow. Vincey falls for a girl visiting from Italy while his older brother has an actual date with her and maybe more. Vincey feels betrayed and the family is struggling with its business. My father was excited it was a play about Italian Americans and thought it boded well for my career. My mother liked that it was about Italian Americans without any mob references. My mother has never seen *The Godfather*. She refuses on the grounds that it glorifies criminals and that Italians have suffered a prejudice based on their last names that is stoked by glorifying images of films about sociopaths. I have to admire her stance, and while I agree to some extent, it's hard to stay away from a good mob movie.

It seemed to me that not only had I gotten back into school but was now being recognized by the outside world. I was soaking up everything I could, trying to be an ideal cast member. It was a nice touch when there were flowers and champagne waiting in my dressing room opening night—from the faculty.

There were reviews, and they were mostly mixed, I was mentioned along with the actress I played with as a "constant treat" in the *Pittsburgh Post Gazette*. That almost sounds dirty. In the hallway, the head of the department said I was the only actor in the show. It was a compliment to me, but a very harsh assessment of the rest of the production.

A few years later, when I vacated my apartment in New York and took what I could throw into nylon laundry bags, one of the many things I left behind was the poster from *Bricklayers* that my family had framed for me. It was my first professional show, and it would have been a great keepsake. Instead it is lost in the windstorm of an ugly break up and serves as a reminder to keep your life in a manageable place. It also reminds me that strife isn't always character building; it's just strife. When it comes in your life, you can't avoid it, but there is no need to go courting it.

It was during the heady time of being in *Bricklayers* and shooting the television project at CMU that I was getting great feedback on my work. The director of the project was trying to tell me that Los Angeles was a better move for me. He said you stood a chance to make a living in LA, but New York was slim pickings. CMU did not have a showcase in LA at the time, so if you made that move, you would be going without a formal introduction. I knew New York and could live at home for a while, so I didn't give it much thought. He was trying to be helpful and was a big supporter. He told his directing classes after the project was edited and screened that he thought I was the only actor who was performing in the right vein for the medium. Directing students were coming up in the hallways relaying the professor's professions.

39

TIME FOR SOME ACTION

There was definitely a let down after the play was over. It ran through part of the winter break, but I was home for the holidays. Christine either stayed in my apartment or went home to see her parents. I was home and had an assignment that I took seriously. Acting class for the second semester was dedicated to the showcase in New York. Over the break, we were to compile at least ten scenes that might work for the presentation. We also had to think about clothes, and I took to the scene procurement with zeal. I rented movies looking for scenes that might work. I transcribed scenes with one hand on the remote and the other writing the words. I scoured the library and had a catalogue from Samuel French, which is one of the companies that publish plays. I knew that I had worked hard to get back to school and the pay off was this opportunity to show my stuff to the casting and agent community.

New Year's Eve was approaching, and this year Kevin had a lead on a party in Harlem. It was in a beautiful brownstone, and Paul and I went to meet Kevin. Zeke was in town, and it was a good party. I was one of the few white people at the party and tried to remain inconspicuous. I accomplished this by dropping a full 40 oz. beer on the floor as the party was reaching its apex. My fumble skipped the DJ's record, and the bottle hit with such velocity that it shattered and shot beer across the hardwood. On cue, the crowd shouted, "WHAT THE FUCK?" So much for me keeping a low profile. I helped the hostess mop up the mess and tried to blend in with the drapes. I was also out of beer, and the guys and I went on a beer run. I think I mistakenly offered to get beer for some partygoers, and it was going to be my treat. We were trying to make it back for the countdown to New Years but left with little time to spare.

There was a bodega on the corner, which is what New Yorkers call convenience stores. It was the first time I encountered the nighttime system of shopping uptown. The door to the store is locked. You ask for what you need through a plexi-glass turntable bank teller thing. This is done to prevent theft at night. If you don't let anyone in the store, it's harder to get robbed. My suburban ass couldn't shut up about it.

We got our beers and headed back to the party. The clock struck twelve as we made our way. We heard a few people hollering Happy New Year and could hear the din of televisions blaring. Across the street we saw a couple of guys milling and seething, and as the New Year rang in, these guys celebrated by pulling guns out of their waistbands and pulling off shots into the sky. Kevin and Paul scattered behind some trashcans. Zeke took off, shouting, "What goes up, must come down," and I kept walking toward the party. I wasn't being bold; it was just how I reacted. I never saw a gun before. I'd never been close to a gun being fired. I'd never been above 80th St., and I reacted by having no reaction at all. The barrage ended, and my friends came out of their hiding places. We made it back to the brownstone, and my nerves finally appeared in the form of my babbling about what had happened. This only made it clear how new I was to this scene and almost eclipsed my dropping the beer as the most awkward thing I did that night. I guess I wasn't as down as I thought.

Getting back to school this time was both a relief and a worry. For the first time, the finish line was in sight. It dawned on me that there was no class above me to say goodbye to, no graduating girlfriend to watch walk away. It was just my class and me; it was our time. I remember feeling different in high school because there was a finite and tactile next step on the horizon. This year, we were staring at the expanse of an unknown future that was as exciting as it was frightening.

We had work to do and the faculty was in full support mode the entire time. That winter break, I received my grades and had a 4.0 for the first, and only, time in my life. I asked my brother, the doctor, who went to Duke and majored in Chemistry if he ever had a 4.0. He joked that he never got close but was learning science and not trying to live off his looks. It turns out everyone in my class got the same grades. It was a gift from the faculty and a way to say we made it.

It was a time that reminds me of those movies set in college, not the party movies, but the ones where the students wear blazers and have cocktails with the professors—like *The Paper Chase* or *A Beautiful Mind* (John Nash the subject of the latter was a CMU graduate). There was a more social element to this year. We had dinner at the faculty head's house, and there were mixers and barbeques, and it was a civilized way to behave. Looking back at it now, it becomes clear that it was all really an elaborate goodbye, but it was a nice way to go about it, and it made me feel grown-up. Christine was by my side for most of these events.

My master plan was to be sure that I represented myself in my presentation as marketable and multi-faceted. I wanted to play-up my East Coast vibe and contrast it with vulnerability and a more vanilla version of myself and show some range. We were all looking for two scenes. Our professors wanted ten choices when we re-convened. I had twenty. It was the first time I noticed that the assignment was just a guideline; the minimum effort would only hurt you in the long run. Some of my classmates were short of scenes. It was finally a time where my having an avid interest in material was put to good use. We spent most of our time reading scenes and seeing how they fit particular people. I also noticed that you had to be an advocate for yourself, and having all these choices gave me more control. I was not going to squander this opportunity. When we went in a circle with scenes, I never ran out. The fact that I had done my research and cast myself well in all the scenes assured a good fit. My choices and the volume of material I had procured forced the other students to get up to speed. The actors who didn't have a clear idea of their strengths were running the risk of being paired up in a scene that didn't fit.

We had made the mistake as a class to get certified in stage combat. What could be mistaken about learning how to fake fight? Other than the obvious uselessness of the whole endeavor, we had to amass a certain amount of hours of practice. The only time we could find was at 8AM three times a week. We were seniors and were supposed to be able to sleep in, but we jammed ourselves up. There is an official sanctioning body in Las Vegas, and after we got our hours, they sent a representative, and we were tested. The problem was we practiced on wrestling mats, but had to test on hardwood floors. What if we had practiced a real martial art? I would be a lot less polite in public places; instead, I need a sword or a quarterstaff to show off any of my skills. When we tested, the auditor told Paul and me that we passed with a "low D," but we were getting the useless certificate because he said, "I could tell you understood the vocabulary of violence." So, we had that going for us.

I will take pride in one accomplishment on the movement front. I was not a good tumbler in gym class as a kid. I didn't have a gymnast's build, but over the years of study I could do Akido dive rolls over people and obstacles with reckless abandon. I would run and dive and come up on one knee and it was exhilarating. I'm not sure my folks invested well if that's the thing that gives me the most pride, but I managed to conquer a fear, and that's something.

On the domestic front, it was becoming alarming how little

contact Christine had with her family. She said there was very little support but that her folks were both doctors, which would lead you to believe they would be on top of their daughter's care. She wasn't working, and things were getting tense.

Christine wore her hair in micro-braids, which are individually woven to a woman's hair and tends to be a low-maintenance style once the time is invested at the beauty shop. It's a great look, but the day at the hair salon is hours long and expensive. At some point she removed her braids and needed a wig. This all backed the story and protocols of someone going through cancer treatment. She wasn't losing her hair. She just wanted the braids out; her not having the money to get braids necessitated me buying a wig as a quick fix. It was a vulnerable moment for her, and I think it was played for effect. Not knowing the ins and outs of what African American women go through with their hair, I believed it was all cancer related. Of course it would be impolite to ask questions; a woman's hair is a complicated thing, so I let it go without a question, trying not to be an asshole.

A black girl from another class asked me if Christine was wearing a wig. I said no, which we both knew wasn't true, and eventually shared the story of what she was going through. Whenever Christine found out I shared her story, she went through the roof. She didn't want anyone to know. This was another clue. It wasn't her wish for privacy that was at issue. It was the scrutiny that level headed questions would bring to the fore. All this gives me an unsettled feeling even to this day. I was on a different planet and don't wish to visit.

My father wrote in his pages that he recognized a certain lack of confidence in his personality. It's memories like this that make me think it may have been passed down. Outwardly, I was confident enough to be at ease on stage, but confidence in relationships was certainly lacking. I'm not even sure that's the way to put it. It goes back to advocating for oneself. Somewhere along the line I thought that wanting things to be a certain way in a relationship and voicing it would lead to that relationship ending. It winds up being a battle of wills, and I found myself subjugating my will to others. My vocal, animated, and perhaps, loudmouth exterior was all bluster and kept most people at arm's length. If I let people inside my reach, they could see I was malleable, and this was not good for me. I think this lack of confidence reared its head in these situations, and I think smart people who wished to could play my nature against my own self-interest. That sounds a little paranoid, but that doesn't mean they're not out to get me.

40

EXILE ON MAIN STREET

When I exiled myself on the Gulf side of Florida, I was attempting to follow a step-by-step method of re-aligning my personality when it came to dating. Any inkling of a negative vibe would send me in the other direction. I remember one date with a girl where we went dancing. Being from New York and thinking I was funky, I hit the dance floor with a vengeance, as if you could dance your way to vengeance. The girl was a bit dim and dour, so naturally, I was attracted at first, and as I was dancing and, in my mind, charming the shit out of her along with the rest of the club, she leaned into my ear to ask, if I was going to embarrass her in public. I think I tried to execute a split and continued to solo for the rest of the night. I wasn't going to let my train get pushed off the tracks. This may not be the best example of me coming into my own, but it was an example of me noticing that when the hackles go up on your neck, you should decipher them and take heed.

The only time I ever jogged for exercise was when I was in Florida. I used the odometer in my brother's car and mapped out a three-mile route. I was not in great shape when I got to Florida, and back in New York I was drinking heavily and smoking cigarettes. I did the run as often as I could, and it never got easier. I've never been a runner. I blew out my knees playing basketball, and my body type doesn't have miler written on it. The runs were almost a way to punish myself and push past a limit that I never before attempted. I never got to the point where I got that runner's high I've heard about. It was a pass/fail endeavor, and I needed it for a while as I put some distance between my self-destructive habits and self-sabotaging thoughts.

The relief I might have felt was tinged with guilt. While it was clear to everyone in my family, I was slow to concede that Christine was lying. My sister-in-law was an investigative reporter at the time and had done some research to help me see that the truth had been stretched. Medical records being confidential couldn't unearth what I needed to hear. I left the situation because the relationship was decomposing; I stayed in the situation because I felt like I had signed on for seeing this person to a finish that wasn't coming.

The information my sister-in-law did find was academic, the fact that there was no record of this person graduating from the university from which she said she held two degrees, started to rattle my illusion.

41

REMEMBER MY NAME

There is a horseshoe curve on the Pennsylvania Railroad Line where you can see both the front car and the back car of the train at the same time. It occurs near the Altoona depot. This train line is the line that helped Andrew Carnegie become the wealthiest man in the world. It is, in part, because of this line that we got the chance to go to the school that our famous robber baron founded. Carnegie Mellon is the first university to grant a degree in drama (back when it was Carnegie Tech) making it the oldest department in the country. The Altoona stop is interesting in the way that the world's largest salt deposit is interesting. It was barely interesting to my classmates and me as we made the turn on our way to New York City for our showcase. We had a classmate from Altoona and were forced to be excited about the horseshoe curve. As the train stopped at the Altoona station, we were greeted by our classmate's family and were treated to sandwiches from a local sandwich shop as his family passed them around before the train left the station.

Playing cards and maybe imbibing a few beers, we felt like a baseball team from the 1930s riding the club car to play the Yankees. All the work we had put in was going to get a literal test, a baptism by fire, and our dreams and fears were going to come in direct contact with each other in a few days.

I was lucky to have a hotel room waiting for me in the city at the Marriott Marquis. My sister-in-law-to-be was working for Marriott at the time and got me a family rate. My classmates were going to be couch surfing with recent alumni or staying with family if they were from the area. The Marriott was over booked that first night, and I got to stay at the Essex House on Central Park South for a couple of nights. I was starting to feel touched. I had my Equity card and had a recent professional credit, and I had two scenes that were close to showing my many sides.

Once I was secure in my room in New York, I realized we were already going our own ways. We were starting to see that our time as a class, as an entity, was coming to an end. I walked around the city with my room card in my pocket wondering what was going to become of me. I was also wondering how I could get a woman up to my room.

Things looked good as far I could see, but you never knew—you could blank after the showcase and be left to your own devices. Stories traveled back to Pittsburgh every year about the people who had the thickest envelopes after the showcase and who met the most agents. My friend Jack didn't even make it back for graduation because within a week's time he was a regular on a soap opera. That was the goal; land a gig right out of the box. The bare-minimum was to come out of the showcase with an agent.

Theatre Row was a row of theatres on 42nd Street between 9th and 10th Avenues. I think there are theatres there now but not in the old configuration. The department had secured the Harold Clurman Theatre for two days; it was what's known as an Off-Broadway house, and we were going to perform there in a few days. We were on our own in the city and for some of my classmates this was a daunting task. We mercilessly mocked our Texas classmate when he said, "No thank you, sir," to a drug dealer asking if he wanted some "smoke" or "sess." Whether it actually occurred was less important than the re-telling of it over and over again.

The format for the showcase harkened back to the difficulty of finding one of those dreaded monologues. We each had two scenes that were two minutes in length. You would do one scene, and it would dovetail into a scene with another actor. I was going first, opening the show. I had a scene from the film *Diner* and a scene from a play I culled from an archive in the library at CMU. It was the scene that Guy had done at his showcase two years before.

My biggest worry was my hair and clothes. The scene from *Diner* had to be edited and had to work outside of a diner. The setting was adapted to having the two guys eating lunch on a table on a construction site. The problem was I was wearing a very sharp outfit with a sports coat and slacks and the directors of the showcase wanted me to be wearing a hardhat as the scene started. I didn't want to be wearing a hardhat when I hit the stage for the first time and didn't think it went well with my outfit. The directors tried to sell me on the idea that we were the architects visiting the worksite of one of our designs. Everyone has to wear a hardhat on a construction site, but you don't wear a hardhat on stage when you are courting representation. We went back and forth for a month before the showcase, and I relented. I would walk on with the hardhat, and take it off as soon as I sat and started speaking. How little it mattered makes me slightly embarrassed to bring up now, but at the time, I was making myself, and anyone in earshot crazy.

The *Diner* scene was to show some comedy and some of that East Coast edge. It was an edit of the scene where one of the guys in the diner yells at the other guy for being indirect when asking for the rest of his sandwich, an early example of how being passive aggressive is exasperating. The second scene was a bit heavier. It was about two hostages that are at the edge of their sanity in captivity. The first line is, "I need a hug." It's a good opener that got a chuckle, but was really about two men who are at the end of their rope. It ends with the two prisoners in a hug, and when we performed it, we got an audible response that I thought signaled the audience understood the pathos of the scene. I had a strong contrast and was really happy with my choices and how I managed to get myself the best showing I could.

The department made a program that featured our photos, names, and the scenes we were performing. They were handed out to the audience, and the members of the industry would receive an additional form to fill out. They would respond to each actor by checking a box that said, "Call for appointment" or "Send picture and résumé." There might have been a "Stay in touch" box to check, but I'm not sure. After each performance these responses would be compiled, with the data to be handed out at a reception at the Carnegie House, after the second showcase.

I was back at the Marriott, and after the second showcase, we had some time to kill before the reception. I invited a small group up to the room. We got food and beer at a deli and piled up food from the salad bar—we were young, and we didn't know any better. Where else were we going to get baby back ribs and tuna salad and beer in one place?

My room at the Marquis had two double beds, so it was big; it also had a great view of the city. We turned out the lights of the room and ate and drank by the light of the skyline. We turned all the chairs to face the large windows, which were essentially the fourth wall of the room. We ate and drank and tried to distract our nerves. We had decided as a class that we would not open the envelopes that would be handed out after the reception until we were alone. We decided this was a private moment. We were also counseled by recent graduates to do it this way because it was brutal on people who didn't get a great response, not to mention classless if you were hooting and hollering about your good fortune. It was a good suggestion.

In the dark, in that room, we were young and bright drama students who'd been through a lot together, soon we would be actors without a schedule to keep or another project on the horizon. We joked and assured each other that we would all find a place in the world we had chosen.

I'm not sure who started it, but at some point and a few beers in, we started screaming at the window, grabbing our crotches, flipping the bird, and telling the city what were going to do to it. I don't know how you go about fucking an entire island, but that was the gist of the boasting we all bellowed out the window of the Marriott Marquis.

We were properly front-loaded before the reception. Wine would have to do to keep our buzz. Some recent graduates were at the reception, and it was a great comfort. Kiera Lyle was there, and it stirred my stomach to see her. I was less worried about my envelope and more worried about how to get her to come back to the Marriott with me. The students and faculty who were assigned to amassing the information were behind closed doors, tallying the results. As the wine flowed and the time wore on, it was clear that this reception was really only a waiting room.

Waiting really is the hardest part. No matter how confident you were, you couldn't help but worry about the response. This was the real reason most of us chose Carnegie Mellon. We knew we would have a leg up in the industry, that if we did well we'd be ahead of every other twenty one year old who got off the bus that year. It was definitely the reason I fought so hard to get back into school. I thought I had a look and the talent, and that the showcase would go well for me. Waiting and drinking wine and seeing recent graduates who had their own stories to tell got me worrying.

There was a balcony, that also had a nice view, and it was hard to fight the urge to tell this part of the city that we were going to fuck it, but today it reminds me of a time when we were walking in certain privileged corridors—corridors that only open for a short amount of time. For some they are always open and for others, they will never get within shouting distance, and some won't need them to be open because they will be marched through and doors will be brought down. Not knowing who you would have to be until the envelope came was maddening.

I flashed back to my summer stock season. A fellow dramat, heading into his senior year, was with us. He hadn't had the best showcase in terms of industry interest, but I knew he would find a way. He was diabetic and during performances at the barn he would sometimes have blood sugar issues. I remember having to ply him with orange juice and candy bars between cues as his blood sugar plummeted. He would never miss a cue and would pull from a deep reserve to get through the show. My dad was diabetic and I knew the seriousness of the disease. It's even more acute in a young person. That summer I thought to myself, this guy really wants this. He'll do what it takes. I need to be more like that. When I heard his presentation didn't yield much, I wasn't worried for him. Years later, when I saw him with a part on *ER*, I was impressed but also reassured.

The moment was upon us, and the faculty and students who were burning the midnight oil compiling our feedback were bleary eyed. We were drunk and eager to get our envelopes. There was some speech about this only being the beginning of our careers, and that there would be opportunities down the line, and not to take any of this too seriously. This was not a make or break situation.

I was thinking, "Did we all eat shit, that bad? Can you just pass out the goddamn envelopes?"

I finally had my hands on mine. What is it about envelopes and their thickness? Mine was thick to the touch, which had to be a good sign. Almost on cue, we broke our pact, and tore open our envelopes. I was on the balcony with Kiera Lyle and she took the sheets of paper out of my hand, her eyes lit up, and she said, "You did really well, wow." Sharing this moment with Kiera was funny, considering what we'd been through. Maybe it was fitting in some way. I snatched my pages back and was less interested in company for the night, and more interested in making my phone calls in the morning. It was a quiet moment of vindication and a proud moment. Kiera got to see how well I did, and it felt good.

A quick scan of the yellow legal sized paper, told me I had done well. There were a lot of "call for appointments," and there were four or five two-sided pages. While we broke our word about opening the envelopes, we tried to remain under control after they were open. I was eager to get back to the hotel and was really excited about getting up in the morning. We had a return trip to Pittsburgh, but it didn't look like I would be able to schedule all of my appointments before that. I kept that piece of paper for years until someone's inane advice about letting go of the past compelled me to get rid of it. Why do we listen to people about shit like that? Yes, you need to let go of the past. That would occur as long as you didn't look at the papers every other week, but having it in a drawer doesn't mean you're stuck. It would be nice to have that paper today, but I listened to New Age advice. I should probably burn some sage.

I remember waking up that morning and shaking off the cobwebs, and trying to warm up my voice so I wouldn't sound groggy when I called the people on my list. What happened next will never happen to me again unless I win an Oscar—my calls were answered. The receptionist said, "Yes, let me put you right, through." I am phone phobic to begin with, but this was easy. I would never be able to work the phones this way again.

My sister had given me a filofax organizer, and I thought I was hot shit as I opened it up and started scheduling appointments. I still have that organizer to this day; am I stuck in the past because they make a quality product or should I chuck it into a landfill? It just dawned on me that awards shows also feature the envelope, and when messages come to your phone, the icon is an envelope, and when you want to email an article to a friend you click on an envelope. The envelope please—how many times have we heard that? There was an envelope waiting for me a long time ago, and it was a great day, and while its impact hasn't quite carried me to the present, it got me far. For that I need to be grateful. Not everyone gets a day like that.

42

MAKE IT HAPPEN

The top priority meetings were with agents, and I had a few to make, but was very eager to see two in particular. The first was the William Morris Agency. The second was Abrams Artists. William Morris recently merged with Endeavor, becoming WME, not to be confused with WWE, which is the moniker for professional wrestling. There were other agencies to meet, but these were the name brands and when you have stars in your eyes, you go for it.

My paper told me that I was the only person that William Morris had asked to call for a meeting. I called the switchboard and was transferred to the desk of the assistant. It turned out that the assistant was the one who attended the showcase and she wanted me to come in and meet her boss and perform some monologues. By now, I had two that I could live with. I was so protective of one of my pieces that I refused to give the name of the play or playwright to a classmate.

The offices for WMA are on Avenue of the America's at 53rd Street. It is a huge building with grumpy important looking people bursting through its lobby. There are banks of elevators and you have to find which one goes to even floors and which one goes to odd numbered floors. I think there is a newsstand in the lobby itself. That always seemed high-end to me. We are so powerful that we moved the newsstand inside, "I'm not going outside for Breath Savers. Are you mad?"

I was on my way to my appointment and felt special. I was going into the offices of an agency that even a layperson would recognize. You didn't have to be in the industry to know who the William Morris Agency was; I was puffed up with this thought and was feeling like all my decisions thus far were paying a dividend. I wish I could remember what I was wearing. I'm sure it was too formal as I was trying to still be the good student.

When you got to the floor that was so high in the sky that your ears could pop, you enter a lobby with a desk that looks a bit like the set to the *People's Court*. There is an attractive woman manning the phones. I approached the bench and told her my name and whom I was there to see. She told me to have a seat and that someone would be right with me.

I didn't wait long when Lisa came out to greet me. She was young and attractive with an athletic body. She told me how much she enjoyed my performance and was excited for me to meet Rebecca, her boss. I was nervous, but when you're being complimented, you gain some momentum over your nerves. I followed Lisa past the guard tower of a front desk and entered a maze of desks and offices. I was led to an office and was introduced to Rebecca who was brunette, fit, and high-energy. She had a Diet Coke on her desk and asked me if I wanted anything to drink. I never know what to do in that case. I usually say "no thanks," but I think I'll take a beverage next time.

We chatted for a bit and she said that Lisa thought I was great, and she couldn't wait to see what I had prepared. I then followed her to a conference room. It was one of those boardrooms where you could sit sixty people, and you could picture the Waterford crystal pitchers every two feet around the table. She wheeled a chair out from the table, and I took some space at the head of the room. She dimmed the lights, so her reaction could be a bit concealed if need be.

I launched into my first monologue, which was the comedic piece. It was short and I was hoping I'd get to do the second piece because it was a killer. I wrapped up the first one and Rebecca stopped me.

"I want to hear your next piece, but before you start, I'm begging you to sign with us." She said.

"Cool." I said.

It was all I could think to say, but now I could relax and really go for it on the second monologue. This one was serious and was about a son who ignored his father at a little league baseball game because he was ashamed his dad was a carpenter. It shows shame and remorse, and it painted a great picture. You can see why I wanted to keep it to myself. I started and was more relaxed; I was playing with house money. When I finished and very dramatically let the last moment hang there, Rebecca was moved. She said, "You made me cry." I'm not sure I saw tears, but I wasn't going to argue.

We went back to her office, and she was all over me. She started typing on the computer and said that they represented John Cusack and that I would go in for everything he passed on, she called a colleague, and he came to the office. He said I was right for playing Anjelica Huston's son, and he'd see if he could get me an appointment later that day. Rebecca said there was a TV show about a guy on the run in a Winnebago, and she thought I could get the lead. My head was spinning. This was like a deal with the devil, it couldn't be this easy.

During our preparations for the showcase, we got some standard advice about how to go about these meetings. We were told we didn't need to mention the other agents who had shown interest. It was suggested that we meet everyone who had asked to meet us, and we were told to be wary of the bigger agencies because you could get lost in the shuffle and not get the attention we needed.

Somehow during this hard-sell seduction I managed to avoid committing right there and then. I wasn't able to keep my mouth shut about the rest of people I had to meet, but I got out of there without having my blood typed.

I was still unschooled in the perils of salad bar dining in the city and as I sat there eating after the meeting, my head was spinning with possibilities and thankfully not botulism. I figured I could meet everyone, head back to Pittsburgh, graduate and come back to make my decision.

My meeting with Abrams Artists was such a pleasure that it didn't feel like a meeting, but more like a get together. I got to meet three of the agents in the office, and they were cool and funny. One of the agents knew a girl I knew in high school, and we talked about Springsteen for half of the time. Of course, I ran down the list of all the agents who wanted to meet me. I know we were told not to, but it gave the present company the knowledge that other people were interested. I didn't think that could hurt me. If they knew I had options they would treat me better, right? They told me to think hard about William Morris, and to remember Abrams offered big agency clout with boutique agency attention to the client. They didn't want me to get swallowed up in a big agency. It all made sense and I told them I'd get back to them after graduation. I shook all their hands and walked to the elevators. As I exited the office, they called me back in.

"Carl, we just wanted you to know that we are very serious about working with you."

"OK, cool." I said.

I really needed to work on my responses, but I was trying to be savvy. What the fuck did I know?

Not every meeting was as enjoyable. One agent kept me waiting for a long time only to ask if I could come back later in the day. I came back later in the day, and she grilled me about what I thought I could do, and why had I kept my sideburns so long. She kept me waiting and now I was stuttering and having a hard time. I was thinking, "You called me in. I didn't bug you for this meeting." When I told friends they said they wouldn't have gone back after I had waited. Again, what the fuck did I know?

Another time I got my appointment time wrong and when they called to see where I was, I was in New Jersey. I hopped on the bus and met with the guy as he was closing up the office. I walked with him to his subway stop and that was how our meeting went down. He was cool and ran a strong mid-level agency; I learned a tough lesson there.

One guy kept me in the waiting room as he held court with a semi-famous TV actor, with the door open. When he finally wrapped up with his client he introduced me to the actor and when we finally sat down to talk he said, "That's what this agency is all about." I didn't know what he meant.

I finally made it back to school on a different train a few days after the school's scheduled departure. News had traveled, not necessarily from me, but from the students who had compiled the results. It seemed I had the hot hand. It was no small amount of pride that filled me—from being cut, to where I was now standing—was a long way.

Being back at school meant being back with Christine. Packing up the apartment and getting ready for graduation was going to put her in a bind as far as a place to stay. My family would be coming out, and it was time to get ready for graduation. I don't know what we did during this time. Did we have things to do or were we just waiting for the day when college would come to an end?

My aunt and uncle would be coming out, and we went to dinner. My uncle was a bit taken-a-back meeting Christine. "I wish someone would have told me she was black." He said. I didn't take much offense; he's a lovely guy—it was just a generational reaction to the way it was when he was coming up. There was a generation gap in my family—he was older than my father, and the only black person he could think of was probably Lena Horne. Why am I giving my uncle a pass when I judged Nancy's father so harshly? He didn't hurl a slur. My uncle didn't have an issue. It was just an adjustment he had to make, and he didn't mean anything other than it would have been nice to know. My father told me he had no problem but worried about the ignorant people who would. My mother was on the record as an opponent to racism; the only issue was whether this was the girl for me.

This was the early 1990s, so it wasn't as prevalent to see an interracial couple, but it rarely came up. We did have a near incident with a group of guys who took exception to Christine being with me, and a group of friends. Unfortunately, Christine didn't take the high road, and it got tense. I was chest-to-chest with a guy I was sure would destroy me. We moved the pile to the foot of a patio at a bar we frequented, and the bartender came out to quell the situation. He was not happy with us. "Don't drag your mess in here. Handle it yourself next time." He had a point, but I needed some back up.

It was moments like that where I could see something dark lurked in Christine's personality. I didn't know what I thought would happen when I went to New York, and she stayed in Pittsburgh. I was more interested in figuring out what I was going to do with my agent decision. God help those around people who are sure things are going their way, especially in the creative fields. It's hard to not think that your activities are the most important thing on the planet. You spent all this time worrying about your work, worrying about your place in the department, worrying about the presentation, and it was hard to have perspective now that the hour was at hand. I'm sure the last thing I was worrying about was my relationship. I'm sure Christine picked up on that. Whether this fueled her next few moves is one question that will never be answered.

I must give myself credit, in retrospect, for how I handled myself during this time period. I would let nothing derail me and I honored the second chance I was given. I made the most out of an opportunity and was impervious to the effects of an unhealthy relationship. It wasn't until things went south that I had a harder time pulling out of the negativity that was spiraling around me like a buzzard circling a carcass.

We all know how the graduation ceremony goes, and we know the format. I don't remember who made the commencement speech, but we were under a huge tent and then the schools and departments broke off into their specific buildings to hand out diplomas.

One moment that I do hold dear is when it was my turn to receive my degree; the head of the department kissed my cheek and said, "Congratulations for turning everything around." It was good to hear those words from that mouth. I noticed Christine giving me a thumbs-up and beaming with pride. It was a good day for all.

It's an amazing process, this whole going to school thing. While you're excited and proud to have graduated, it's a crummy thing saying goodbye to people. It would be the last time I would ever see some of these people and years before I saw others. Some I would see and grow closer to in the real world, and one would be lost too soon. We were a company of sixteen and we were going our own ways. It was both exhilarating and lonely. My brother took a picture of me walking across the quad to return my gown. I'm still wearing my mortarboard and the gown is draped over my arm, the wind billowing the fabric like a plume of smoke. I'm alone, and coincidently there is no one else in the frame. The campus was buzzing with activity, so an empty frame was statistically hard to come by. My head is down. I didn't know the picture was being taken, but seeing it puts me in that emotional state in an instant. It was my last official act as a student at Carnegie Mellon University. It had the look of an athlete walking off the field for the last time and the feel of a man's first step into the unknown.

That melancholy is part of an actor's life, I think. Every time I close a show I walk the stage for the last time and say a prayer that I get another chance to perform. Even with TV and film, you have to say goodbye to the process. The busy actor knows this as well as the struggling actor, maybe even more so, but leaving all that work behind and that struggle and victory behind was a hard lump to get down my throat. Having appointments in the city and a bright future only blunted the emotion. I guess this is why they warn you to enjoy the Halcyon days.

There was a final reception fittingly on the main stage where convocation occurred. It was a chance for families to meet friends and for some of the faculty to mingle. A professor walked up to me and asked about William Morris; there was a lilt to his voice like the advice to avoid a big agency was a theory that hadn't been tested yet. He was impressed and said go for it. I told him I still had to think about it. I'm sure I stressed over the decision as I know no other process. There was a wish to put the brakes on, to freeze the frame for a moment, but that is a childish wish.

It was the first time in my life that I was the graduate in the family. I had been in tow for all of my sibling's graduations. This time, I was the one in the robe holding up my degree for the camera. They were there for *me* this time. I thought it would feel different. I had been thinking about this since I was a kid. I remember being in a hotel room and opening presents, my brother joking that I didn't have to react to every gift with the same enthusiasm, and trying to escape a feeling of emptiness. All the summers where I needed a moment to process or to re-insert myself into some kind of routine were nothing compared to how I was feeling at this moment. I wonder if I am alone in this feeling of being vacant. I felt like a house that was just moved-out-of, empty of its contents, but still alive with the spirit of recent evacuees.

I'm not sure how I got home, and I'm not sure how long I stayed in Pittsburgh. I had to shake off the blues and get down to the business of getting down. I had a second meeting with Abrams where I got to meet a west coast agent, and I sat with the gang again. The woman who knew a girl from my hometown told me she found out that they used to call me Joe Actor in high school. It was another great meeting, and I was torn. The only thing I could think of as a negative was that they were actively telling me William Morris would be a bad idea. I didn't know if they were looking out for me or badmouthing someone. I left that meeting less than sure.

Rebecca, from William Morris, set up a meeting for me with a visiting agent from the west coast, and he started out by saying, "I heard you made Rebecca cry?"

"I guess I did." I said.

I still wasn't warmed up with my comebacks, but I was saying more than one word at a time. The office he borrowed had signed pictures of Tom Hanks on the wall. I was also introduced to the commercial department and was moving closer to a decision.

My folks were good sounding boards, but it was outside their sphere of expertise. I was home now, and the faculty was no longer at our disposal. I talked to recent graduates and tried to get a feel. The prevailing wisdom was you would only get lost in the shuffle if you weren't talented, like when a college coach tells you you'll start at quarterback as a freshman. After all the debate, I went with William Morris.

43

NEW YORK MINUTE

The creepy feeling I got from living back at home was balanced by the excitement I was feeling about my decision. I was in the city everyday and going on general meetings with casting directors or going on auditions. Checking in with friends who were just getting to the city, I knew I was hitting the ground running. It was a good move. I was meeting casting directors who worked on big projects. The meetings were set-up by William Morris, and I would go in to talk or sometimes do my monologues. It was the middle of summer when things were slow in the business, but I was being introduced to the people I would need to know in the future.

Lisa, the assistant, was my lifeline. I rarely talked to Rebecca. I was able to bounce stuff off of Lisa, and she would always take my call. She taught me a simple thing about the city that I should have already known. This was before Mapquest, so finding addresses wasn't always so easy. New York is on a grid, and it is easy to figure out once you know which direction you're going. I was OK on the West Side, but when I would get downtown addresses or have to go to the East Side,

I would have to bug Lisa. She told me that Fifth Avenue demarcates east and west. One side of Fifth Avenue is east, and one side is west. If you have an East Side address with a low number, it's close Fifth Ave. but on the east side of the street, and vice versa for west. It was silly that I didn't know this already, and thank God none of my classmates knew about my ignorance, especially since I perpetrated a street-smart savvy.

It was a time in my life where I was battling feelings of uselessness. What the fuck was I able to do? If you dropped me in the wilderness, I would dehydrate looking for a payphone and an ATM. I was bouncing between panic and confidence daily. If I didn't get an acting job, I would have to go back to school to learn a trade.

When I had to pick up a script for an audition, I would pick it up in the lobby; there was a house phone you could use to call the back office. Once in a while, I would buzz back and see if Rebecca was around. Often she was busy. I figured she was busy working for her other clients and me, and I didn't need to bother her.

The agency was broken into departments, and this is where the lost in the shuffle worry made the most sense. Rebecca was my agent, and she was in the motion picture department. I knew a lot of CMU graduates had found work in the "soaps," so I inquired about it. Lisa told me that "soaps," were in the commercial department and not under Rebecca's radar. I had been sent out for commercials, which can be great supplemental income, but not for the "soaps". Lisa also told me that they were trying to keep me out of the "soaps" because they were thinking I was headed for something better. While flattered, I thought it had more to do with the way things were billed in the office. At the time, I bought the reasoning. I had no deep desire to be on the "soaps," and I didn't think I was pretty enough to be considered, but I could play a cop or an orderly and maybe make some money.

Trying to figure out how I was going to live in the world at large and how I was going to get out of my house was a daily worry. I needed a job, but what would I do? I got a reprieve from my worry when I booked a Tylenol commercial. I was relieved that I had made good on an audition, and I knew it would pay a pretty good rate. The audition was a good indicator that some of this stuff was random. I was unable to pronounce acetaminophen, and it was in the text of the commercial. I was lucky that people were running late and was asked to stay in the room as the only male of my type available. With every new audition I found new ways to butcher the pronunciation of the active ingredient in the product. It was like a blooper reel, and the casting people thought it was funny. Having a couple of cracks at it and loosening up helped me win over the room; my temporary speech impediment was forgiven.

The commercial shot in Philadelphia, so there was travel pay, and it was a two-day shoot. It was the first time I received per diem money, which is an amazing thing. When you are out of town, you are given money for meals. One of the actors was a familiar face, and I was excited to be on the set with him. I was playing a medical student making the rounds with the doctor. The guy who played the doctor had most of the lines, and he was struggling with them. We had many takes. Toward the end of the day that put us behind, but upped our pay, so we were cool with it. The actor, however, was unraveling. The crew had to write his lines on cue cards to help the Doc get through it. We wrapped for the day and went back to the hotel. I was fired up. I had money in my pocket, a hotel room, and I wanted to go out. None of the other actors were as excited as I was to spend a night away from home, probably because their home wasn't still the home they grew up in. I managed a decent meal and a couple of beers at the lobby bar.

Seeing myself on television was great, but seeing that first check was even more satisfying. My dad wanted to see my pay stub, and my mother was telling him to leave me alone. It wasn't enough to move out, but it was a larger sum than I had seen in a while. My dad stole a glance at the check and said, "I bet you could get used to a couple more of those."

It was hard not to feel like things were going my way, that I would have one of those rare, seamless paths to success. I watched TV with a discerning eye, thinking that I was now part of this world of entertainment, and it would be a matter of time before I was working regularly. I was getting good feedback from the meetings, and one casting director, in particular, was a big supporter. He actually stopped me when I was doing my monologue and asked me to make some adjustments, I thought it was going badly, but Rebecca actually called to tell me the guy loved me. He carried weight and worked on prestigious projects. It was all lining up.

Occasionally, I was put on tape to be sent to the west coast, and I was told that I was on hold for a movie of the week about a swimmer who is seduced by an older woman. Can you imagine being paid to be seduced? I checked my messages hourly.

When you're with a big agency, you get the whole script when you have an audition. Every few days, I would head into the city and grab my script. It was uniformly bound with a blue William Morris cover. I would go to lunch or coffee and try to flaunt my script to the eyes of strangers who didn't give a shit. I was still piling it on at the salad bar these days, so nobody paid me any mind. I was learning how to kill time in the city without an apartment to go back to. I would use the bathrooms and the bank of phones at the Marriott Marquis. I felt at home in the 7th floor lobby. This was where it all got started. It felt like my rightful place.

The money was running out, and I really needed to get a job. A classmate of mine had found work at a fancy fitness club in the city, and I initially wanted to learn the trade of personal training. Unfortunately, they needed a trainer on the floor for the opening shift, which started at 6AM. I couldn't find a bus that would get me there at that time and had to take a job at the front desk. I was barely breaking even with the commute and the low rate of pay, but I wasn't looking to work in New Jersey; my work life and social life were happening in the city.

Christine had found a place to live with my friend, Clancy, who worked with me in construction the summer before my senior year. I think he had a roommate, and she actually took the couch. Clancy knew about her situation and was being a nice guy. I was making maintenance calls to Pittsburgh and breathing a sigh of relief when the calls were over. I wasn't paying much attention to the situation or my relationship. I was more interested in how things were shaping up for me on the career front.

The hindsight goblin really kicks me in the ass on this one. How easy would it have been to break-up over the phone? All the standard lines applied, "It's not practical being in two different cities." "It's a time of transition for me. I need to focus on my career." Or how about, "I'm out of this, because I get a nauseating feeling in my stomach every time I think about the relationship." Of course, I said none of this and was burying my head in the sand, figuring it would work itself out.

It didn't work itself out. It became a mess and led me to the shores of St. Pete Beach where I tried to get my life back on track, away from everyone I knew and everything that was familiar. To steal a title, I was less than zero.

Working at the fitness club was a crash course in multi-tasking. I would have to answer the phone and transfer calls. I'd have to swipe cards of members and get familiar with forms that made me wonder how a gym could have so much red tape. There were forms to freeze your membership and forms to change how you paid your dues. There were no forms to cancel a membership; that would take an act of congress. I could workout for free but usually worked-out in the rougher gym in New Jersey.

I was making friends in the gym and was trying to find an answer to the riddle of finding a place to live in Manhattan. It was a time where it felt like I lived in the Lincoln Tunnel. It was also a time where I felt a weight around my neck, a weight that was tugging at me from four hundred miles away.

While I was working in the city and getting my life started, a list of hardships befell Christine. Whether they were convenient for the purposes of keeping me in the relationship or an actual avalanche of misfortune is still up for debate. By debate, I mean they either occurred or didn't; my apprehension in calling them false was a carry-over of guilt that I couldn't shake. I'm unsure even to this day because the array of events were serious, and the thought of them being fabricated is almost harder to swallow than the idea of having to live through them.

At some point, Christine told me that Clancy was acting in an inappropriate way, meaning that he was hitting on her. She assured me that they were unwelcome advances but wanted me to know what kind of friend I had in Clancy. Soon after, she found a room with some female drama students who knew her through me.

I didn't talk to Clancy for years after that misinformation, not until I was in Florida trying to find answers and evidence of Christine's lying.

The next event was so thorny and woe inducing that I'm actually bracing as I prepare to explain. Christine told me that she had been attacked and raped on the way home to her new apartment. I was stunned and didn't know what to do. This horrible development fell on the heels of a terrible turn in my life back in New York.

A week before the incident, in Pittsburgh, I got a call from Lisa at William Morris. She said she had Rebecca on the line. Rebecca took over the call and told me that William Morris had merged and taken over another agency (Triad) and that her client list was expanding, and she would be too busy to help develop my career. She said she would keep me on until I found a new agent, but we were done.

I took this blow harder than the news of my girlfriend's incident, and I hope God will forgive me. Maybe I had some level of discernment and didn't believe the incident in Pittsburgh was true, or maybe I was that self-involved.

I had made a couple of good friends at the gym, Ingrid, and a woman who was a celebrity fitness trainer. I was struggling with the loss of my agent and the news from Christine. My new friend came up to me and said, "I know you have a bright light in you, but it's very dim, right now. I want to do something to help you. I'm going to buy you a plane ticket to see your girlfriend." I hadn't told anyone the news about the attack and I thanked my new friend. I had to get to Pittsburgh to comfort Christine, but it was out of obligation and a fear that I was losing my humanity. That my new friends were black made me want to do right by my girlfriend so it would be clear that I was "down."

Everything about that trip to Pittsburgh was plagued with woe. I made all the requisite gestures of a concerned boyfriend; I was acting in a scene that was out of my depth. I didn't bother to visit the campus or seek out a professor. I was ashamed that things had fallen apart so fast. Christine was glad to see me, and we tried to be a couple. I also didn't seek Clancy out, and we stayed in this awful bubble for the rest of the weekend.

Coming back from that trip, I was less than re-energized, which is what I needed if I was ever going to rebound from being dropped by my agent. I mailed headshots and résumés to the agents that showed interest in me after the league presentation. I called Abrams Artists, and they asked if I had been submitted for a certain role on a soap opera. I said I had not, and I was asked to come in and talk. This was good news, and I was hoping to get back on track with no interruption.

I went to the meeting eager to make the decision that I should have made in the first place. I met with the main guy I had talked to before, but not the rest of the gang. I brought him up to speed on what had happened and he did his best not to say, "I told you so." He said we would have to meet again, with the rest of the crew, and I should call in about a week. I walked out thinking I would be able to bounce back with an agency that wanted me, and wasn't just taking me out for a test drive like WMA had done. A week later I called Abrams, ready to get started, and was told that it wasn't a great time for them to sign new talent, but good luck.

The lesson from this episode could be summed up with a thank you note. Had I sent thank you notes, I might have had a chance to re-group. It also dawned on me that I had wasted a lot of Abrams time. Meeting with them three times was supposed to be my introduction to the company. I was not supposed to say *no* after being feted in such a way. This is pure speculation, but I think I was being taught a lesson in the workings of the entertainment business.

My remaining ally was the casting director who had shown interest in me during one of the general meetings William Morris set-up. I called his office, and he took the call—a good sign. I brought him up to speed, and he told me to come in and talk in a week's time.

The casting director entered the room, and we shook hands. He looked over my list of agencies that I had contacted and made a suggestion. He mentioned an agency that wasn't on my radar, and he said he would make a call for me and that it might be a good fit. He said that they might need you as much as you need them. If this book ever sees the light of day I wish I could thank this man in person. He gave me a lifeline when it looked like I was dead in the water.

The agency had a big reputation and went by its initials. It wasn't one of the three letter agencies, but it used four letters, DGRW. I waited in the lobby and tried to manage my stress. I was fighting feelings of desperation, and it was something I knew I had to reign in before it stunk up my interview. Once I was in the office, I spoke with one of the "initials," and it was going fairly well. I was hoping to get to the business of getting to business. At one point, another agent walked by the office and said he remembered me from my presentation and that he thought I was good. This was six months later, and I thought that was a good sign. I turned back to my interviewer as if to say, "You saw that, didn't you? Now let's sign and get this party started." The agent said that a new client had to be a unanimous signing, that all the partners had to agree; I needed three more initials. I took this hard. He told me to let him know when I was in a production, and he asked me if I had any videotape of my acting. I took his last words as a blow-off and left the meeting feeling like I was finished before I started.

What I know now is that that meeting was a first step, and that there was a relationship being started that if I were willing to nurture, could have led to an earned and healthy working relationship. I had tape of the television project and I was regretting not having a bigger role. I could have made a copy, and that would have given me another reason to call the office and have my name come up again. I could have found a production, which would have given me another reason to call. I was spoiled by my early access and was now starting to see what an actor's work really is. Building relationships and finding work are your jobs. The agent helps you find paying jobs, but you have to be working to find an agent. The presentation was a lucky thing to have gone through, and I was one of the luckiest of my year, but when I ran into bad luck, I became paralyzed. I had to ask myself if I wanted this as much as the diabetic actor I had worked with in summer stock.

Sometimes your mental limitations are more debilitating than the physical. I was taking this all the wrong way. It didn't help that my relationship was also something to contend with, and I was losing the stamina for it all.

44

CROSSROADS

The collapse of my early career was now about to be magnified by the presence of Christine making a move to New York. Apparently, she had family who lived in Far Rockaway, which is aptly named, as it is the last stop on the A line of the subway and, with all the stops it takes, it feels like it's three hours before you get there. It is a beach community but is also known for being a pretty tough part of the world. They have what I now know are dollar vans waiting by the subway. I hopped into one to get to one of the beach streets and didn't know what to pay. I wound up over-paying by four dollars and was lucky I didn't get rolled. I think Christine was staying with an aunt and uncle and I went out to visit. They were all very nice, but I think Christine was also being untruthful to her family. She was constantly relocating to other relative's houses in different parts of the city—a cousin in Crown Heights, a grandmother in a different part of Brooklyn. She was all over the place, and I started to wonder how she could leave her care at the Falk Clinic in Pittsburgh.

Her lack of funds coupled with fierce pride or unwillingness to work left her at the mercy of others to find a place to stay each night. I had met her parents at a barbeque, and they seemed nice, so I couldn't imagine it being hard to ask for help or their being unfeeling to a child in need.

Christine also began to stay at my parent's house and the shameful part is we basically ignored their wish for an unmarried couple not to sleep in the same room. It sounds quaint, but it was what my mother would have preferred. How I managed to be so inconsiderate is still something I regret.

I didn't feel like I had a relationship so much as a responsibility. We were not physically involved, and I had started looking elsewhere for affection. I am not trying to soften the blow by speaking euphemistically. I know I had a girlfriend, in the technical sense, and being unfaithful wasn't virtuous, but I felt like I was carrying a burden, and I stepped out of my relationship. This would also complicate things down the line and lead to more tangled webs in our saga.

The story got worse for Christine. She said that she couldn't stay at her cousin's anymore for some reason, and she said she couldn't stay at her grandmother's either because her grandmother lived in section eight housing which prohibits anyone not on the lease from living there. I asked her, "What have you been doing?"

"Riding the trains at night." She said.

Here I am messing around, and I have a cancer-riddled girlfriend who is riding the trains like a guy I avoid on the street. What the fuck? I remember one night staying in Crown Heights with another cousin, and Christine flipping out and accusing someone of stealing some of her jewelry. I wondered how she would think a relative might do such a thing and wondered how this awkward situation could get any worse. I remember watching an HBO comedy special and laughing at Jon Stewart and wondering how I would ever get my life back on track. We had to relocate in the middle of the night to an apartment project across town. When we got off the train at the Utica station, transit cops stopped us and said, "Get to where you're getting and get there fast." None of this was enough for me to bail out.

While I was trying to avoid getting involved with someone outside of my relationship and while I would keep our rendezvous chaste, I would tell the new girl about my woes, and she would praise my loyalty and concern for my girlfriend. It did little to make me feel better about the situation and did little to stop me from reaching to her in an effort to find some calm in the storm. I had known Keesha from the gym and might have located a phone number from the membership database after I heard she might be interested. This is not ethical or maybe even legal. I took a shot because I didn't think it would be an unwanted abuse of the system.

I was happy with Keesha; she was different than Christine. She was a native New Yorker, a real sister, not suburban like my girl. I thought she was exciting and sexy. She was a singer and a working songwriter, and I was bottomed out in my career. She was also a fitness fanatic, and I would make my rounds as a front desk manager and find her stretching in an aerobic studio.

In this mess I had managed to write a screenplay about an interracial couple, and I shared it with her. I was trying to show some of what might attract a woman, even as I was feeling lower in spirits than I could remember. I was trying to let her know I was "down," and I wanted her to think I had a chance in the world. We went to a Barnes and Noble bookstore, and we found seats, which is no small feat in New York. She was returning the script and we were going to talk about it. I suggested we read it out loud, and we read some scenes. I was trying to throw my acting out there to get some mojo going, and it worked. She was impressed and it was our first step toward a romantic entanglement.

I was hanging out with some college friends talking about how little money I was making, and someone made a fateful suggestion. They said I would make a great bartender, and that some bartenders make more than stockbrokers. I gave it some thought but was clueless about how to break-in.

Here comes another confession that I'm not so proud to share. It's another secret that I keep—I went to bartending school. This is a deep secret, especially as I have tended bar for years on both coasts and in Florida. In no city in the world is it remotely acceptable to admit such a thing. Résumés with a bartending school listed are thrown in the trash. Going to bartending school is like going to acting school; wait, I did that too. I've been fucked from jump-street. Friends I have known for years don't know this. It takes away all my street credibility. The thing is, you learn from doing, but how do you learn what the hell you're doing? You lie about your experience, and you try to survive your first job.

My friend Jordan and I decided to go to this school near Port Authority. Jordan was also barely scraping by, working at the same gym. He had the opening shift and had to be there by six AM. We had fun in the classes, and truthfully they gave you a good bit of knowledge. I remember being mocked on the bus back to New Jersey when I ran into a classmate from high school. She was ultra hip, and I think she now lives abroad. She saw my index cards with drinks on them and asked me what I was up to.

"I'm going to bartending school."

"Oh, Carl, you don't need to do that. You just get a book and lie and get a job and figure it out." She said.

I tried to explain that they had job placement (which was a crock of shit) and that I needed the study help they provided. It was a feeble attempt, and it made me feel like a dullard. A year ago, I was a student at a prestigious university. Now I was riding a bus trying to remember what was in a Singapore Sling.

My friend Ingrid also worked at a restaurant that I would frequent. She would always get me a couple of free beers, Rolling Rock, I think. She was a hostess, at Tattinger's, and it was a cool place to have a friend. Tattinger's had live music and would clear out tables on the weekend for dancing, which wound up not being legal and had to be stopped. It turned out they were looking for someone to work Sunday brunch. She introduced me to the woman who owned the restaurant.

"Do you have experience?" She asked.

"Uh, yeah, back in college, and I went to bartending school." I said, and instantly regretted it. Her face crumpled in a combination of impatience and pity.

"Why don't you come in on Monday, and we'll talk."

I skulked back to the hostess desk and told Ingrid to tell the lady something good about me.

I got the job and realized that Sunday brunch was the worst shift, other than any dishwashing shift. I had to set up the bar, cut all the fruit, make Bloody Mary mix, and I had to be there at ten. After all that, I would stare at the nine people who came in. It was a learning shift, or it was simply impossible to staff. I was sure I knew enough and quickly found out I didn't.

There was very little damage I could do with such a quiet shift, but I would find a way. The night guys were animals. They were seasoned grizzled bar veterans, and they would give me grief about my set-up. They were also pissed that I was such a green horn because they needed me to pick up night shifts, and I wasn't ready.

Eventually, I befriended one of the younger guys on the staff, and we wound up hanging out with the boss one night. We went to a club that had those inflatable sumo wrestling suits, and I dominated the mat. We wound up back at Tattinger's for a nightcap. I was not sure this was a good idea; in my nerdy mind, I thought hanging out with the boss could be a bad idea. It wound up being a good move. Turns out that everyone knew I was clueless, but the question was would I fit in. There was not a lot of turnover with the bar staff and breaking in a new guy was always a tough match. I guess I passed.

I was brought along slowly and eventually went live at night. I got roughed up but got a high at the end of the night when I was cut into the pile of cash we had earned. My inexperience was forgiven because my personality was my biggest asset. It's something I wish I had learned earlier. Back at the gym, I was made a manager and was

approached by the sales manager to see if I wanted to sell member-
ships, which could have been quite lucrative. I was focused on getting
my career back on track and was worried about the job's possible lack
of freedom. I passed on the job and would wait for shifts to open up
at the bar.

The biggest lament of bartenders is that they wish they could get
out of the business, but they can't afford the pay cut, or they can't
see working longer for less. It becomes a golden handcuff situation.
A casting director spoke to us at Carnegie Mellon and warned us that
the restaurant business was debilitating and that we should try other
survival jobs. I was starting to see her point. Had I taken the sales job
when I didn't have auditions, I would have learned a new gig and when
I did have an audition, I would have found a way to work it out. Also,
learning sales is an essential skill for the artist to master. I would also
have been working in the daylight and in a healthier environment.

As they say it's too late to turn back now, and while I think there
are other ways to support oneself in the arts, I feel like I have learned
some good things being a bartender. If I weren't street smart before, I
am now. The cross section of humanity I have come across is impossible to duplicate in any other field. I've been hustled. I've broken up
fights. I've met pimps. I've chatted up celebrities. I've cut people off.
I've protected women from unwanted advances. I've also seen people
destroyed by alcohol. I've met life-long friends. I've entertained both
strangers and family. I developed a personality that helped me onstage
as a comic. In some ways, I found myself as much behind the bar as
I did in drama school. I've also lost myself, and trying to keep from
unraveling when you work in front of the public can be excruciating.

Things were becoming excruciating. Keesha, from the gym, frequented Tattinger's on Sunday nights because there was an incredible
open mic for singers, hosted by one of the best singers I had ever
heard. I had been working a double shift on Sundays, unable to get
rid of the brunch shift. Still commuting form New Jersey, it would be
a twenty hour roundtrip and that was if I were lucky enough to make

the four AM bus. If I missed the 4, I would have to wait until six AM. On one of these long nights, I managed to hop in a cab with Keesha and we headed to the Bronx, where she kept an apartment. The inevitable was about to happen, and I wasn't going to stop it, complications be damned.

The cliché in movies is that the guy will never leave the wife or the girlfriend for the other woman, and in many cases, that's true. In this case, I was sure I needed to move on, but who breaks up with a girl with cancer? Who is that cold? I was clear about my wishes with Keesha but was saddled with what I thought were my responsibilities. It became unmanageable. Christine came to the gym, once, and I was stuck with a horrible situation of introducing her to Keesha. It caused a lot of strife with Keesha, and I had to agree it was unnecessary, but Christine was telling me she had trouble finding a place to lay her head at night. I was sick to my stomach much of the time.

One morning, lying in bed with Christine in my parent's house, I was at a precipice. Christine asked me a pointed question.

"Do you ever think of being with someone else?"

"I already have." I said.

She was struck by my confession and we left the house to talk. We made our way to a place that I used to visit in happier and romantic times. There is a cobblestone street a few towns over from my house. It is a steep, hilly, romantic road rarely used by cars. There is cover from many trees, and there is a cobblestone wall that you can sit on and peak at views of Manhattan through the foliage. I had been introduced to the wall by Maria Castillo back in high school and had brought maybe one or two women there since. Why I chose this place to have this conversation with Christine is a mystery. I suppose I was feeling guilty and wanted to sully a special place with a negative memory.

I told Christine that I wanted out of the relationship, that I needed for us to be over, that I was caving into the pressure, and that I wanted to be happy with someone else. At this point, she tried to scale a fence and was attempting to jump down the hill that abutted the cobblestone wall. I pulled her back over and tried to get her to calm down. If I wanted to have any special memories of this place, I had ruined that possibility.

"You need to take me someplace, so I don't hurt myself." She said.

45

RIDING THE STORM OUT

We boarded the bus and made our way to Roosevelt Hospital on the west side of the city. She said she needed to check herself in and had to talk to a doctor. We are talking about a psychological evaluation. I handed her off to a nurse and sat in the waiting room feeling shame that I have yet to feel again. I broke up with this girl and now I'm putting her in the loony bin. I felt as low as you can feel. I felt so bad that I couldn't imagine being able to shake it. The darkness of the moment left my emotional visibility at zero. A smile was miles a way. A day without a knot of guilt was further away. A healthy relationship and affectionate handholding were not in the building. I wanted to wretch but didn't want to draw attention to myself.

A doctor came out to talk to me, and I refused to step into his office for further conversation. My brother told me in Florida that the doctor probably would have told me to avoid this person because she was a sociopath or a borderline personality. I was too ashamed and couldn't imagine anyone trying to comfort me, the monster that left his girlfriend to climb the walls.

I don't know if I ever told Keesha that I had come clean. I think I did, and I felt free if not a little dinged-up emotionally. It was only a mirage, this feeling of coming out of the dark. I got a call from Christine from the mental ward. Today, the term might be the Psychiatric Unit; either way, she was on the unit, floor, or ward and calling from a payphone. She needed a few items and asked me to bring her some magazines and things. I was worried about having any contact at this point and encouraged her to call her cousin. She didn't want to do that, and this is where I begin to see the method to her madness. She was isolating herself and isolating us as a couple. Every chance she got, she would put us on an island and not tie the boat to the dock. She tried to put a wedge between my friend Paul and me; she made Clancy out to be a louse. She didn't want me to share her business. She was doing what cult leaders do—isolating the cult member from people who would offer an alternative view. Making me feel like I was the only person in the world to whom she could turn to was another tactic, and I bought it hook, line and sinker.

I agreed to bring her a care package and was resolute as I signed in and hit the button for the elevator. On the floor, I walked into a scene straight out of a dark drama. The *Cuckoo's Nest* reference doesn't work here. It was like any other floor in a hospital except the patients milling and seething, were afflicted with mental maladies, and some physical ones, to boot. It was a dismal place, and to say I wanted out would be using a criminal lack of scale to the situation.

A patient approached me and handed me some Monopoly money and said, "I am the Pope, and I want you to have this money."

"Thank you," I muttered and he took his phony bill back. He proceeded down the hall to pass out and retrieve his papal blessing to any of the willing or able in his flock. There were patients bellowing in their rooms, and I was fearful of catching something that would affect my already ragged psyche.

I handed over the bag of necessities to Christine and tried to speed up the proceedings. As hard as it was, I reiterated my desire for this to be over and told her she needed to reach out to family.

When Frank Sinatra says what he says about having few regrets and too few to mention, in the song "My Way," I think a generation of people decided to live by a no regrets policy. I have often said that if you don't have any regrets, you weren't swinging for the fences. Even Frank said he had a few, not zero. What happened next is definitely one of my regrets, where I veer off Sinatra's course is that I am now choosing to mention it. I could also quote Robert Frost because I was at the edge of two divergent roads in a yellow wood and being one traveler, long I stood, and instead took the road only a fucking moron would take.

Christine was asking for another chance. She was in her hospital gown with the Pope down the hall, and she was asking me to take her back. I got up from the bench where we sat and told her no.

I was so close. I made it to the elevator and she was on my heels, begging. It would be cruel to say that I was dragging her down the hall as she clung to my leg, but it was the emotional equivalent. She kissed me and said please with a level of depth I could not conjure in my best performance. I relented and said we would talk when she got out. It only gets worse, and the writing is now making me sweat. I've told the story a handful of times, but this is the first time I have sat with myself and conjured the moment.

In truth, I would have said anything to get off that floor. I was sure I could renege on my pledge to meet again. I don't know where I went after that. I might have wandered the streets.

I had picked up some steady shifts at the bar while still living at home. I was stockpiling cash at a brisk pace. I was beefing up my wardrobe and was able to make up for lack of a New York address by spending freely at restaurants and bars. It was retail distraction at best.

Christine called, and we made a plan to go to dinner and somehow I was convinced to get a hotel room in the city. Dinner was painful, and I was looking for a way out of this deplorable situation.

I drank quickly and with a purpose, which is not recommended. We got to the hotel room and relations that had all but ceased resumed in the biggest moment of weakness in history. It was my first sexual out of body experience, because I was watching myself making the biggest mistake of my life.

Winter was upon the tri-state area and Christine was still struggling to find a steady place to live. She was back to her treatment and was telling me that her doctor was saying if she didn't get out of the cold, the complications could be disastrous. I never went to a doctor's appointment with her or asked much of the particulars. She threw around words like molescum, lupus, anemia, walking pneumonia, and I was just trying to maintain. I just knew that I was expected to get her off the street.

We combed the want ads and started looking for an apartment. I had amassed a good chunk of change that could have been used on any number of things that could help my career, but I sunk it into an apartment in a shitty building with someone I wanted to break-up with.

At this point, I had to tell Keesha that I was back on with Christine. It hurt me as much to hurt her as it did to forsake a chance with her. I felt rotten, and when I signed the lease it felt like I was signing my death warrant.

I remember packing up my stuff, and the feeling in my house was about as bad a soldier shipping off the next day. I was the walking dead. I wanted out of my parents' house, and I guess I thought I could work out the rest once I got in the city.

We tried. We weren't doing much together, and I was working a lot and drinking a lot. It was a bleak winter, and I remember thinking how does someone on chemotherapy gain weight? Seeing apple pie in the fridge didn't dawn on me. She said it was the radiation. Christine was also smoking and drinking. I was thinking she had given up and was wondering how long I would have to support this person.

The only creative outlet I had was going to a friend's bar in Alphabet City after hours and drinking and being funny and being encouraged by this great friend whom I knew briefly at CMU. This was years before "Bet City" was gentrified and the bar was a shady dive that would have been too shitty for Charles Bukowski. Johnny Sosa was an intense writer and a very inspiring dude who I was trying to siphon some life force from. I bought a micro cassette recorder in an effort to stoke some writing or comedic embers, and I would tape our conversations into the wee-small-hours.

I would get home at five or six AM, fall into bed, and wake up with just enough time to get to work by four PM. It was like *Trainspotting* without the heroin and the comedy.

On a few occasions, I would ask a waitress at my job to come with me to meet Johnny, and we would stay up late and eventually made it back to her place and fell into bed. There I go again, trying to soften the blow; I was falling apart. It wasn't the ideal situation. She was married for a green card, but the guy had feelings for her and maybe some mob ties. She thought I had a lot of positive energy, and I was shocked anyone could see anything but my decline.

Getting up for work one day, I saw a post-it note taped to my micro cassette recorder. It read, "Play me."

I pressed play on what was a tape of me riffing with Johnny, and not sure if a female voice was heard. Christine recorded a wake up message over my late night bull session.

"This is what the fuck you call writing? Sitting around talking shit. I'm gonna tell you this now, if you cheat on me again, I'll kill you." She said on the tape.

I was less worried and more pissed about losing the material. Hadn't she heard of Studs Terkel? This shit was gold. I would use it someday, and now I had a death threat in the middle of a drunken rant.

I carried on and was also forced to get an AIDS test by Christine, which after Magic Johnson had me stressed. It is always a good idea to do that, but she said I had tried to kill her by having sex outside of the relationship. It was a heavy tone at the homestead, and I was close to losing it. I passed the test and, like Chris Rock, I passed with a D.

My family had come into the city to visit the apartment, and it was as lame a visit as could be imagined. My middle brother got married months before, and I was his best man. I still don't look at wedding pictures because Christine made it into the frame. He was with his wife during the visit.

At some point, my brother in Florida drew me out and I told him I was close to bottom. He told me that the family was worried; he said that I was the only one who believed Christine had cancer. He said I was being worked over by a very sick person, and I needed to get out of the relationship. I felt like saying, "Yeah, no shit."

He said he would buy me a plane ticket, and I could come stay with his wife and him. I relented and now had to get through telling Christine. I also needed a minute. I had an apartment. I had a job; I had a vague notion of getting my act together.

When I told Christine, I made arrangements to sleep somewhere else. I was going to avoid being in the apartment with her. She came to the bar during my shifts and acted like nothing had happened, which scared me more than her threat. She just sat there sipping beer and smoking cigarettes.

Weeks before she said she ran into Keesha. She said that Keesha had followed her to our apartment with some friends and was threatening to kick Christine's ass, banging on our apartment door. She said she talked to a cop and even had his card. I went to the precinct to talk to the guy, but he was out that day, and I didn't follow-up. I confronted Keesha, and she almost slapped me for the accusation. Who wouldn't?

For a few nights I had to scramble for a place to stay. I hung out at a diner until morning one night. I hung out at a bar where I knew the owner. They were closed but let me in, and we hung out until sun-up. I thought it was funny that I was "riding the trains" while Christine slept in my apartment. Did she ever really have a hard time finding a bed?

We had a meeting at work one afternoon. I hadn't been home. Christine stopped me on the street. She told me she had vodka and all of her pills, and she was going to take them and kill herself. It was a wrenching decrepit scene. I knew enough not to take the bait on a threat of suicide, or maybe I just didn't care.

Keesha was pissed and told me she was going to let people know that I wasn't this nice guy everyone thought I was. She was going to tell my boss that I had swiped her number off the computer, which was a criminal offense. I was getting it from every direction. I tried to head off any action at the pass, but I was wearing the same clothes and had to plan my escape. I felt awful. Keesha was right to be mad, and her reaction did, at first, make me question whether or not she harassed Christine, but she was pissed. We were on our way to a relationship, and now she had a shit storm on her hands.

I didn't know what to do. I called Jimmy Carver and asked him if I could stay with him but not to tell my parents. I felt like I had fucked up and was paying the price.

I had a plane ticket and had to make some arrangements. I told my boss at the bar. We had become close as a crew, and I was part of the family. She was worried for me and accepted my resignation. The apartment would be the other hurdle. Christine was not going to vacate, so I had to get my shit and leave her to deal with it. I was on the lease, and I had to let the landlord know. He gave me an earful, and I told him I'd be in touch.

Part of me dreamed I could break-up and keep the apartment and live in the city and be happy. My brother took the reigns and told me not to prolong the move and not to get too close to Christine.

I called the one guy I knew could help me, my buddy from Jersey City and the Governor's School. We went to fourteenth-street, and I bought six nylon laundry bags. I told him we were going to go over to my place, and we were going to fill the bags with all the stuff I needed. I told him not leave me alone in the apartment. I used my key to let us in, and she was there and irate. She asked me to give my key back, and I refused. She cursed and punched me in the chest repeatedly. I figured I deserved it. We went through the apartment and looted the place like we were stealing.

I got what I could but left important artifacts and mementos. I thought the smoke would clear, and I would be able to get the other stuff out. I left televisions and furniture, a mountain bike and my favorite chair. I like my things, and this is how badly I wanted away from this person. She screamed and cursed and haggled about the things I was taking, still playing me, still manipulating. I kept my key and left with what I could carry and what I thought I could live with as the remnants of this ordeal. It was the last time I ever laid eyes on Christine.

46

AFTER THE FIRE

If you've seen the John Sayles film *Brother From Another Planet*, you can picture how I was operating the first few days in my new world. I was reeling from the mess I made and still unsure I did the right thing, but there I was. It was warm in winter and there were lizards instead of roaches. I was walking around like a feral human, a wolf-boy, as everything was new to me.

The night before I left New York, before my great migration, I sat at a booth at my soon to be former place of employment. I was drinking and smoking, and I saw Keesha walking my way. She sat at the booth and talked calmly. She heard that I was leaving town and maybe still had some sympathy for me. Conversation was odd. We danced around things for a while, I bought her drinks, and I chain-smoked. Finally, she addressed the large mammal in the room.

"Do you really believe I could do what she said I did?" She asked.

"If I believed that, we wouldn't still be talking." I said.

"How could you think that?"

"I don't know."

I wanted to tell her that if she would have me I would scrap the plan to leave New York. I wanted to apologize and tell her I knew for certain that I was being lied to, but I was still reeling and feeling guilty as the guy who would break-up with a girl with even the remotest possibility of having cancer. This isn't another regret I mention, but one of those beautiful achy moments of drama we live through. I wanted to reach out and kiss her, try to woo her to bed and still make my exit, but I'm not that good, and I knew I had caused her some pain. Someday, I would have to let her know how I really felt, but sitting there double fisting my vices wasn't that day.

"Good luck." She said.

"Thanks."

We stood and I offered my hand. We shook hands like old war buddies on Memorial Day, glad to see each other, but reminded of the tough times behind us.

Lying in my brother's bed, not with him, but the bed in his spare room, I fought the urge to smoke and the urge to reach out to Keesha, the girl I left behind in New York.

Adjusting to life in Florida was not easy. There were not a lot of places to go where you would see black and white people together. I found a hotel lounge that had an R&B band and that had a predominately black crowd. I had no friends to roll around town with and not a lot of money either. I posted up at the bar and stuck out like Nick Nolte in *48 Hours*. The band was proficient, but a far cry from the music I would hear at Tattinger's every Sunday night back in NYC. I've learned that trying to re-create New York in places that aren't New York is futile and frustrating. It is a hard place to get over if you fell in love with it. No place can measure up and certainly not Tampa and certainly not a Ramada Inn in Tampa.

One of the few links to normalcy and one of the few things I could talk to my father about during this time was the football pool at the *New York Times* sports department. I had been allowed to compete along-side the writers and reporters and editors and my dad. They figured my money was as good as any, and they didn't think I would pose much of a threat.

Every week I would call my dad and make my picks based on the point spread in the *New York Post*, which thinking about now, was a funny resource. I don't think the *Times* even prints the betting line, so we were forced to pick up the tabloid every week. I was doing well. I had won two weeks outright and my overall record was at a seventy five percent winning rate. I was at the top, and the guys in the office were not happy about it. My dad loved it. It was that little window where we could share a moment as men.

In need of a job in Florida, I lucked into an acting job where I worked on an industrial training video for a chain restaurant. It was through a friend of my brother, and it was my first time reading off a teleprompter. I never saw the finished product, so I never got to see how well I read or if my eyes were following the words. It paid a decent rate, and it gave me a little wiggle room. I joined a gym and that was my main event of any given day. I was running out of funds when the end of the football season was approaching. I was still at the top of the board, and with a week left, there was only one opponent within striking distance. The guy asked my father if I wanted to sit out the last week and split the pot.

My father said, "I told him no dice, that you were going to play out the last week."

"OK with me." I said.

"Ted Williams could have sat out the last game of the season, in '41, and coasted to .400, but he took his cuts and went 6 for 8 in the double header; he finished at .406." He said.

It was funny to hear the Joe DiMaggio biographer tout Ted Williams as the standard bearer.

I took my chances the last week of the season and won the whole pool and a tidy sum that would buy me a few weeks of breathing room in Florida. My father also used some of my money to buy pizzas for the guys in the office, which made me look magnanimous. "I figured you wouldn't mind," he said.

I didn't mind and bragged to whomever would listen. The next year I lost my shirt in the pool. I guess that's why they call it gambling. I blamed it on not having a subscription to *Sports Illustrated*. It made me miss my folks and made me feel more remorse for having lost my way.

These small infusions of cash were not enough to keep me afloat, but I tried to stretch them to their limit.

There was a small professional theatre in St. Petersburg. It was an Equity house, and they were doing a production of Neil Simon's *Lost In Yonkers*. I called to arrange an audition and went in to do a monologue and read a scene from the play. Looking at my résumé, the director was impressed or maybe curious how I had found my way to these shores. We spoke for a while, and she said she'd be in touch.

A few days later, she called to say that I was too young for anything in their current production, but that the company had been doing Shakespeare in the park and assured me I would be part of it with a major role if I would be interested and could wait it out. I thanked her and tried not to take it too hard that I wouldn't be working in the current show.

This left me with no choice but to hit the pavement looking for a job, and the only recent experience I had was behind the stick. There were not a lot of bars in St. Pete, but there was the beach, and across the bay, there was Tampa. Not having a car, I had to be sure I could get to the job. That left me on the St. Pete side of the bay, which was more sedate and had less nightlife.

I hadn't given up hope, but I was low energy and I couldn't quite explain how I was feeling. I was being prodded to be angry and not guilty about the situation. Christine had done a number on me, or so I was told. I needed answers.

My brother, the doctor, was telling me that if Christine had any of the combination of the maladies she claimed, she would not have lasted six months. I reached out to Clancy and asked him if he ever took Christine to an appointment, he said no. I also apologized for ceasing our friendship. I told him I was led to believe that he had stepped out of line. He was cool about the whole thing.

There were some loose ends to tie up, and I had to make a call to Christine's father. I told him it was not my responsibility to take care of his daughter, and that I needed her out of the apartment, or I needed my security deposit money returned.

My paranoia led me to get a post office box so as not to expose my brother's address, and I wanted to keep my whereabouts unknown. Somehow I managed to get some mail forwarded, and I received an envelope from Christine. It was a manila envelope completely covered with words in marker, curses and taunts and suggestions to go to hell. It was a dark angry scrawl, like the graffiti of an angry mob. I took it in stride. My sister-in-law and brother found it disturbing.

I went to a shrink and brought the envelope. She said it might have reflected an angry person and someone on the edge of a manic cycle. She couldn't diagnose a person she hadn't met. I was looking for answers. I needed some proof that I was being lied to, and my family's assurances were not enough. I had found a letter that Christine received rejecting her claim for disability. It didn't have the word cancer in it and should have pushed me to the truth. The letter cited the facts that while there were emotional problems and a chronic bladder infection; she should be able to work.

The truth was I needed out of the relationship, and the truth is I will never know what really afflicted Christine. All you know is I left, and if she was sick, shame on me. If she wasn't, shame on her, but I wanted out and her family would have to bear the responsibility. As time carried on, I just wanted all the grief behind me. I'm sure it was maddening for her. I was gone; there was no more arguing and no way to lash out at me for taking off—just a post office box in Florida.

47

COME IN OUT OF THE RAIN

While I was regrouping and missing New York, I felt like I had a chance to start anew and to give myself some grace in moving forward. I was also trying not to be a nuisance in my brother's house and may have taken it too far. My brother and his wife were almost newlyweds, and I was grateful to my sister-in-law for opening up her home. I was still a night owl and wanted to be quiet while people slept. The house was a ranch style house with sliding doors on the bedrooms instead of the hinge-type doors. The doors made a lot of noise as they opened and closed. One night I had to go to the bathroom, which would have me sliding the door making all that noise and heading to the bathroom on the other side of the house. I had a couple of red Solo cups near the bed, and I decided to relieve myself in the cups, so as not to make noise, thinking I would empty the cups in the morning—psychotic, I know.

Returning home later that next day my sister-in-law was not her usual bubbly self.

"I don't know what that is next to your bed, but you need to deal with it." She said.

I had forgotten to get rid of my pee cups, and now I was exposed as the biggest freak on the planet. This was not the way I wanted to get to know my brother's wife, or something I have shared since then. It's not exactly the kind of anecdote to break the ice.

A few weeks later, I landed a job at a fancy hotel in St. Petersburg and was avoiding eye contact with my sister-in-law. It was a classic pink Spanish stucco resort and tennis club. It was more formal than I was used to, and it was a big adjustment. I was not used to working day shifts. I was not used to wearing a bow tie and was not used to having an escort to the bank room and to my register, something that was called a code fifteen by a rent-a-cop department called loss prevention. I had to have three interviews and was already worn out when the job started.

My boss was a young guy who was the food and beverage director, and had recently transferred from Hawaii. He wasn't my direct manager, but he was the last guy I had to meet. One night, I was on a double date and it turned out that my new boss was on the other side of the table. Ted was a good guy, and he might have been straining the boundaries of his position by dating a girl in his employ, but he wasn't worried.

The date was not going well on my side of the table, and when the girls excused themselves to the bathroom I was relieved.

"This date is a disaster." I said.

"Yeah, mine too." Ted said.

"I don't know anybody in this town, and I need a road dog, you game?"

"I don't know anyone either; let's bring this to an end, and we'll go out without them."

"Done."

It was the first time I asked a dude if he wanted to be friends since childhood, and it was the first time a date had been so lame that I ended it early, but this was the new me. If it wasn't going to work out with this girl, I'd be better served having a partner in crime to go out and meet some new girls. That he was my boss was an asset I seldom abused.

As we started going out at night, some of our mornings were rough going at work. Ted could hide in his office, but I had to stand in this grand ballroom and pour mimosas. The boss would make his rounds, and we would try not to laugh when we saw how roughed up the other guy was.

"I heard you were late today, Mr. De Gregorio?"

"Yeah, sorry about that boss." I said.

"Don't let it happened again." Ted would say.

A minute later, he would call the phone behind the bar, and we would make plans for that night. One of my responsible managers found out I was friendly with his boss.

"I didn't know you were tight with the big man?" he said.

I didn't abuse the situation, but I didn't mind the feeling that someone was looking out for me, and the managers left me alone after that.

The girl I had worked with on that training video told her agent about me. I got a call from the local agent, and she started finding auditions for me. I started getting some commercial work, and I was motivated to head to Orlando to meet bigger regional agents.

I had shot a commercial and gotten friendly with one of the actors, and when I made my way to Orlando, I gave him a call, and we made plans to grab a bite after I had cold-called a few agencies.

I walked into an office of an agency and explained my situation, and I was asked if I could perform something. I had a monologue from the Ken Burn's documentary about the Civil War, and it was a beauty. It was a letter from a husband to his wife on the eve of a great battle. He tells her to look into the breeze on a spring day if he does not survive, and that the breeze will be his breath from beyond. It is a stunning letter. I broke it out in the middle of the day with phones going off and the agent barely looking at me, and when I was done, I was handed a contract for representation. I walked out puffed up and feeling like maybe I could get my mojo back in the Sunshine State.

My actor friend was stunned that I had managed to land an agent he'd been courting for years in one door-knocking afternoon. He offered to let me crash that night at his house, and I met his mother and slept on a pullout couch.

This was the beginning of my re-awakening. I was auditioning and booking jobs at a high rate of success. While I never admitted it, I had given up hope in New York. I tried to swallow the anesthesia of domesticity and a fridge full of beer. I had no plan to get back what I had lost.

In the small pond of Florida, I was seeing some of the allure of being able to throw my weight around in a shallow pool.

Part of an actor's life is to keep your foot on the accelerator when momentum starts to aide your way. Sometimes you run out of gas, and you have to push a jalopy in neutral to a filling station. Sometimes that filling station is miles away in a humid part of the world. Florida was re-invigorating me—I was an actor again, and all was not lost. The pull of New York, though, was magnetic, and I was having a hard time staying patient and adjusting to a slower pace of life.

Within weeks of landing, I had a job, an agent, and a show on the horizon. I think they call it a "geographic" and it can be effective, at first. Finding yourself in a different city forces you to tackle a big to-do list; that's why people do it, to kick-start some productivity and to help you forget.

It might have been an easy corollary, but once the negative influence was removed from my life, there was room for me to see daylight

Whether I applied the brakes or pressed the gas would now be up to me, but for the first time in a while, there was some open road.

When you get off track and have to re-align, you get to see your life as an open session. The empty feeling of what to do with a day off, or who to call when you don't know anyone was constant and not altogether unpleasant. While I was hard wired to behave in a patterned way, I was now in a new orbit, and it was liberating. It was a time when you could follow so many divergent tributaries, unsure where you might wind up.

It was also important to me not to fuck-up again, and I was cautious with a more selfish protective shield. I wasn't tentative, but I was voicing words of self-preservation by rote as if I needed to practice my pitch for not getting myself into another mess.

This was also the time when the call from the theatre company came. I was counting on the call but also scared it might not be coming. I spoke with the director and was asked to come in and sing. I thought it was Shakespeare, didn't remember any jams in *Julius Caesar*. Turns out that they did Shakespeare in the park with a twist. They added songs and production numbers. I was making my comeback in a musical. I guess they needed some kind of hook to get Floridians to watch the Bard other than the ability to bring a cooler of beer to the park. It was culture light. I was thrilled.

It was a small professional theatre contract, but it would qualify me for health insurance when you factored in the rehearsal and the run of the show. What that does for an actor's soul is immeasurable. Being paid for your work is a boost to the psychological immune system. Providing for yourself with your art is a great feeling.

Being asked to pose for the full-page ad in the *St. Petersburg Times* was a great way to get started. We were doing *As You Like It* set in the 1920s gangster era. I was in the ad with a Tommy gun, another gangster, and a pretty blond. Nothing stokes the actor's ego more than a good picture of oneself and getting some ink in the local rag.

We began rehearsal with the usual table read. I was playing Sylvius and was looking forward to meeting the actress playing Phoebe. Sylvius and Phoebe are the comic preview to Romeo and Juliet. The play had small scenes where I would be running after the woman I loved. I was playing the lovesick young man, and I thought if the actress playing Phoebe was hot, we might get to do some offstage character research.

As the first scenes began, I was scanning the room and when an attractive woman read lines that were for another character, I would sink a little. When I read my first line and waited for the reply, I didn't know where it was going to come from. When the dude who posed with me in the newspaper ad spoke Phoebe's first line, I tried not to say 'fuck' out loud.

The room erupted in laughter. This group had worked together before, and I was being set-up for a reaction that I played perfectly. The read-through got back on track and I was waiting for some hot young chick to come in and take over the role from my mustachioed counterpart. It didn't happen. That was the concept. Phoebe would be a man in drag—so much for a backstage romance.

My discomfort in the playing the love interest to a drag queen was more disappointment in not having a real woman to chase around the stage. I was looking forward to a chance to flashback to my high school days and have make-out sessions behind the scenery—unless I wanted to jump the hetero ship, that wasn't going to happen. There were other women in the play, but, you know, when your characters are in love, it's almost a given you get to hook up with your partner, right? That's why a straight guy gets into theatre in the first place.

Rehearsals were during the day, and I had day shifts at the hotel. I had to quit, but wanted to have a job when the show was over, so they worked with me. I was thrilled to be an actor for eight hours a day and not a bartender. It was almost a direct dividend being paid. I was feeling better about being where I was. I was still missing New York, but the actors in the play were all jobbed-in from the city, and I was comforted to hang out with a new crew.

The rest of the cast was curious what I was doing in Florida. Before we got to know each other, they were joking behind my back that I killed a man and was on the lam in St. Pete, hiding in a theatre company for cover. I was still in and out, emotionally, and I might have given off an air of mystery instead of trying to make friends. Soon I would tell them the story, but for a time I enjoyed the mystique.

Being in rehearsal went a long way to make me feel like I was making good on the help that I had been extended.

It was also a time when I thought I could subvert the system and maybe get on TV before I left the state of Florida. My agent in Orlando was getting me good auditions for TV shows being shot in the area, and I was getting called-back. In some cases, I was only brought in for the callback. I was getting close. At one audition, I was wearing a jacket I bought from a uniform supply store in New Jersey. I bought it because it looked like a jacket that Treach from Naughty By Nature wore. It was a quilted black nylon number. The director told me to wait for a minute after an audition, and he came back with another guy. I took this as a good sign.

"Whatiya think of that?" he said to the new guy.

"Yeah it could work."

I was standing there thinking that *it* had a name. Then I realized that they were talking about my jacket.

I told my brother, "If I can't employ myself, maybe I can employ my clothes."

The play was close to opening, and I was having trouble with the steps of a dance number. I had dislocated my kneecap, again, in my brother's kitchen, when I pivoted and caught my patella on the handle of the cupboard under the sink. It was popped out and I was screaming and going pale. My knee reduced itself back into its socket just as the paramedics arrived. I waived off a trip to the hospital and walked around tentatively for a while. Dancing was exacerbating the instability of my joint, but there is no way I was going to let a musical theatre injury hold me back. It was not exactly a Willis Reed moment, but I did manage opening night on one leg. It got better as I learned the choreography.

Opening night was a complete surprise. Being in a park, we had to wait for the sun to go down to get started. We had trailers for dressing rooms, and the stage was built and resembled a stage at an outdoor rock festival with stairs leading to the stage.

I was glad to be working, but I didn't know there would be two thousand people a night to watch a re-imagined Shakespeare musical. It made me feel good about this little city that I had run away to and made me feel like I was part of the world again.

There are few things better than an opening night party. By the time the play is up and running, you are hopefully a band of gypsies who get along and already have an annoying amount of inside jokes.

My nickname was Cha-Cha, for the duration of the production after the character in *Grease* with whom I share a last name—Cha-Cha De Gregorio, the best dancer at St. Bernadette's. She is clearly a slut, and I almost didn't mind the nickname or the inference that I was a slut.

The party was held at the house of a benefactor of the theatre company. If I'm not mistaken, the production marked the tenth anniversary of the park series. It has grown over the years to packing in 20,000 people and transformed from Shakespeare to big Broadway musicals and has become a smashing success.

I sat by the pool after an overwrought thank you to the producers of the show. I wanted to tell them how far away this moment once felt, how I wondered if I would ever work again, how important this opening night was for me. The producers were gracious if a bit uneasy with the intensity of my comments.

One of my cast mates, the girl who dubbed me Cha-Cha, approached me poolside.

"Cha-Cha, are you ever going to tell me the story?" She said.

"Which one is that?"

"What the hell you're doing down here?"

"Did I kill a man in self-defense?" I joked.

"Yeah, that story." She asked.

I told her the short version and shook off my moodiness and headed into the party.

A few weeks into the run, I received some mail from Christine. It might have been a stack of bills—I'm not sure. It included an audio-cassette, and it had a sticker reading, *play me*. I was sure it bore little resemblance to the talking tapes that I shared with Kate back in the Oberlin days. Instantly, my stomach lurched back to the days when I roamed the city.

After the show that night, the cast went out, and I asked my friend if I could talk to her. I showed her the tape.

"I got this in the mail today."

"Did you listen to it?"

"No, do you want to listen to it with me?"

"I don't think you should." She said.

She pulled my arm, and we walked out the back door of this barbeque place where we were drinking. We were out back with the stacks of empty beer boxes and empty kegs, and my redheaded friend pointed to the dumpster behind me.

"A long time ago a friend of mine gave me some good advice." She said.

"Yeah, what's that?" I said.

"Keep the drama on the stage." She said.

"I hear you."

"*That* is drama." She said referring to the tape.

I looked at my friend for a moment, absorbing what she said. I started pulling the tape out of the cassette and made a pile that looked like a curly Halloween wig by the time I was done. I crushed the plastic cassette carcass under my foot, threw the bundle of tape in the dumpster, and gave my friend a hug. We walked back into the bar, and I bought her a drink.

48

COUNTRY ROADS (TAKE ME HOME)

March 24, 2011: John Denver is a fucking asshole. By all accounts, he was a great man, a great musician, and a real good guy. He's also been gone for a long time, and I don't mean to speak ill of the dead. But, if you are trying to keep your shit together and not cry in the sorrow of the news of your father's terminal illness, and someone puts on a John Denver record, you know what I mean when I say, "Why don't you just kick me in the balls." When he sings "Sunshine On My Shoulders" when you're trying to chop vegetables, and you start blowing snot, you know that you are helpless against emotion.

Years ago, my father was hit by a car walking in a crosswalk in the city on his way home from the Times. When he was home and healing, he listened to *John Denver's Greatest Hits* everyday. He used to tell me that Sinatra thought the world of Denver, and you can hear Ole Blue Eyes saying, "That hick kid Denver is a great artist; get me another scotch." At that time it couldn't get any less hip than having a father in a bathrobe rocking out to John Denver.

When you grow up and shake off the coil of coolness, you hear music in your bones and in your soul. Being home to take care of my dad, those songs broke me down. I was powerless against the tide of their simple beauty. Knowing what the songs meant to my dad and hearing them with heartsick ears was stunning. The pain of "Leaving On A Jet Plane" was like a back alley beating. My father was in a bathrobe again, trying to get well as he sang along to "Country Roads," and I was trying to stifle my tears. I sat on the porch and my dad came out and said, "Don't take it so hard." He was comforting me from a place I have never known—sad for himself, but empathetic to a son in sorrow. It makes you wonder where people come up with such spirit, makes you wonder what else there is, makes you wonder how John Denver knew so much. It makes you appreciate art and humanity and makes you feel small and fragile.

I would like to be able to say that I completed this book in the six months my father battled cancer and that I got to place a copy on his lap as he sat in Zerilda's Chair. That didn't happen, but it was the impetus I needed to get started. I came home the first time after the diagnosis with a draft of a screenplay that he poured through in his fatigue. Upon completion, he said, "It's good. It needs work, but it's good. That one character is funny." It wasn't my best work, but I wanted him to know that I hadn't given up.

My father got to see me perform; he got to see me on television and told me it went well when it didn't. Actually, he blamed the other performers for trying to overshadow me, but he still got to see my name across the screen 3,000 miles away. He got to know that I was cast in a movie. He got to fall in love with the woman I fell in love with. He got to read my words and helped me produce my play.

He didn't need to see me finish this book because he knew I would. While I battled inertia at points in my life, my dad knew I was a finisher. One thing I know I will do is finish this book before the anniversary of my father's passing. Not finishing it would be taking too long, belaboring my grief, which I can already tell will last my lifetime.

When people rub your back and try to calm your tears, they tell you how proud your father was of you. I knew my father was proud, but I wish I could have let him know that I was always happy and that my worries were behind me. While I met a few of my goals in his lifetime, I never had that foothold on my future that would have put him at ease. I know he worried 'til the end about all of his children and my mother, and maybe that's the nature of being a parent. That we were by his side as he drew his last breath is a gift that someday I will be grateful for.

When my father drew in his last breath and exhaled for the last time his face twisted in a way that said, "I really don't want to go; this is bullshit," not in a tragic way, but in a way that made me love him more. He was vital until the end; the way he fought and stayed kind was a lesson to live by. His wanting to stay said to me that he still had life left in his soul, and wanting an instant more is the way we should all be at our final hour.

Only someone who lived well can still fight for a moment or two of the beauty and agony of our time on Earth. My father left nothing in the tank. He lived with diabetes for thirty years, and suffered with spinal stenosis, but still refused to get a handicap placard. He was tough in that generational way that makes us wonder if we're getting soft as a nation.

While I worry about my age and my chase for success, I have to remember that my father made an impact on people's lives for every moment he was here. There was no acceptance of his fate and no wish for this life to be over. He wasn't biding his time in his old age; he was busy living and sometimes yelling and writing.

Denial is a powerful mechanism; sitting in a restaurant, crying into the phone, and hearing that my father's kidneys had failed and that he was being stabilized enough for people to make it home and enough for him to be brought home for his final days, I still thought there could be a late inning rally. There wasn't. When I arrived in Newark and rode home with my brother, I was told my dad was no longer able to speak. This was news to me, and I guess I fantasized about a final exchange of words. I had to recall the last words my dad said to me. Sadly they were over the phone. I was on my way to do a set somewhere, and I was just checking in.

"Give 'em hell, son. Give 'em hell."

Those were the last words I heard my father utter. When I dropped my bags and came to my father's bedside, he came to life and squeezed my hand, and I cried and stared into his eyes trying to burn my thoughts and feelings into his soul.

He stayed with us for one more day, and I know it was his last act of will. He wanted to hang out for one more day.

When a book is good, you read it until the last word. My father wrote and lived his life until the last page turned. That he would have been able to say a few more words is the legacy he left me. It got me to my last page. Scene.

ACKNOWLEDGMENTS

It pleases and daunts me to acknowledge those who have helped me along the way to this book's completion. Pleases for obvious reasons of gratitude, and a harkening back to the timeframe of the book. It daunts me mostly for the omissions both in name and honorifics that come along with sitting down to remember who I might thank.

As a reader I seldom read acknowledgements. A rare exception led me to see my father's name in Richard Ben Cramer's book on Joe DiMaggio. I was reading it in secrecy, because I didn't want to upset my father. His biography of Joe D. preceded Cramer's bestseller by many years, and while the acknowledgement confirmed my father's savvy as a biographer, it was bittersweet for him.

It is my hope to let a few specific people know that I was thinking of them and not to leave people off the list. I believe everyone we encounter has an effect on our lives.

Firstly, I thank the population of my life so far, and the population of the book, whose names are changed, who taught me so much as friends, and more.

To my family, the spine of any human, and any story, I thank you for bringing me here.

To my mother, who passed her passion for reading to me, and who's early reading of the book, buoyed my journey to completion. Thank you, mom, for getting through your initial discomfort, and taking in the story, as the keen observer you have always been.

To my brother, Barry, thank you for your support and for the laughter that soothed my worried soul on so many occasions.

To my brother, Steve, thank you for your empathy and for always having my back. Thank you for sharing your talents whenever I asked.

To my sister, Karen, thank you for your unwavering loyalty, and for your esteem even before it was deserved.

To my father, the reason this book came to be. It will never be easy to not have you here. My eternal love and gratitude.

To my teachers, too many to name, but most notably, Roberta Blackenhorn, Marceline Decker, and Don Wadsworth, I thank you.

Mentors and friends, Paul Urcioli and Kevin Kittle, thank you.

Friends, Bill Carter, Sean McElroy, Inga Ballard, thank you for still being in my life.

Kat DiTomasso, thank you for your expertise, effort, and encouragement.

To Sedonna Norman, my love and gratitude can never be fully expressed. I shudder to think where I would be without your love and support. I love you.

Carl DeGregorio is a Carnegie Mellon University graduate, still plying his trade as an actor, comedian, and dramatic person. He has appeared in film, television, and on stage and in comedy clubs around the country. For more information visit www.carldegregorio.com